HARD
EASY

Other Books by Arthur F. Coombs III

Don't Just Manage—Lead!
Human Connection: How the "L" Do We Do That?

HARD
EASY

a get-real guide
for getting
the life you want

BY ARTHUR F. COOMBS III

Copyright © 2020 by Arthur F. Coombs III

All rights reserved, including the right to reproduce this book, or portions thereof, in any form. No part of this book may be used or reproduced in any manner whatsoever without written permission from the author, except in the case of brief quotations embodied in critical articles and reviews. The views expressed herein are the responsibility of the author and do not necessarily represent the position of the publisher. For information or permission, write: Arthur F. Combs at www.ArtCoombs.com.

This is a work of creative nonfiction. The events herein are portrayed to the best of the author's memory. While all the stories in this book are true, some names and identifying details may have been changed to protect the privacy of the people involved.

Editorial work and production management by Eschler Editing
Cover design by Brian Halley
Interior print design and layout by Marny K. Parkin
Ebook design and layout by Marny K. Parkin
Published by Scrivener Books

First Edition: 2020

ISBN 978-1-949165-16-6 (Paperback)
ISBN 978-1-949165-17-3 (Hardcover)

DEDICATION

To my children and bonus children. I trust you'll all live long, healthy, happy lives. You have heard verbal snippets of Hard-Easy more than you wanted. Now that this is completed, I will back off the Hard-Easy lectures. Okay—I just lied. I love you way too much to back off. Point of fact, I am guessing you will not read this book because of the anxiety it may conjure from those previous Dad speeches. Therefore, if other readers do not tell you about this dedication, you will never know. And that will be easy-hard or hard-easy. Just depends on your perspective.

To my wife, Barbie, who I know will read it. Why? Because you love me that much. You have been the very definition of supportive throughout this process. Thank you for allowing me to discuss, debate, and share most of these ideas with you. Thanks for your contributions. They mean the world to me because your unconditional love is my world. I trust as we move into the winter of our years that the sweet joy of easy will fill our home and hearts with laughter, love, and peace.

CONTENTS

FOREWORD	xi
PREFACE	xv
What the Law of Hard-Easy Is and What It Can Do for You	
INTRODUCTION	1
The Cattle Drive	
CHAPTER 1	9
The Parable of the Summit: Learning from the Wisdom of Others	
CHAPTER 2	13
Walmart at 2:00 a.m. and Finding Your Why	
CHAPTER 3	23
Neanderthals Don't Have 401(k)s: The Genetic "Hard" Wiring of the Instant-Gratification-Craving, Easy-Hard Brain and How to Beat It	
CHAPTER 4	33
Seduced by Easy: How Easy Tricks You and How You Can Fight Back	
CHAPTER 5	53
A Brief Warning about Crisis Highs	

CHAPTER 6 — 57
The Case of the Intelligent Idiot
and the Value of a Wisdom Lens

CHAPTER 7 — 65
Lessons in Physics and Natural Laws:
Flywheels, Compound Interest,
and Microdecisions

CHAPTER 8 — 73
High-Profile Case Examples of
Easy Crashing into Hard

CHAPTER 9 — 87
In Praise of Grits

CHAPTER 10 — 97
"I Can't Because . . .":
The Top Excuses of All Time

CHAPTER 11 — 113
A Few Practical Ways to Help You
Identify and Purge Excuses

CHAPTER 12 — 121
Silencing the Toxic Whispers of Shame

CHAPTER 13 — 135
Invasion of the Brain Snatchers:
How the Quest for Instant Gratification
Robs Us of Free Will and True Joy

CHAPTER 14   145

    Garlic against the Instant-Gratification Vampire:
        Defenses for When Instant Gratification
        Tries to Suck Your Attention Away from Hard-Easy

CHAPTER 15   157

    You Need a Purpose, a Plan, and a Vision:
        In Other Words, You Need to
        Become a Salmon Person

CHAPTER 16   167

    Invest in Value: A Deeper Look at
        Time, Assets, and the Parable of
        the Banker and the Fisherman

CHAPTER 17   179

    The Decision to Jump Is Made on the Ground:
        Or What I Learned While Plummeting
        14,000 Feet to the Earth

CHAPTER 18   195

    Goal Setting for Those Who
        Think They Know How to Set Goals:
        The Five Principles of Big-Picture Goals

CHAPTER 19   205

    The Five Friends You Need and
        the Five Friends You Need to Avoid

CHAPTER 20   221

    Relationships

CHAPTER 21   239

    The Ten Commandments for Achieving Academic Success for Those with (or without) Dyslexia: Hard-Easy Lessons for Academics

CHAPTER 22   259

    Death

CONCLUSION   269

    This Moment Is Yours: Spend It Wisely

ACKNOWLEDGMENTS   275
NOTES   277
NOTE TO THE READER   283
ABOUT THE AUTHOR   285

FOREWORD

I've always known having Art as one of my best friends growing up had a big influence on me, and now I can put my finger on exactly why that was. As I read early drafts of *The Law of Hard-Easy/Easy-Hard*, I quickly recognized the concepts Art's not only lived but encouraged me to embrace during the past fifty years we've been friends.

Art is a master observer of human behavior. He notices trends, then experiments with them in his own life. He also sees the best in people and genuinely wants them to achieve their highest potential. This gives him a unique ability to find and push the right buttons to help others realize that potential. I have experienced this button pushing many times, and I'll admit it's sometimes annoyed me, but I also have to admit that his observations were usually correct and I'm a better man for it.

A good example of this is when, at Art's suggestion, I started wrestling during my freshman year of high school. I'd played several sports in junior high—soccer, football, track, etc.—but I wanted to invest real time and effort in a single sport. Art's suggestion hit home, and I found that wrestling appealed to me because of its individual and team aspects. Simply being on the team was no guarantee that I would compete against other schools. I had to work for a spot to compete and then defend my spot once I had it. Therefore, I quickly learned that my success in wrestling was directly connected to the effort I put in—the foundation of Hard-Easy.

In wrestling, it's simple to find the Easy. Much of the training focused on weightlifting and conditioning, and I was often tempted to do just enough to get through practice (choosing Easy). However, Art, also a wrestler, worked extremely hard in practice and drove me to choose Hard and never let me slack off, and yes, it annoyed me from time to time. Even so, I remained on the JV squad my junior year, a position where I remained undefeated in the regular dual matches. This made me a bit overconfident going into the district tournament at the end of the season. Art tried to push me to keep working hard until the end, but I took it easy and chose to go skiing the week before the tournament. I did fine in the early rounds, but in the semifinals, I lost to an opponent I'd beaten before.

This was Hard-Easy in action. I had slacked off on conditioning and lost my edge, leaving me without the stamina I needed to defeat my opponent. I can't say for sure, but chances are my opponent had chosen Hard prior to the tournament and maintained, or even improved, his technique, stamina, and confidence to give him the advantage. During the final round, I had to sit in the stands and, frustrated, watch two wrestlers I had previously beaten compete for the title. I could only blame myself. I'd chosen Easy, ignoring my friend's encouragement and example to choose Hard.

Art has used the law of Hard-Easy throughout his life, and I've used it in mine. Through it, we've both achieved successes that bring us joy in many areas: family, career, health, etc. One of the best endorsements I can give for the value of the law of Hard-Easy is as a parent. My greatest wish for my grown children and young grandchildren is their genuine happiness. I know they can reach this by learning the importance of Hard-Easy and putting it to use in their own lives. Art has the same hopes for his own children's happiness. Ultimately, he could have chosen Easy and talked one-on-one with each of them about Hard-Easy, but one of Art's amazing qualities is his desire to leave the world better than he found it, one person at a time. For that reason, he chose Hard and has dedicated many hours to writing, revising, and releasing *The Law of Hard-Easy/Easy-Hard* into the wild so it can benefit a much wider audience than just the one in his own home. We both hope you'll embrace the Hard-Easy model and use it to create the same happiness for yourself.

It's difficult to separate Art from the law of Hard-Easy, as it's practically part of his DNA. His work ethic and the successes that have followed can make him seem more intimidating than your typical guy next door. So I want to introduce you to the Art I know, whose friendship I have cherished since childhood to the present day, where I work with and for Art as chief technical officer of KomBea Corporation, the company he founded.

He and I truly clicked as children, and from then and into our teen years, we spent countless hours together. We saw each other at school, participated in sports together, and then hung out when we didn't have somewhere to be. We often spent this spare time at his house laughing, talking, baking cookies, and being typical American teenagers. We rarely had pocket change to go do much, so we had to get creative to find activities that wouldn't get us into too much trouble. In hindsight, we must have had someone looking out for us because as typical teenagers, we didn't always make the best decisions.

As we grew in both age and common sense, Art and I began going on long outdoor adventures together. What started in Boy Scouts turned into a tradition in college and beyond. The law of Hard-Easy was born on these fifty-mile hikes, where we spent days with whatever provisions and equipment we could carry. We worked hard to prepare for these hikes, which were not only physically demanding but also dangerous, even with proper preparation. As Boy Scouts, our preparation often led to us taking turns carrying the gear of our less-prepared troopmates in order to avoid having to turn back. As young adults and on our own, that preparation gave us the endurance and knowledge to push through challenges, which in turn gave us opportunities and experiences casual hikers will never have. One of the rewards was the taste of McDonald's after a week of hiking and eating freeze-dried meals.

So, who is Art Coombs? He's a typical man I'm lucky to have encountered and formed an enduring friendship and professional relationship with. Chances are he's a lot like your best friend. Despite the challenges he's faced and faces, he is an ordinary guy who has achieved extraordinary things. That's Art with the law of Hard-Easy, and with this law, you too can achieve extraordinary things.

Putting the law of Hard-Easy to work will be uncomfortable. To make it work, I have had to accept the consequences of my Easy choices and live with what might have been had I chosen Hard. Reflecting on our imperfections is extremely difficult, and Art has undertaken an intricate task in guiding you to this examination with love, humor, and a sincere desire to help you be the version of yourself you want to be. When Art pushes your buttons (and if you're doing this right, your buttons will get pushed), remember that this is a natural response to true self-reflection, and know that Art is your biggest cheerleader as you shine a light into the embarrassing corners of your life and start cleaning them out.

Good luck on your Hard-Easy journey. It will be hard and uncomfortable, but I urge you to stick with it and reap the rewards.

—David Peachey,
Chief Technology Officer of KomBea Corporation

PREFACE

WHAT THE LAW OF HARD-EASY IS AND WHAT IT CAN DO FOR YOU

First, if you are looking to improve your life, this book is for you. If you are looking for someone to coddle or absolve you of poor decisions, you will be disappointed—and this book is not for you. This book is for those who embrace self-improvement. It is for those who want to take a candid look at their reality, not escape or avoid that reality. It's for readers who want to better their lives and are not looking for a silver bullet, magic pill, or hot, trendy success secret that, like a fad diet, won't lead to lasting, positive change.

And second, I am *not* telling you to instantly accept anything in this book as doctrine.

I'll explain.

Sometimes we hear an opinion—especially if it's from someone we respect or consider an authority—and accept it as religious dogma without rigorously probing the idea to see if it stands up to our core beliefs, ethics, and values.

When we fail to give philosophies and ideas due diligence before we agree with them, even if we think we're following a principle to help us improve, we may be doing more harm than good. We can fall into the trap of adopting ideas as sacred truth—no matter the source—without thoroughly inspecting the idea to make sure it aligns with our core values and ideas.

The same goes for this book and my ideas. I expect you to not instantaneously accept them as absolute truth. My ideas deserve your scrutiny. I want you to reason with your head and then listen with your heart. Because I know that when the heart is convinced that the head has it right, you are motivated to move. Please forgive the author's inadequacies, give these ideas due process, and then make your verdict.

Now, onward.

The Law of Hard-Easy . . .

§ is sequential and causal. The effort we put in determines the outcome. The harder we work initially, the easier we'll have it later (Hard-Easy). When we take easy shortcuts, we're postponing the hard work, but it's likely compounding interest in the meantime (Easy-Hard).

§ is an accumulation of small decisions over time. We make hundreds of decisions every day. If we examine them through the Hard-Easy lens, we begin to recognize that many of our seemingly inconsequential decisions gain significance as they pile up. For example, spending two dollars each workday on a coffee doesn't seem like much when you're handing over the two dollars. You're getting the cheap drip coffee, not the latte, after all. But that small expense adds up to ten dollars each week and forty dollars each month. In a year, you'll have spent around $500. But that's just money. What about the ten minutes you spend each day playing a game on your phone when your child is in the living room? That adds up too, but when time is gone, it's gone for good. You don't get a redo with your kids' childhoods.

§ is directly related to our choices, not our circumstances. The universe is notoriously unfair. The easy thing is to compare ourselves to others and end up in a negative place. Maybe we believe the universe has been so unkind to us there's no reason to try—we'll never achieve our dreams. Or maybe we look at someone who is the victim of the universe's unfairness and judge that person—after all, they're just not trying as hard as you, so you each are getting what you deserve. Part of living Hard-Easy is avoiding the comparisons that lead to negativity. Control what you can control—your choices—and support others on their journey.

💰 is a natural and universal law, just like gravity. It affects everyone equally, regardless of how much or how little they know about it. The advantage goes to those who are aware of it, because we can invest that two dollars or ten minutes each day rather than waste it. We can use this law to benefit ourselves and those whose lives touch ours.

My Challenge

The point of this book is to help you learn how to make this natural law of the universe work *for* you instead of *against* you. This is a journey that requires sacrifice, confronting unpleasant thoughts, and other hard things. Before you decide I'm an unreasonable taskmaster; there's something you should know about me.

I'm dyslexic.

Maybe you don't know a lot about dyslexia, so let me give you just a glimpse.

A person with dyslexia might suffer headaches or stomachaches and even get dizzy while reading. Some dyslexics see movement while reading or writing to the point of motion sickness. Some lack depth perception and peripheral vision. Letters, numbers, words, and sequences can get repeated, transposed, omitted, or reversed.

In school, most dyslexic kids can read, but few comprehend what they're reading—at least the first time through.

And then there's math.

Some know the answers if they are allowed to count on their fingers. Others can count verbally but not objects (even their fingers). Some can do basic arithmetic but not word problems, algebra, or higher math.

Dyslexia is a spectrum of brain malfunctions.

Science has demonstrated that someone with dyslexia has a disconnect in the part of the brain responsible for reading, writing, and arithmetic—the classic "three Rs." Today's technology lets researchers watch all the jumbled-up synapses misfire in real-time.

Meanwhile, the synapses for creativity and innovation are firing on all cylinders. While the three-Rs part of the brain got faulty wiring, the creativity part got a Formula-1 engine with high-octane fuel.

The cruel irony is that no one typically notices your creative genius if you struggle to read, write, or count. Dyslexics often aren't far enough behind to get real help in the school system; instead, they're labeled dumb, careless, immature, or lazy.

My teachers constantly misjudged me as lazy and stupid. I hid my dyslexia, terrified that someone would find out. The best way I can describe my feelings during those years is sad-mad.

I was lucky to have a father who not only believed in me but who also had a PhD in education from Stanford University. He understood dyslexia. He didn't necessarily know how to "fix" it—no one in those days did—but he understood it. Most importantly, he understood me. His influence created an environment in which I could more easily tackle the major obstacles thrown in my life's path.

Day in and day out, he showed me how to live. And though he shared his wisdom and guidance, he never let me forget that, ultimately, it was up to me to decide what path I was going to take in life—disabilities or not.

Okay. Enough about my dyslexia. I didn't tell you so you'd feel sorry for me. I told you because it's important for me to be open about my personal set of challenges. Each person who holds this book has a unique set of circumstances, and I know how tempting it can be to use such difficulties as an excuse to give up and settle.

Some readers will see the universe as being incredibly cruel to me. Others will scoff and declare, "Dyslexia? That's cute. But I have *real* problems." Remember, the law of Hard-Easy is not about comparing ourselves to others. The only comparison that matters is who you are now and who you want to become. I know the law of Hard-Easy will be a powerful tool that will bless your life or curse it, and only you can decide its role and your fate. However, I promise, no matter your circumstances, you can be the person you dream of being.

Your First Goal

One of the major concepts of the law of Hard-Easy is delayed gratification. If while reading this book you become eager to get started *now*, I urge you to delay that gratification. First, get all the information so you can make informed, strategic decisions.

At the end of each chapter, you'll find a shortlist of reflection activities. These activities will help you gather your thoughts and formulate bigger plans.

Now that you have an idea of what you're in for, let me tell you a story about the time I first learned about the law of Hard-Easy. Well, perhaps in some ways I have always believed in Hard-Easy, but I had never heard or thought about it this way.

Storytelling is a remarkable conveyor of knowledge, reaching clear back to ancient oral traditions. It takes complex ideas and boils them down to their simplest form. We'll be doing a deep dive into the nuances of the law of Hard-Easy in this book, but at its heart, the law is simple, as my own introduction to it will illustrate. While reading my story, consider how the law of Hard-Easy has affected your life in small or large ways.

But for now, just imagine me (an avid horseman but not a cowboy), some rugged cowboys with decades of experience, and a whole bunch of cows.

INTRODUCTION

THE CATTLE DRIVE

My horse's name is BigDog.
    He's a big yellow palomino. Majestic. Powerful.

A few years ago, we were on a cattle drive, and we had been on good terms. Until now.

I'm an avid horseman, but I'm no cowboy. However, I love riding the trail with my cowboy friends. It's miles of hard work through vast, unpopulated stretches of rugged, high desert mountains. The rhythm of the days and nights leads me to Zen-like meditations, opening my mind to insights and epiphanies.

It was a cool fall day. We had been riding since five-thirty that morning, and now the sun was high in the sky.

I was helping my friend move 1,200 head of cattle across a rugged range south of Loa, Utah, to a new grazing area.

That's a lotta burgers on the hoof.

We moved through the crisp mountain air to the sounds of the drive echoing off the mountains: riders slapping their chaps with rope to encourage the cattle to keep moving, hooves clomping across the rocky trail, the cattle lowing and bellowing, and the wind faintly hissing through the aspens and evergreens. The smell of sweat, leather, and pine was a constant as the sun climbed to its zenith and we logged mile after mile.

I watched my horse and others instinctively and lovingly drive the cattle. These horses were "cowy" horses—those who watch, track, and rate cows. They know their job and are excited to do it. BigDog was very cowy. He could read the herd and direct the cows, making my job almost effortless. It's quite magical.

At last, we came to a stream. Everywhere, pine trees shot up from the rocky soil. Where we stood, the creek was about thirty feet across.

The cowboys drove the cattle across the shallowest point of the fast-moving stream, where it was only about two feet deep. After everyone had crossed, it was just BigDog and me.

Things had been going fine. But now BigDog and I had a disagreement: where to cross the deep creek, the churning current blocking our way.

I gave the muscular Palomino a gentle kick in the ribs, but he pulled up short and refused to budge. I kicked him again with a bit more energy, but he was stubborn. Then he trotted to the spot where he wanted to cross.

I could see why he preferred his spot—it wasn't as wide from bank to bank. Maybe fifteen feet. But it was clearly deeper.

At least it was clear to me—that's because humans have excellent depth perception, whereas horses have minimal depth perception: a horse's eyes are set far apart, so their ability to see depth is limited. From most angles, horses cannot get a left-eye/right-eye view of the same object in one glance. As potential prey, they're built for peripheral motion detection at the expense of depth perception.[1]

BigDog could see the surface of the water but not how deep it was. It could be an inch or a mile deep. For him, what made the most sense was to cross where the distance between the banks was narrower. He couldn't see that the water there was nearly four feet deep—nearly to his cinch—and flowing much faster. It would be much more treacherous.

I turned BigDog around and led him back to my spot. But just at the water's edge as the stream burbled over rocks and logs, he stopped and refused to cross, resisting the reins and jerking his head as if throwing a tantrum.

Back and forth we argued about where to cross. It was an utterly ridiculous horse-and-rider spat. One I was losing.

As the minutes passed, I grew concerned that the herd and other riders were getting too far ahead of us. I rolled my eyes and said to BigDog in disgust, "Fine, jackass! Have it your way. We'll cross where you want to cross. You're wrong, though. You'll probably end up scared as hell and soaking wet, with both of us swept downstream."

Yep. I was talking aloud to my horse.

As I spun BigDog around to let him cross at the deeper spot upstream, I saw Gordon on the other side of the river, sitting high in the saddle atop his gorgeous bay quarter horse, General. Gordon is a gritty, veteran cowboy and well respected on the trail. He had come back to watch me argue with my horse.

As I was about to give in to BigDog, Gordon's gravelly voice cut through the crisp mountain air: "Coombs, you can live easy-hard or hard-easy. It's your choice."

Just what I needed—a heckler to mock my horse handling.

Annoyed, I yanked the reins hard. BigDog snorted and stopped.

"Gordon," I shouted. "I have no idea what you're talking about."

Gordon had the slightest hint of a grin on his face. I could tell my horse and I amused him.

"The easy way is to let your horse choose where to cross," Gordon shouted back over the sound of the creek. "That is, it's the easy way *right now*. But if you take the easy way now, you'll have to live *hard* later."

I did not have time for this cowboy-fortune-cookie horse shit.

Seriously—why didn't Gordon tell me something useful, like "If you spur him while singing 'Stairway to Heaven,' he'll obey you."

Gordon must have noted my frustration. He shifted in General's saddle, leather creaking and spurs clinking. "Coombs, if you don't stick to your guns and make that horse cross this stream where you want him to, you'll have this fight with him every time you come to a stream. But if you do the hard thing now by forcing him to do it your way, it will be easy later. You should not care if it takes you all day. Make that horse cross where you want him to cross."

I figured Gordon knew what he was talking about.

I figured it would be a smart thing to take his advice.

So I whirled BigDog around, pointed his nose over the edge of the creek where *I* wanted to cross, loosened up the reins, and gave him a good kick in the ribs.

Nothing happened.

Great. Gordon was just making this stuff up. It was probably some elaborate cowboy-hazing ritual.

Cicadas whirred in the tall grass. I licked my lips and tasted salty sweat.

"C'mon, now," I said to BigDog and gave him another firm kick.

And that was when my horse surrendered in our battle of wills. He dipped his butt, launched into the stream, and doused my boots, pants, and chinks with water.

And thus I had plunged into the concept of the law of Hard-Easy.

We pushed cows from 5:00 a.m. to 8:00 p.m., and both BigDog and I were exhausted. It was time to go home. I loaded BigDog into his trailer, and off we drove.

I made a pit stop, however, before settling in for the long drive. Just on the south side of Loa, Utah, there is a Sinclair gas station adjoined by a Brian Farm Service Center Country Store. You can get all the typical stuff—sodas, beef jerky, candy bars, hot dogs. But at this gas station, you can also grab feed for your livestock, fertilizer for the crops, barbwire to repair a fence, or the latest Makita belt sander.

I filled up the tank and went inside for a large Diet Coke and a snack. At the checkout counter, five customers stood in front of me, including a young mother with two toddlers about ages three and four. As we waited in line, the toddlers spotted the candy for sale—gum, candy bars, Starburst, Skittles, gummy worms. All those goodies were placed there to create an impulse buy. And it was working: the kids were feeling some impulses.

Both reached for the candy. And their mother quietly said, "Not today."

The mom wasn't going to win that easily. Those kids wanted their candy, and they wanted it now. And being told no only made them want it worse.

They whined. They pleaded. They got louder. They reached around their mom for the candy.

"No," the mother said more firmly but still under control.

And every no was a cue to the toddlers to escalate their tantrums.

Now everyone in the checkout line was focused on this battle of wills.

Would the mother give in? "I told you no candy today," she said, prying the candy from her kids and putting it back on the rack.

A father myself, I felt for this fellow parent's struggle. If you're a parent, you've been there—you've been this mom with these kids.

And that was when I saw the law of Hard-Easy in action. Fresh off the trail, now I heard Gordon's voice in my head: "You can live easy-hard, or you can live hard-easy. It is your choice."

This was another situation illustrating the principle I had been introduced to less than twenty-four hours previous. The principle dictated that if the mom did the hard thing now, it would be easier for her with these kids later. *If you give in to their demands now, you will only be showing them that the louder they scream, the higher the probability that they will get their way later.*

The kids were really causing a scene. I could see her will begin to wilt. I am sure she was feeling some silent, social pressure to get her kids under control in a public place. She was, no doubt, feeling embarrassed and judged. I remembered the times my kids had meltdowns in public and I would sometimes do the easy thing to quiet them.

So when she caved, I completely understood.

"Just this once," she said.

Did the screaming stop? Yes, it absolutely did. Just as if the toddlers had flipped a switch to nontantrum mode.

But how would that moment affect those two toddlers and their mother a few days, weeks, months, or years down the road? Could such a small choice make much of a difference?

As I paid for my snacks and drove off, I thought, "You can live easy-hard or hard-easy. It's your choice. It's your life."

After that trip, I began to see examples of the law of Hard-Easy in everyday situations. Once you notice something you've never noticed before, you begin to spot it everywhere. Like if you never noticed how many people say "um" in their speech patterns, when someone points it out to you, you suddenly start hearing it everywhere.

What Gordon taught me—that you can choose to go easy-hard or hard-easy—was more than a lesson about horses or mere cowboy wisdom. It was nothing less than a natural law, just like gravity. And just as gravity affects us regardless of whether we know about it or not, so does the law of Hard-Easy, regardless of whether we know about it or not. I saw that at the gas station when I witnessed the mother in her battle of wills with her kids.

My mind has spun on Gordon's wise words and their implications for years. I have spent countless hours contemplating and articulating ideas about the law and gathering evidence of how it works.

Gordon was right. What if I had given in to BigDog that day at the stream? I'd still be giving in to that horse—and things would be much harder now.

Even though my horse and I had some occasional squabbles in the past, they're few and far between now. BigDog was a lot more inclined to give in and agree with me after just a little gentle persuasion. It was hard then, but it was easy for the next fifteen years we explored the backcountry together.

Chapter Recap

Key concepts and takeaways from the preface:

- The law of Hard-Easy is simple: putting in the hard work first makes things easier down the road.
- The reverse is also true: choosing Easy first makes things harder down the road.

- Now that you've been introduced to the law of Hard-Easy, you'll begin to see it being played out all around you, in your life and in others' lives.

Pause and Think

- Where do you see the law of Hard-Easy in your experiences?
- Can you identify a Hard-Easy choice you've made today? Yesterday?
- If you had been that mom in the store, how would you have handled the situation? Or if you had been me, what would you have done?
- If you've faced similar situations where you were able to choose Hard in dealing with the kids, what thoughts or beliefs helped you to choose Hard instead of Easy?

CHAPTER 1

THE PARABLE OF THE SUMMIT

Learning from the Wisdom of Others

Accumulating wisdom is good. Applying that wisdom to help yourself and others to make the best possible choices while avoiding pitfalls is ideal.

What is wisdom? And why should you listen to me about this Hard-Easy thing?

I conducted a rather unempirical poll on social media to find out how people define wisdom. Most definitions featured common denominators, and I was able to boil it down to this: wisdom is the synthesis of knowledge and experience yielding insight into making the right choice.

With both knowledge and experience, one can better see the big picture.

While some young people may possess great knowledge, I would say that most simply do not have adequate time, experience, or perspective to be truly wise. (Bear in mind, some youth are precociously wise, and some of those who are forty-plus are shockingly unwise.)

On the cattle drive, Gordon was wise, saw the big picture, and helped me see it, too.

In a way, I'm writing this book for my kids and future grandkids and great-grandkids (in addition to the vaster audience of humanity)—to help them see the big picture of Hard-Easy and share all the things I think I've learned about this natural law.

I heard a slightly different version of the following story many years ago. The original author is unknown to me, and yet it has always stuck with me. In the following chapter, I mold it into a story I hope captures the essence of wisdom and how wisdom operates—and why it's difficult for those who can't see the big picture to sometimes trust the voice of wisdom in their lives.

The Parable of the Summit

If you have read my other books, you know I live in Utah at the base of a mountain that towers nearly 12,000 feet (3,600 meters) above the valley floor—Mount Timpanogos. My home sits at about 5,000 feet, on the foothills of the mountain.

I have hiked to the top of the mountain many times. And I have ridden my horse along the switchback trails high on its slopes. Its beauty and majesty are awe-inspiring.

From the highest reaches of the mountain, I can see all the way across the valley. I can look down the slopes and spot my house. When I use binoculars, I can easily see the grill in my backyard. I can watch my horses trot across the pasture. I can see the dogs lying in the shade, and I can watch the pesky magpies stealing fruit from my cherry trees at the edge of the property.

As I pan my binoculars across the valley, I can also see I-15. It runs north-south through the valley.

From the top of Timpanogos, when the weather cooperates, it's not hard to see twenty miles in either direction on the interstate.

In this modified parable, I sit on the summit of Timpanogos with my binoculars. I'm scanning I-15 because I know that my oldest son, A.J., is driving it right now, on his way to Salt Lake City for a job interview. He wants to make a good impression and be there on time—a little early, even.

I can't immediately spot him and my little white car through my binoculars, so I call him. "A.J., where are you right now?"

"I just turned onto I-15."

I train the binoculars south toward the on-ramp nearest our house to find the familiar vehicle. "Are you near Provo in the middle lane behind a large semi-truck that has a yellow J.B. HUNT sign on the trailer?"

In a surprised voice—and wondering how his stalker-dad has found him—he asks, "Dad, are you following me?"

"Nope. I'm at the top of Timpanogos with my binoculars."

He laughs, and I can hear him roll his eyes through the phone. "Wow, that is sick." Translation: cool.

As we're talking, I notice flashing lights farther north—police, fire, and ambulance. I can see a major, multicar accident on I-15 about ten miles ahead of A.J.

Traffic has already begun to back up near the accident, but it hasn't affected A.J. yet.

I can visualize exactly what A.J. sees—smooth sailing ahead. He thinks he'll make it to the job interview on time, no problem.

Because of my position and perspective, however, I can clearly see A.J.'s future and the consequences of staying on his current course. I also know how to help him navigate around this challenge.

"Son," I say. "There's an accident about ten miles up the interstate. They're closing down the entire freeway."

"Oh no! I really wanted to be early and make a good impression. Do you think I can get there a different way?"

"Take the next exit and get on the Geneva frontage road. Then you can then jump back on I-15 in Lehi and still make your interview."

That parable conveys a simple truth—when you combine knowledge (I knew A.J.'s location and where the accident was) with experience (I had driven multiple routes in the area), you have a different perspective—you can see the big picture (the many possible outcomes of A.J.'s situation and the best possible route to take). It's like setting up a complicated pool shot—you can see the chain reaction of the collisions you'll set in motion and what balls will sink.

Or it's like a chess master who looks at the board and calculates several moves ahead. She can see how a single move will likely be countered and how she will counter that counter, and so on.

In my parable of the summit, this is represented by my ability to see a nasty collision from my vantage point, a collision my son could not possibly know about.

Even if he had been using a real-time GPS tracker, he would not have had time to make the adjustments as quickly as he could through my coaching based on my knowledge and experience. My wisdom allowed me to guide him through those obstacles and still achieve his goal of making a good impression at his interview.

With all that in mind, let me tell you about my younger son, Kai, and our trip to Walmart. You'll hear all about it in the next chapter.

Chapter Recap

Key concepts and takeaways from chapter 1:

- Wisdom is the combination of knowledge plus experience.
- Wisdom typically develops with age.
- Listening to the wisdom of those you trust can be beneficial.

Pause and Think

- Are there times in your life when the wisdom of others helped you make a good choice—or avoid a poor choice?
- Are there times in your life when you ignored the wisdom of others and later discovered you wished you had followed their advice?

CHAPTER 2

WALMART AT 2:00 A.M. AND FINDING YOUR WHY

We can't impose wisdom upon or force someone to make wise decisions. Likewise, wisdom cannot be imposed upon us. Although we might or might not listen to mentors whose advice can guide us, we always need to arrive at our own wisdom. But how?

I'm a big believer in communicating the why. I try to incorporate this principle in much of my writing. If people understand why they're doing something, they're much more likely to value the task and to give it their best. In this chapter, I'll introduce this concept more fully and show how knowing the why can help us embrace the law of Hard-Easy.

I shook my son Kai awake.

It took awhile. He's fourteen years old. And it was 2:00 a.m.

"What time is it?" he asked groggily.

"Two in the morning," I said.

"What? What's wrong?"

"Nothing. C'mon. Let's go."

"Go where?" He rubbed the crusties from his eyes and smacked his lips around his funky morning breath.

"I want to show you something."

"Show me tomorrow." Kai pulled his pillow over his head, burrowing away from me like a grub.

"I can't show you tomorrow. I have to show you tonight."

Curiosity got the better of him, and he peeked out at me. "Show me what?"

I smiled. "C'mon. I'm taking you to Walmart."

Kai and the Great Homework Lie

In many regards, the apple does not fall far from the tree. Kai hates doing homework and is exquisitely skilled at procrastinating. I can't blame him. I, too, was the master of homework avoidance when I was his age.

While Kai was in eighth grade, I would pick up him and his sister Mac from school. I'd ask both if they had homework. Both always had the same answer: "No, not me, Dad."

Suspicious after several days of getting the same answer from both, I would sometimes ask follow-up questions. But Kai and Mac always had slick responses:

"I did it during break time."

"We had a substitute, and they didn't give any homework."

"I got it all done yesterday."

"Oh, I mean, I do have some homework, but it's not due for a few weeks."

The list of excuses went on and on.

Then the end of the semester rolled around. Reckoning Day.

Mac's report card was fine. I was very proud of her.

I opened Kai's. Not so fine.

Kai had several Fs, along with a few Ds and Cs. His GPA that semester was a dismal 1.25. Heavy sigh.

After talking to his teachers, I was assured Kai was a bright young man and had done reasonably well on tests. However, he was missing many homework assignments.

I was stunned. He had been lying to me about his homework.

As a parent, I was disappointed and frustrated. I knew he was better than the grades he'd gotten.

I was also frustrated with myself. I'd thought myself a better parent than that. I'd thought I was more in tune—a cool dad who was asking all the right questions as I encouraged, trusted, and nurtured my kids into adulthood.

Illusion burst.

It was time for me to up my dad game.

For Kai, this was not an ability issue; it was an issue with his focus and will. How could I reach him and mentor him toward success?

Be the Gordon

When this story took place, I'd been mulling over this law of Hard-Easy for quite a while. And in my head, the truth of it was self-evident. When I was trying to help Kai get better at doing his homework, I'd channel my inner Gordon and tell him he could do things easy now but it would be hard for him later.

Unfortunately, Kai was taking after BigDog—being stubborn, insubordinate, and refusing to cross the river where I wanted him to.

During our many homework debates, I would often say, "Kai, you can live easy-hard or hard-easy. It's your choice and your life. The easy thing to do now is play video games all afternoon and ditch the homework. Your friends come over, and you have a great time trying to get to the next level and defeat the big boss.

"But if you continue on this course, you will soon have to live hard. It's not something I believe—it's something I know. And you can't control it. Nobody can. It's a natural law. Same as if you jumped off a cliff at Canyonlands: once you leap, you have no choice but to submit to the law of gravity and the results of your actions.

"So the arrival of Hard may come during the next test. And again when you apply for college. It may snowball and hit you again when you try to get your first big job. As sure as the sun rises every morning, if you do not alter your course on your homework, you will encounter Hard down the road—and likely keep encountering it. And when Hard comes knocking, it will be monumentally difficult to make any course corrections. You will be stuck living with the consequences of your actions now."

Pretty good dad speech, right?

Kai would roll his eyes. "Dad, not again with the Hard-Easy thing. I hear that one more time, I think I'm gonna puke."

"Kai," I said. "Sure, you've heard it, but I don't think you've really *heard* it. If you had, your actions would change. So until you truly understand and your actions reflect that, your good ol' dad will continue to give you the speech."

How could I get him to get it?

A Peek into the Future: The Consequences of Living Easy-Hard

Kai is a great kid. He's not a couch potato who lazes around the house and does nothing but play video games. Whenever I ask him to help me with yard work, feeding the horses, unloading the dishwasher, taking the garbage out, cleaning his room, getting the mail, and many other nonhomework chores, he never complains. In fact, quite the opposite—he always responds to my requests with a cheerful "Sure thing!"

Occasionally he says, "Just after this one game." Then he finds me in five or ten minutes, just as promised.

But when it came to getting a straight answer from him about homework, for whatever reason, Kai was always running a con game with me.

I quickly learned that all his teachers posted their homework assignments online. I could log in and not only see the homework assigned, I could track Kai's progress.

Now I had the ability to spot a homework fib and could tactfully call Kai out. I had equipped myself with knowledge (Kai's current academic status) and experience (with Kai avoiding his homework).

Interesting point: even when Kai knew that I knew about his homework, he would *still* evade it at all costs.

Homework became a constant battle between us. On the grade front, it got a bit better, but he was still getting a few Ds, several Cs, and a B or two. That was improvement, sure, but those grades did not reflect the potential student I knew Kai was.

As eighth grade morphed into ninth, the Great Homework Struggle continued. I started to do what I think most parents do when confronted with heavy, consistent resistance about doing homework—I kicked into deeper, more militant micromanagement.

I set aside blocks of time for schoolwork. Then I placed restrictions on exactly where that homework would be done and who he could do it with.

I regularly confiscated his cell phone, computers, video games, and the other devices I knew were pulling him away from homework with their siren song.

I even used food as a motivational tool. "You can't come out for dinner until these three pages of homework are done."

His grades moved in the right direction, with Cs, several Bs, and some As.

So, I had done it, right? I was a success, wasn't I?

Not really.

It was a relentless, daily battle—one I dreaded. Our homework saga raged on. I grew increasingly frustrated and tired. Our relationship grew strained. No matter how many times I gave Easy-Hard/Hard-Easy speeches and talked about Gordon, BigDog, and the screeching, we-want-candy-now kids from the gas station, it fell on deaf ears.

What was I doing wrong?

Perhaps, I told myself, *this is just what parenting is—the relentless management of your kids until they leave the nest and live with the consequences of poor choices made in their youth.* And then when they visit for Thanksgiving dinner, you get the pleasure of hearing them gripe about how hard it is for them now, and you can triumphantly say, "I told you so."

Is that really what it's all about?

This situation troubled me for months on end. I do not know who was more excited for summer—the kids or me. At least during summer, we wouldn't have our nightly homework tug-of-war.

Remember in the parable of the summit how my older son, A.J., was heading toward the traffic jam on I-15? Now, metaphorically, Kai was in that car, but he didn't want to take Dad's word on what was ahead. For a while, I tried towing his car and dropping him off on the roads I wanted him to be on. But then he'd start working his way back to the ease of I-15, and I'd have to hitch the car to my tow truck again. What I really needed to do was to get him up on that summit with me and hand him my binoculars. Kai needed to see for himself the closed interstate and the different routes he could use to avoid it.

Then, one night in bed, I realized that all this time I'd been overlooking the obvious. I was managing my son to the hilt. If you have read my first book, *Don't Just Manage—LEAD!,* you know that the main theme of that book is that people do not want to be managed. They don't want to be controlled. They resent being told what, how, when, and where to do a task.

They want desperately, however, to be led.

Leading is all about the why. When you give others the why and they buy into it, you do not have to focus on the how, when, where, and who.

Kai had no why.

He didn't have the big picture. I'd been focusing all my wisdom on the smaller task of his homework and hoping he'd see the big picture.

I thought, *Art, you teach others the difference between management and leadership all the time. Hell, you wrote a book about it. Why are you—of all people—managing and not leading? Kai does not want to be managed; he wants to be led.*

Then I heard it like a voice from the heavens:

Give Kai the why. Help him see into the future and truly understand the consequences that will hit him twenty, thirty, and forty years down the road.

Like a flash, I knew exactly how to accomplish that. I jumped out of bed and got dressed.

It was 2:00 a.m.

Perfect.

I went downstairs and woke Kai up.

And that is how we found ourselves driving to Walmart in the few hours before dawn on a Wednesday.

Once we got in the car, a groggy Kai asked, "Dad, where are we going?"

"You'll see," I said. "I promise this will not take more than twenty minutes. After that, you can get back to bed and sleep in as long as you want."

Two miles down the road, we pulled into the parking lot of a Walmart Supercenter. This store is always open.

Working at Walmart from 11:00 p.m. to 6:00 a.m. are employees who struggle to find work elsewhere. Sure, there are some doing their best to make ends meet—young and old (though not retirees, who work only the day shifts), different backgrounds and ethnicities. These individuals are engaged, happy to have work, and working hard to advance. They want to be there, and you can see it in their eyes, in how they carry themselves, and in how they speak.

But the vast majority working this shift tend to be employees who truly don't want to be there. Their body language is different. How they interact with you is different. The look in their eye is different.

I suppose every job has this phenomenon to varying degrees: those who want to excel, those who don't want to be there, and all points in between. But you tend to see more of this segment working the graveyard at Walmart. If you don't believe me, go to a Walmart or any other twenty-four-hour retailer or department store at 2:00 a.m. and see for yourself.

I want to be clear here—and you'll see how I phrased it to Kai in the next paragraph—I am not poking fun at anyone here, shaming anyone, or otherwise trying to be mean-spirited. I have deep empathy for all those working jobs they may not enjoy in less-than-ideal circumstances. But many are there because of the choices they made in an earlier phase of their lives. If you can get a few to open up and talk to you candidly, their stories reveal this truth.

As we parked, I said, "Kai, listen. I am not in any way trying to be demeaning, disrespectful, or belittling to anyone or any organization. But we're about to go inside, and I want you to observe. You will see men and women in their thirties, forties, and fifties stocking and cleaning to prepare for tomorrow's rush. I don't know any of these people. However, I am betting that when they were asked at your age, 'What do you want to do when you grow up?', not one of them said, 'I want to restock shelves at 2:00 a.m.' or 'I want to push a broom for hours every morning before the daily rush.'"

With that, we got out of the car and walked across the near-empty parking lot to the brightly lit entrance.

As we walked through the sliding glass doors, it was as if I had called the manager, told him what I was going to do, and asked him to stage his early morning workers for maximum effect.

There were people cleaning, preparing food displays, restocking shelves, sweeping, and mopping. We could spot many whose body language seemed to say they had limited choices in their lives and weren't happy about having to be there. It was as if they were stuck and wondering, how did I get here?

As we got to one aisle where we had a little privacy, I said quietly, "Kai, many of these people do what they do because they have limited options. Some were limited by their circumstances, but many were limited by their choices. You're fortunate in that your circumstances are not a limiting factor, so it will all come down to your choices. When you choose to live Easy-Hard, you limit your options. When you decide to live Hard-Easy, you maximize your options to have endless opportunities, including the ability to accomplish your dreams."

I could now tell the wheels in Kai's head were spinning—fast.

We continued our tour of the store. At another point, I slowed down and quietly said, "Kai, life is a long road, and I want you to not only be happy traveling it but to also love each and every step. Listen, there's nothing shameful about working hard, no matter what you do. If you're truly happy in a job like this, then I'll be proud of you. I want you to make the floor as clean as you possibly can and create the most organized, gorgeously stocked shelves anyone has ever seen so you're proud of your work. I love you no matter what. I just want you to be happy."

I paused. "But, son, I don't believe this is the future you envision for yourself."

He slowly shook his head. "It's not."

"But this is the future you are pursuing—and you don't even know it. This is what I'm talking about every time I give you the Easy-Hard or Hard-Easy speech. You have every opportunity at your disposal, so it's your choices that matter the most. What do you really want?"

As we walked outside and got in the car, it was deathly quiet. Neither of us said anything.

As we neared home, Kai looked at me and said, "Dad, I get it."

Kai now had his why.

I smiled and said, "I love you."

Aftermath

How is Kai's homework now?

He's not getting straight As.

But now he gets mostly As, a few Bs, and an occasional C. And that's good. He has even been asked to join the honors math class as he starts his sophomore year in high school. Not bad for a student with a GPA of 1.25 just a few semesters ago. But you know what's better?

The father-son wrestling match we used to have every day has stopped. I do not tell Kai when, where, and how to do his homework. He manages it himself.

Is he perfect? No, but he is far better at self-management than when I was doing it for him. Now when I ask him about homework, and if I can help, he will often say, "Dad, I got this."

And now I believe him.

Occasionally I have to nudge him in the right direction, and I do it with one word. I just have to say, "Walmart." He will smile and say, "Dad, I'm on it."

Chapter Recap

Key concepts and takeaways from chapter 2:

- While you cannot impose wisdom on others, you can help them find their why.
- The concept of Hard-Easy is simple, but it's easy to ignore or take for granted.

Pause and Think

- In what areas of your life are you most resistant to living Hard-Easy?
- What whys can you identify that encourage you to live Hard-Easy in spite of that resistance?
- Are you more like A.J. and trusting of wisdom, or are you more like Kai and want to see things for yourself?

CHAPTER 3

NEANDERTHALS DON'T HAVE 401(K)S

The Genetic "Hard" Wiring of the Instant-Gratification-Craving, Easy-Hard Brain and How to Beat It

Living Easy-Hard is a constant temptation. A big part of that temptation is our human desire for instant gratification. In this chapter, we'll discuss where the impulse for instant gratification comes from and how it operates in our lives. When we have this knowledge, we are better able to overcome that impulse.

Imagine you are a Neanderthal.

Prominent brow. Big, jutting jaw. Hairier than your old uncle Dmitri. You smell rank—an intense, musky blend of body odor, grime, smoke, and bodily excretions.

Toilet paper and cologne have yet to be invented.

And here you are, doused in mud, with the rest of your band of hunters—eight of you.

Kronk, the oldest, has seen enough winters that his hair has turned the color of snow. Morch, the second youngest, is missing an eye, ear, and two fingers.

You're waiting for the mammoths. You can see the sun glistening off their wooly pelts and the white plumes of their breath. They're coming closer—closer to your ambush.

When the hunt is over, the entire tribe comes to feast on and harvest the meat.

Your first item of business is clear—gorge. Then you rest a few hours and gorge again.

This manner of eating is key to your survival. It's also why it will take you hundreds of thousands of years before one of your descendants comes up with the idea of a 401(k). The hominin brain is *hardwired*—or *easy*-wired, in this case—for an Easy-Hard life.

The Evolution of Instant Gratification

From *Australopithecus* to *Homo erectus* to Neanderthals to *Homo sapiens*, our brains have evolved to seek instant gratification.

And until saber-tooth tigers stopped snacking on us and microwave pizza pockets were invented, that do-it-now impulse helped keep our species—and progenitor species—alive.

You just killed an antelope? Gorge on it, because you don't know when your next meal will come.

We all still have that primal part of our brain firing its powerful, impulsive imperatives across our synapses.

If evolution had stopped tinkering with our *Homo sapien* brains, we might still be running around like instant-gratification heat-seeking missiles. But instead, nature added a new wing onto our brains: the prefrontal cortex.

Introducing Your Prefrontal Cortex

The prefrontal cortex is the newest section of your gray matter. It's like the responsible adult of our brain: it has the power to override the older, feral regions of the brain that kept us alive by demanding we eat, drink, mate, and fulfill our wants and desires *now*.

But impulse control doesn't happen automatically. It's like a muscle—the more you exercise it, the stronger the prefrontal cortex's ability to control your impulses becomes. The less you use it, the more it atrophies. People who don't practice restraint jeopardize a future they can't even conceive is possible.

Our primal lizard brains and our prefrontal cortexes, as science and psychology demonstrate, are locked in a constant tug-of-war.

Jackpot—Lottery Winners and Losers

"Okay," you may say. "Some people simply get lucky. They are the outliers who live Easy-Easy."

Remember, the law of Hard-Easy is a natural law. You jump off a cliff, gravity immediately jerks you downward. You hit a baseball, it rockets in the opposite direction of your bat with an equal and opposite force. You live Easy-Hard, at some point Hard catches you and all the Easy dies on the vine.

Let's look at lottery winners.

When their number comes up, defying all reasonable odds, these people get handed a check for more money than they could have earned over several lifetimes. Surely, for the rest of their lives, they are on Easy Street. Right?

But that's not typically what happens. Because, like all of us, lottery winners have little Neanderthals inside their heads.

Approximately 70 percent of large-jackpot lottery winners go bankrupt. Apparently, the huge amount of money dropped into their laps is so vast the value of the cash becomes an abstraction void of meaning. It would be easier for them to count the grains of sand on the beach than to count the money they just received. There seems to be no conceivable end to their newfound wealth.[2]

Therefore, it is *hard* to pay attention to how much they're spending and *hard* to budget.

It's *hard* to turn away the money-grubbing near and distant relatives who show up to ask for cash—they don't want to seem selfish.

It's *hard* not to spend their money on all the luxurious indulgences they've ever fantasized about but could never afford.

It's *easy* now! They have all the money in the world, practically.

Easy living gives way to hard living when all that money evaporates and the lottery winners can't figure out why they're forced into filing Chapter 11, financially poorer than before they won the lottery!

And it's not just lottery winners. Think of the athletes, entertainers, and business people who earn a fortune in a relatively short amount of time only to fritter it all away and end up bankrupt.

Why does that happen?

The Hard-Easy Paradox

There tends to be a direct correlation between how difficult something is to obtain and how much we value it.

That applies to money, material goods, and life experiences. If your rich friend gets a brand-new car for her sixteenth birthday and you don't get a car but have to get part-time jobs and save for a year and buy your own used car when you're seventeen—who do you think will value their car more?

Let's take it a step further: What if you both wreck your cars? Your friend's parents are going to buy her a new one. You will have to spend another year working to earn money to buy another used car. Which of you will miss the wrecked car more? You will, the person who had to *work for it*.

And that's where winning the lottery goes bad. Very, very bad. The winners tend to take the money for granted since they did nothing to earn it. And so they spend it like it means nothing until they have nothing left.

So, are we just doomed to impulsive, Easy-Hard living thanks to our genetic inheritance? No. Fortunately for us, we have a way to beat the Neanderthal brain.

The Gift-Card Study

In 2004, researchers at Princeton University headed up a multidisciplinary study involving four universities. The team consisted of four heavy-hitters: Jonathan Cohen and Samuel McClure, at Princeton's Center for the Study of Brain, Mind, and Behavior; David

Laibson, professor of economics at Harvard University; and George Loewenstein, professor of economics and psychology at Carnegie Mellon University.

The four wanted to see which neural systems were involved during problem-solving and how the resultant behavior competed or cooperated between these neural systems. In other words, they wanted to see how the pathways in our brains thrive or short-circuit as we try to make a decision.

Fourteen students were given gift cards ranging from five to forty dollars. They could take the gift card immediately, or they could wait between two to six weeks and get a gift card in a larger amount. They were given several minutes to think about it and then choose. While they decided what to do, their brain activity was mapped using an MRI.

Here's what they found: The students who surrendered to instant gratification (Easy-Hard) and took the gift card immediately registered the most activity in the part of their brain where emotion originates. They displayed weak activity in the part dedicated to abstract, analytical reasoning. They did not allow their analytical side to engage and take part in the decision.

The students who decided to wait for gift cards loaded with more money showed diametrically opposite brain function. Their analytic pathways lit up like a Christmas tree, and their emotional brainwaves gave off nothing more than a dim glow. They kept the emotional side in check and did not allow it to hijack their decision-making.

The researchers concluded that when impulsive decisions are made, emotions choke out reason. (I can personally attest to this when the decision involves whether or not to binge on chilled Thin Mint Girl Scout Cookies.)

Harvard's Laibson had this to say:

> Our emotional brain has a hard time imagining the future, even though our logical brain clearly sees the future consequences of our current actions. . . . Our emotional brain wants to max out the credit card, order dessert and smoke a cigarette. Our

logical brain knows we should save for retirement, go for a jog and quit smoking. To understand why we feel internally conflicted, it will help to know how myopic and forward-looking brain systems value rewards and how these systems talk to one another.[3]

Carnegie Mellon's Lowenstein went on to say:

Our results help explain how and why a wide range of situations that produce emotional reactions, such as the sight, touch or smell of a desirable object, often cause people to take impulsive actions that they later regret.[4]

Such psychological cues, according to Lowenstein, are known to trigger dopamine-related circuits in the brain similar to the ones that responded to immediate rewards. It also helps explain some aspects of addiction, such as why drug addicts become so focused on immediate gratification when they are craving a drug.

Did you catch that? Those who live Easy-Hard—who give in to instant gratification—trigger a dopamine-induced euphoria on par with drug addiction.

That's probably what was happening in Kai's brain when he avoided his homework in favor of playing video games or spending time with his friends. It's hard to fault him for wanting to chase that high, but it was imperative to teach him the importance of recognizing and controlling those Easy impulses before the Hard caught up with him.

Addict Yourself to Hard-Easy

As the gift-card study tells us, impulsive behavior is not the only way to get your brain to release dopamine. You can get a sense of euphoria—although not quite to the same intensity—when you delay gratification (living Hard-Easy). When you delay gratification and exert self-control, the parts of your brain responsible for analysis are stimulated (remember the prefrontal cortex), and you get a pleasurable sensation, a kind of euphoria.

The more you use those pathways, the stronger they become. Until one day you find it's easier to make the better choice for the situation, even if it's hard.

Let's look at money for a moment. They say money can't buy happiness, but using delayed gratification and saving it just might.

In a survey of 1,025 American adults, it was found that saving money could have a significant positive impact on your happiness. Of those who had a savings account, 38 percent reported feeling extremely or very happy, compared to 29 percent of those without a savings account.[5]

Savers indicated that setting money away for a rainy day made them feel better about themselves. When asked why, they said it helped them face the unknown, gave them inner peace, and made them feel proud and in control.

The only habit that trumped saving money on the happiness meter was enjoying strong relationships with family and friends. (More on this in chapter 16.)

Practicing (delayed gratification) doesn't always make *perfect*, despite the cliché. But it does create patience, strong character, and new opportunities. You may even become an expert, as we'll soon learn.

The Ten-Thousand-Hour Rule

More than four decades ago, Herbert Simon and William Chase published a paper on the nature of expertise in chess. They wrote: "We would estimate, very roughly, that a master has spent perhaps 10,000 to 50,000 hours staring at chess positions."[6]

Let's put that number in perspective. Imagine practicing the tuba. You do it twenty hours a week, fifty weeks a year. That seems like a lot. But at that rate, it would take you ten long years to achieve expert-level mastery of the tuba—or any given skill.

After Simon and Chase's publication, more research followed looking at expertise in a variety of fields and the time it takes to reach varying degrees of excellence and mastery.

In his book, *Outliers*, Malcolm Gladwell coined this as the "ten-thousand-hour rule."

There has been a great deal of debate about this rule in recent years—about whether it's valid or not and about what exactly it signifies. So let's clarify those counterarguments before I make a Hard-Easy point about it.

First, there are some skills that, no matter how much we practice, we may never master. For example, I will probably never become a master brain surgeon, Olympic-level sprinter, or theoretical mathematician. So ten thousand hours isn't the magical threshold to mastery, regardless of skill. More likely, you will become a master at a skill in which you have natural aptitude by practicing it that many hours.

Another addendum to the ten-thousand-hour rule comes from journalist and author David Epstein, who says the rule becomes the rationale for people to hyperspecialize at something from a young age (think of Tiger Woods golfing from age two). Angela Chen of *The Verge* said, "Epstein gathered studies that looked at the development of elite athletes and saw that the trend was not early specialization. Rather, in almost every sport, there was a 'sampling period' where athletes learned about their own abilities and interests. The athletes who delayed specialization were often better than their specialized peers, who plateaued at lower levels." So if we agree with Epstein, Tiger was an anomaly.[7]

Caveat notwithstanding, if you do devote that amount of practice to skills you don't have an aptitude for—or are simply terrible at— you will get better than you were. But most likely you will not attain expert level.

When it comes right down to it, you don't need MRIs or Ivy-League professors to prove the science behind forming habits and behavioral patterns. Common sense tells you that the more you repeat something, the easier it becomes.

Aristotle figured it out 2,400 years ago when he said, "We are what we repeatedly do. Excellence, then, is not an act but a habit." That applies to living Hard-Easy, too. It is a skill, and the more you practice delayed gratification to pursue the Hard path, the better you will get—and the better it will feel each time.

Do you have to be an expert-level Hard-Easy master with ten thousand hours' practice in saying no to your Neanderthal brain?

No.

The more you exercise your analysis-based neural pathways by exerting self-control and triggering euphoria for delayed gratification, the better you become at Hard-Easy.

So it appears Aristotle and my friend Gordon are on the same wavelength.

Embrace Boredom and Find Excellence

"Repetition can be boring or tedious, which is why so few people ever master anything."[8]

As a kid, I played baseball. My father played semipro and had visions of me carrying on his love for the game. He pitched to me constantly. As I got older, he would take me to batting cages where pitching machines would pitch me ball after ball.

At one local batting cage, there was an old, salty manager. For over twenty years he watched endless youngsters try to learn to hit a baseball. He occasionally gave my dad coaching tips to help me be a better hitter.

One day I overheard my father say, "I am sure you have seen endless kids learn to hit." He smiled and said, "I've seen 'em all." Then dad asked, "What one attribute, more than any other, guarantees a great batter?" I will never forget his answer. "Easy—the mental fortitude to handle the monotonous boredom of practicing every day for hours." He went on: "Many come because it is fun, but soon the fun of hitting fades and the hard part of perfecting your swing sets in. That's when they quit."

If you seek greatness, you have to commit yourself to mastery, and that can be hard. If you are dabbling, you are not fully committed. Perfecting a skill is hard and sometimes boring. Push through the boredom and find Easy in excellence.

Chapter Recap

Key concepts and takeaways from chapter 3:

- Our brains are genetically hardwired for instant gratification.
- We have the ability to resist impulses and delay gratification.
- You can make a habit of Easy-Hard or Hard-Easy. Both yield euphoria.
- The more you practice resisting instant gratification, the easier it becomes.
- Embrace the boredom of Hard and find the excellence of Easy.

Pause and Think

- When we procrastinate, we're usually seeking instant gratification by putting off the hard task. What kinds of things do you tend to procrastinate? Start with areas such as relationships, spirituality, education, career, retirement, and travel.
- From your procrastination list, pick out the trends that will yield the future results you most want to avoid.
- Narrow your list to two or three ways you tend toward Easy-Hard. Keep this list close at hand.

CHAPTER 4

SEDUCED BY EASY
How Easy Tricks You and How You Can Fight Back

Easy haunts us in many ways and can even trick us into thinking we're living Hard. This chapter will help you understand Easy's tactics so you can avoid falling for them. It will also equip you to fight your way back to Hard-Easy.

Easy is a boldfaced, seductive, dirty liar.

Easy tells you what you want to hear and lets you off the hook instead of holding you accountable.

Easy is not to be trusted under any circumstance because it takes your fears and uses them against you, and it's a master marketer, making a pitch that sounds amazingly good to our Neanderthal brain.

The Hard Path Brings Failure and Pain: Temporary Stops on the Way to Easy

Every day, several times a day, you'll find yourself at a crossroads. The Hard path and the Easy path await you. The Hard looks unpleasant. Swamps. Quicksand. Terrifyingly steep cliffs. Hailstorms and darkness.

And then there's Easy. This path descends gently down through a sunshine-filled meadow. There's no resistance, no obstacles, nothing intimidating.

So, the question is, how do you look Easy in its come-hither eyes every day—and turn away to face the often-excruciating, terrifying path of Hard?

In Frank Herbert's book *Dune*, an organization uses a litany to combat fear. It begins, "I must not fear. Fear is the mind-killer."[9] Fear is also one of Easy's minions.

Ordinary people accomplish mind-blowing feats of success all the time. But if they're ordinary, how do they achieve the extraordinary? They're not more intelligent, wealthy, capable, or courageous than the average person. They feel all the fear and doubt the rest of us do.

What enables them to accomplish great things is that they do the hard things that brighter, richer, more capable individuals don't have the discipline to make a reality.

Choosing to live Hard-Easy doesn't immunize us from failure and disappointment. The more difficult something is to accomplish, the higher the rate of failure.

But here's the radical difference in your mindset when you commit to the Hard path. When we live Hard-Easy, we see failure not as an impenetrable wall but as a stepping-stone to ultimate success.

Focus on the Fix

Striving for the reward won't take away the pain, exhaustion, or trials staring you in the face. It will, however, provide motivation to keep going. In the previous chapter, we talked about addicting yourself to Hard-Easy. I want you to crave the high that comes when you achieve your ultimate reward—and when you reach the smaller goals on the way to the finish line.

It's the endorphin rush after the long run, the view from the summit after climbing a mountain, either literal or figurative.

I think a lot about the fix because I like to take action when things aren't going as well as I'd like.

Some of the people who have literally changed the world are the ones focused on the fix. A great example? Thomas Edison—someone we should think about every time we walk into a dark room and reach for the light switch.

Edison made more than ten thousand prototypes before he hit on the right combination of materials and processes to create an efficient light bulb. When mocked by a reporter for how often he had failed, Edison famously quipped, "I have not failed. I've just found ten thousand ways that won't work."

Edison lived Hard-Easy.

But imagine if he had chosen the seductive Easy-Hard path at any point along the ten-thousand-prototype journey.

At prototype #2—or prototype #9,999 for that matter—what if Edison had said, "Damn, this is way too hard. I can't believe I've wasted all my time on this. I could have been playing badminton with my neighbor Mr. Davis or taking great naps in my hammock."

However, he didn't. Every day, he ignored the siren song of Easy and stepped purposefully onto the thorny path of Hard.

And his light bulb became the cornerstone product in the rise of General Electric. Edison is a legendary figure—an archetype of genius and success—even in our day. But if he had given up after one of his ten thousand failures—if he had not focused on the fix and instead played more badminton—we probably wouldn't even know his name today.

"Many of life's failures," Edison said, "are people who did not realize how close they were to success when they gave up."

Or, in the context of this book, those who failed are those who chose the sexy, nearly irresistible allure of Easy.

Words Matter

Think of disappointment, discouragement, and doubt as a pack of velociraptors. They all hunt together to bring you down on behalf of their master, Easy-Hard.

Just because you start down the path of Hard-Easy doesn't mean Easy-Hard has given up on you. It still wants your soul.

How do you get these snarling, razor-toothed predators to transform into elation, courage, and belief—creatures that serve you instead of hunt you?

What I'm about to say will sound overly simplistic at first. But it's how you begin to condition your synapses for a Pavlovian Hard-Easy response in the face of those velociraptors who prefer you as the docile prey of Easy-Hard.

You can begin to dispel disappointment, discouragement, and doubt with a phrase that hardens your resolve and sharpens your focus. That phrase is to remind you to choose, and stay on, the hard path. That phrase is: "Bring it, Hard!"

You were probably expecting some ancient Egyptian incantation that summons supernatural forces to propel you to success.

Nope.

Here's how "Bring it, Hard!" works.

Have you ever watched a boxing match where one opponent lands a devastating blow?

Then the just-punched opponent flashes a sinister grin and slowly shakes his head as if to say, "Is that the best you got?" He wryly gestures to his opponent to come forward and try again. It's a reaction aimed at disheartening, deflating, and demoralizing his opponent.

It's also a phrase that can infuse the boxer who was punched with a rush of determination, confidence, and defiance.

Nothing will demoralize the velociraptors more than you staring them in the face and saying, "Bring it, Hard!"

It's a rallying cry. Sports teams have their versions. Militaries have theirs. Everyday people have still others. But "Bring it, Hard!" is mine. It's a motto that sums up a sense of resolve and is designed to stoke the emotions that bring out the fight in you. Since this book is about Hard-Easy, we'll make our phrase one that invites Hard to give us its best shot.

Embodying the Attitude of "Bring it, Hard!"

The following story captures the attitude of "Bring it, Hard!" and the art of psyching out the forces opposing you.

In June of 1973, Secretariat (lovingly known as Big Red), jockeyed by Ron Turcotte, entered in the Belmont Stakes for a chance at winning the Triple Crown and indisputably going down as the best Thoroughbred racehorse ever. Secretariat's primary opponent was Sham, ridden by Laffit Pincay.

Horse-racing aficionados (i.e., owners, trainers, writers, etc.) believed Turcotte would stalk the other horses to the far turn, then let Secretariat loose for a triumphant sprint to the wire. Secretariat was bred for speed, while Sham was bred for endurance. Pincay's strategy was to go out hard and use Sham's long-distance breeding and stamina and an early fast pace to take the fight out of Secretariat. The experts watched, their mouths open in utter disbelief, as they were soon to be proven wrong.

Secretariat held the rail, thundering past his challengers until he was eyeball to eyeball with Sham as they entered the first turn. The roaring of the crowd quieted. I am sure many were wondering, "Did Turcotte push Secretariat too soon?"

Sham and Secretariat raced side by side around the turn, but then Sham took the lead by a head, then a neck, then a half-length. Pincay was driving Sham at a world-record pace.

Would Sham at long last have his day in the sun? Would his strategy to go out fast win the day? Would Sham's long-distance pedigree drain Secretariat's strength during a flat-out sprint over Belmont's gruelingly long one-and-a-half miles?

At the midpoint on the backstretch, it seemed as if Secretariat was pulling even with and looking directly at Sham. Both jockeys indicated later that it was at this point the race was decided.

Secretariat, with one eye-to-eye glance, seemed to say to Sham, "Is that the best you got?"

You could almost see Sham's resolve and fight melt. You can find the race on YouTube—check it out and watch for that moment.

Pincay said he stopped pushing Sham, who had nothing more to give. In fact, Sham faded so much the pack of horses that had been many lengths behind the two leaders caught and passed him. Sham finished in last place.

After passing Sham, Turcotte loosened up on the reins and let Secretariat run his race. Secretariat pulled ahead, first his head and neck, then his powerful auburn-colored chest. Soon, spectators could clearly see his muscular hindquarters methodically driving him forward with increasing power and speed.

Secretariat finished the race at 2:24—the fastest Belmont ever, shattering the track record by an absurd 2.6 seconds and setting a new world record for 1.5 miles on a dirt course—a record many believe will never be broken. The second-place horse, Twice a Prince, was a mind-blowing thirty-one lengths back.

I know I've talked about velociraptors and racehorses in this chapter. The point is, when you face the terror or dread of the obstacles and unpleasantries clogging the path of Hard, don't shy away from them. Don't let doubt herd you in the opposite direction. Don't let the specters of past disappointments melt your resolve.

Utter these magic words, even if you don't quite have faith in them yet: "Bring it, Hard!"

Is Saying "Bring it, Hard!" Easier Said Than Done? Is It an Easy-Hard Solution?

While it is true that things are easier said than done, we have to start somewhere. The truth is that *after* you've said "Bring it, Hard!", you'll still have days, months, years, and sometimes even decades of Hard ahead of you—you won't be Secretariat in all of your races. But by uttering these words, you start to change your mindset. When you change your mindset, you change your thoughts. When you change your thoughts, you change your actions. When you change your actions, you change *you*.

Remember, words matter. Self-talk matters. If you're feeding your synapses negative words and ideas, that has an effect on who you become. People who live Easy-Hard often beat themselves up with regrets over mistakes. It's important to not beat yourself up.

Self-Sabotage: The Victim Mentality

Another type of negative self-talk that leads to a negative mindset and negative actions is assuming the victim mentality.

Let's be clear: I am not saying those who are victimized are not justified in feeling like victims. What I'm talking about is a type of feeling that undermines our agency and enslaves us to an incapacitating belief—that we are victims and therefore nothing can be done. This is regardless of how justified the belief may be.

As long as you believe you are a victim—no matter how justified you are in that belief—and you believe your circumstance is something or someone else's fault, *you have no ability to change it.*

But don't take my word for it.

Elizabeth Smart

Elizabeth Smart was fourteen when she was kidnapped from her bedroom in Salt Lake City, Utah, at knifepoint. Her abductor, Brian David Mitchell, took her into the foothills above Salt Lake. There, she was held captive—chained to a tree—by Mitchell and his wife, Wanda Barzee. Mitchell raped Smart daily. He also threatened to kill her family if she tried to escape.

Nine months later, in Sandy, Utah, someone spotted Mitchell and called the police. Smart and Barzee were with him and wearing disguises. Smart wore a gray wig, sunglasses, and a veil. But she was recognized. At last, she had been rescued.

This part of her ordeal was over.

But now she was facing the post-traumatic stress, the guilt, the shame, the anger, the terror, the helplessness—everything a victim of sexual assault and abduction must face.

How could she overcome it?

Let her tell you.

Speaking at Chicago's Sage YMCA in 2018, Smart said she does not let the horrifying experience of the past rule her today. "We all have a story, we all have a past," she said. "We all have extra baggage."

And despite negative experiences—and how easy it is to get stuck in them and allow the trauma to keep victimizing us—Smart said, "Ultimately, it is not what defines you."

After the first rape—on the first day of her captivity—this fourteen-year-old middle-schooler said, "I felt ruined, beyond help. How could my parents want me back? There was no light, no hope, nothing to hold on to, nothing to survive for. . . . How could this happen to me?"

After her rescue, still dealing with these feelings, as all victims of abuse do, Smart's mom's words helped her to refuse victimhood. She told Elizabeth to "Be happy . . . live your life. Don't allow them to steal more of your life."[10]

Smart has refused to let Mitchell and Barzee steal more of her life. At the time of this writing, at age thirty-two, she is married and the mother of three. She is also an activist, journalist, and author of the *New York Times* best-selling autobiography *My Story*.

That's not all.

- She has testified before Congress to support legislation against sexual predators.
- She spoke at a women's conference hosted by Maria Shriver on overcoming the obstacles in your life.
- She founded the Elizabeth Smart Foundation to support the Internet Crimes Against Children Task Force and educates children about violent and sexual crime. The foundation is combining forces with Operation Underground Railroad to fight human trafficking.
- She was a commentator for ABC News, specifically reporting on missing persons.
- She testified in the Utah State House of Representatives in favor of a bill creating an optional curriculum that trains kids on preventing and reporting child sexual abuse.
- She was a correspondent on the show *Crime Watch Daily*.[11]

She's done all that and more. She has followed her mother's mantra: "Don't allow them to steal more of your life." And she encourages others facing the depths of uncontrollable, challenging times to follow that mantra too.

As reported in *People* by Eunice Oh, Elizabeth advised fellow abduction and rape victim, Jaycee Dugard, "[Don't let] this horrible event take over and consume the rest of your life. I would just encourage her to find different passions in life and continually push forward and learn more and reach more for them and not to look behind, because there's a lot out there."[12]

Some might think it's easy for Smart to say, "Don't let this horrible event take over and consume the rest of your life." Easy to say, much harder to do.

Yes, quite true.

Smart knows what types of feelings and thoughts filled her head and threatened to destroy her.

She gave one example of this in a speech on human trafficking at Johns Hopkins University in 2013:

> I'll never forget how I felt lying there on the ground. I felt like my soul had been crushed. I felt like I wasn't even human anymore. How could anybody love me or want me or care about me? I felt like life had no more meaning to it. . . . I felt so dirty and so filthy. Who could want me now?
>
> I remember in school one time, I had a teacher who was talking about abstinence. She said, "Imagine you're a stick a gum. If you have sex, it's like you're being chewed. And if you do that a bunch of times, you're going to become an old piece of gum, and who's going to want you after that?" I thought, "Oh, my gosh, I'm that chewed-up piece of gum. Nobody rechews a piece of gum; you throw it away." And that's how easy it is to feel like you no longer have worth, you no longer have value. Why would it even be worth screaming out? Why would it even make a difference if you are rescued? Your life still has no value.[13]

Side note: I am quoting Elizabeth Smart. But I must make it known that I (along with Elizabeth Smart) adamantly disagree with her teacher and the gum/sex analogy. In my opinion, this is shaming at its worst, and individuals and organizations who encourage this type of psychological shaming are absolutely misguided. They give no hope, no mercy. Simply put, they are evil. We have to stop these shamed-based ideas, which do far more harm than good. (More on shame in chapter 12).

These feelings and thoughts tormented her during her captivity and were the demons she had to defeat daily after her rescue.

To connect Smart's experience back to our idea of "Bring it, Hard!" It's not difficult to imagine the phrase "Don't allow them to steal more of your life" as Smart's rallying cry. Her power phrase. Her way of looking fear, abuse, shame, and doubt in the eye and saying, "Is that all you got? I'm *not* going to let you define me or control me. I'm not allowing you to steal more of my life."

Elizabeth used that mantra to propel her forward, to keep her head and heart clear, and to use her experience and voice to help others.

Rejecting the Victim Mentality and Discovering What Success *Really* Looks Like

What does it look like to reject the victim mentality and take the Hard-Easy path? Here are a couple of case studies that illustrate that battle within.

Case Study #1

Let me tell you about one of the most successful people I know. She's a single mom who works a full-time, midlevel management job at an insurance company. She loves her children, works earnestly at a tedious job that would put me in the loony bin, and lives within her means. Here's something else you should know about her: she's always had a passion for photography.

It would certainly be easy for her to tuck her passion for photography away in the midst of all the demands and pressures of life. It would also be easy for her to blame life for not giving her enough time to pursue her passion.

But she doesn't.

She packs her digital camera in her oversized purse everywhere she goes. As she walks through a parking lot, she sees what no one else would even notice. She takes pictures that frame the mundane as extraordinary.

But she doesn't stop there. She turns her pictures into posters and prints. She doesn't make much money selling her pictures, but guess what? She's selling them. She has customers. People buy her prints, and she receives little boosts of validation.

She's taking steps to fulfill her dream of being a full-time photographer. Even better, she's happy since she's nurturing the artistic imperative in her heart.

Was it hard for her to save up for the camera equipment she wanted while providing for her family on her own? Most definitely. Is it hard for her to carry her equipment with her as she rushes to appointments, meetings, and her kids' activities? Yes. But she does it.

She shouts, "Bring it, Hard!" at her obstacles. True, there are things she has no control over. Quite a few things, actually. But how she *reacts* to her obstacles—that's all on her. She doesn't run from them. When doubts creep in, and failure strikes a blow, she does not retreat or quit. She digs in, regroups, and pushes back with greater force upon the forces opposing her.

That's rejecting the victim mentality and choosing not to let the bad circumstances of life steal another minute from you. That's a huge success.

Case Study #2

I talked to a therapist friend of mine about the Hard-Easy/Easy-Hard concept. She readily admitted that it was a "cool" concept. She even said she might start using it in her individual and group therapy sessions. But she had her doubts, too. "It might just be too tough for some people to do," she said. After all, it couldn't possibly work for everyone.

Then she started telling me some of the stories she's heard from the people she works with, like the women who have suffered years of sexual abuse (she did not give me names, yet she wanted to share various situations without violating client confidentiality). She talked about evil acts perpetrated on the innocent—acts that stunned my soul with shock and anguish.

One woman was repeatedly gang-raped by her father and uncles. Another was tied up by her cousins and forced to watch pornography as a young child. There were more—every story a portrait of unfathomable cruelty.

My emotions bounced from sad to incensed and back again.

As she related their stories, she told me these women were living Hard-Hard. Every day. There was no Easy—not even any hope of Easy down the road.

At first, I was speechless. I couldn't even relate to the kind of devastation these women were enduring.

But I still believe that, contrary to what my friend hypothesized, they were doing something hard right now in the hope that they might heal and make things easier in the future. They had reached out and decided to seek help. They had resolved to meet with a therapist and share the stories that had seared them with a sense of shame for decades. For many, that was undoubtedly a hard choice. But they did—and were doing—it.

In an unfair world, Easy is a relative concept. Easy isn't always *easy*, but it should be *less hard*. So, in a sense, my friend and I were both right, and it came down to a matter of semantics. These women had started down a path of Hard-Less Hard, the same path I'd named Hard-Easy.

These survivors now had a harder choice to make: the same choice Elizabeth Smart speaks of—surrender to the abuse and continue to allow their abusers to steal more of their lives, or fight and refuse to let their past and their abusers define them going forward.

Their mantra could be "I will be happy." Happy is the reward for doing the Hard. Survivors who succeed at this do so by taking control of their lives and doing the things they need to do to be the people they want to be.

That is the Hard-Easy thing to do. Perhaps the hardest thing to do. But I believe it can make all the difference. And in my opinion, these women had already started down that path by seeking therapy.

Fast-forward several months, and I was thinking about those women again—the ones my therapist friend said lived Hard-Hard. I asked her how they were doing.

Amazingly, they were taking steps in a positive direction. They were making progress. They'd realized an important truth: those hard times were temporary. They were over. Though these women may relive the trauma innumerable times in their heads, they could do things that allowed them to grab the reins and take the horse to the best place to cross the stream.

I realized something else about those women. Not one of them was facing her demons alone. They were able to draw strength from others. They had cheerleaders who stood with them, propped them up when they felt they couldn't go on, and encouraged them to move forward. They were doing the hard work and facing each day with courage, determination, and strength.

A Final Word about Anguish and Persevering When Persevering Sucks

When you suffer a loss or are victimized, can you discern what the hard path is? What do you do when you get help and do all the hard, or "right," things, but it's just not paying off, and meanwhile everyone is telling you that you just have to keep doing the hard things and stop seeing yourself as a victim—what then?

The best advice I can give you is to continue to lean into hard and trust that the miracle of time will soothe your heart and that the peace of Easy will soothe your soul in the long run. It sucks when bad things happen to good people. But we each ultimately have the power to choose how these ugly events will affect us.

Easy comes over time. Giving yourself time to heal, grieve, mourn, rage, and crumple is not being a victim. It's part of the process. Just remember the advice of Elizabeth Smart: "[Don't let] this horrible event take over and consume the rest of your life."

The Paralyzing Nature of Complacency

Complacency is another subtle way Easy-Hard lures you down its path—without you even realizing what you're doing. Complacency is the carbon monoxide of the soul—odorless, tasteless, and invisible—a mindset that permeates your life and suffocates your ambition.

Complacency is a form of fear. That might sound weird. You think of fear as something that terrifies you and gets your adrenaline pumping. You think of complacency, however, as something more chill than chilling. Nothing terrifying. No adrenaline. Just the sense that things are okay enough not to have to change anything.

But therein lies the fear. Complacency means you're afraid to change something. You might be in an easy stasis in your life. Status quo. You've got the routine going, you've found your comfort zone, and you're afraid to change it up.

Your life might, in fact, be good enough. You might have everything you've ever wanted. You might be blissfully happy. You might run five miles a day, have no debt, contribute to a dynamite retirement plan, love your job, and do volunteer work. So what then? Isn't that good enough?

If that's you, let me ask this: What if this version of your life is really just prototype 9,999 and if you give up now you never get to prototype 10,000—your "Edison light bulb" of a life?

The Complacent Mouse

The desert snake has an interesting problem. It can't out-slither the rodents it hunts, so it must ambush its prey.

The snake lies patiently in the shade of a rock, relatively out in the open. It doesn't move.

The mouse can often see the snake, but as long as it stays out of range of the fangs, it's not in danger. If the snake makes a move, the mouse knows it can outrun it.

The mouse might be on high alert at first, peeking over every now and again just to make sure the serpent hasn't twitched.

It hasn't.

Some mice grow accustomed to the snake's presence and begin to take for granted that it won't move. Over time the mouse becomes more desensitized to the danger posed by the snake.

One of these mice might take small steps toward the snake to pick up a yummy seed, then closer still to snag a small piece of cactus fruit. Tiny step by tiny step, it moves closer to the serpent.

One step by itself does not matter. Perhaps two don't. But over time, each step accumulates and closes the distance toward the snake.

Then, when the rodent least expects it, WHAM, the snake strikes. The attack is hard, fast, and without warning. The fangs sink in, the venom squirts into the body, the mouse shrieks and convulses—and it's over. The rodent pays a harsh price for its gradual accumulation of unwise choices.

So it is with us. Another aspect of complacency is that when we make poor choices, we become more and more comfortable with the danger we put ourselves in.

One more cigarette will not kill me. One more night of partying with drugs and alcohol will not hurt. Skipping this homework assignment is not going to keep me out of college. Fudging this year's tax return won't be a big deal—I did it last year, and no one caught me.

Seemingly small but bad decisions are not that big a deal. The sky is not falling; the serpent has not struck us. At times we may even find that we are experiencing success despite our poor actions. Because the snake never seems to move, we naively go from day to day, completely blind to the law of Hard-Easy, making the same mistakes and taking the same shortcuts, with no apparent consequences. The snake did not strike yesterday, so obviously he will not strike today. Nothing bad has happened, ergo, nothing bad will happen.

Going back to our mouse friend—suppose the very first time it took a step toward the distant snake, the snake struck out at it. The snake would have been too far away to hit, but the mouse's survival instincts would be on high alert. It would instantly change its behavior—sprinting as far away from the danger as possible and not inching another step closer.

If you got a ticket every time you went even one mile over the speed limit, you would have an immediate legal punishment indelibly linked with speeding, and you would take fast and proactive steps to correct your bad judgment. In fact, if this were the case for all of us, there would be no speeding at all.

But that's not how it works. We go one or two miles over the speed limit and never have a problem, so we push it to four or five miles over the speed limit. Still no problem. In fact, we have even cruised by the state trooper occasionally. He was cool—all he did was wave. No harm done.

Speeding obviously does not matter, we tell ourselves. We are safe. So we grow more and more complacent, more and more careless. Now we are regularly doing ten to fifteen miles over the speed limit. And one day we see those flashing lights in our review mirror, and our heart starts pounding. The consequence has caught us.

And getting a ticket is the best possible consequence you can get. What if while speeding you misjudge a curve, hit black ice, nod off for a moment, or get distracted for a split second with the "important" text you have been waiting for? Wreckage of machine and body, and even death, may await you and others. At that moment you will be like the complacent mouse who has wandered too close to the snake and now feels the fangs sink in.

Take Your Complacency Temperature

In those moments when your life seems devoid of chaos—when you think you're truly happy—is when it's more important than ever to do some intense self-examination.

Ask yourself why your life is good enough. If you can think of plenty of times in the last six months where you've congratulated yourself on achieving a goal or being happy, perhaps you're not complacent—you're just at peace with the results of your trek along the path of Hard-Easy.

On the other hand, if your inventory seems crowded with "I wish I could have" or "I put up with that, but it's okay," your complacency detector is beeping. And you should take notice.

I have a dear friend of thirty years who smokes like a chimney. Whenever I tell him how much his smoking worries me—which is often—he tells me, "I'm as healthy as a horse, and I've been smoking forever. Why should I stop now?"

Because he is complacent, it's easy for him to maintain his unhealthy habit. It allows him to reject a path that, deep down, he really fears: giving up something he enjoys and something his body and brain are addicted to. My friend is aware of the cravings, withdrawals, and other side effects he would face on this journey. Why go through all that pain?

I have another friend who is extremely overweight. For many years I have watched her consume bags of Doritos while downing a two-liter of Dr Pepper for breakfast. Her pantry is filled with the worst of the worst when it comes to junk food. She has told me she doesn't like the way she looks or feels, and she immediately follows this admission with "I don't know if I want to go through the pain of losing weight." Every time I've suggested she do just one small thing to make a change, she counters it with "I don't have the energy."

Her complacency is allowing her to avoid a path that, deep down, she really fears: giving up the delicious junk food she loves and craves, facing down hunger, and putting her body through potentially painful exercise. Changing her diet and activity in order to change her life will be hard because of the many years she's been living complacently in Easy. Why go through that pain?

Complacency at its most malignant is when you know you need to change but you've already given up. You've conceded the victory because you believe that changing your course is just too hard.

If you've fallen into the complacency trap, listen to me: you *are* worth the extra effort.

Don't believe me?

Ask the people in your life. They'll tell you that your value far exceeds any of the growing pains change will cause.

My friend who smokes? I want him around for another thirty years. I wish he could see in himself the value I see in him. If he did, he might make an effort to quit, hard as it is.

My friend who needs to eat healthier? Recently she has started to make efforts to change. She has lost about eighty pounds and is looking more alive, healthy, and happy than I have seen her in years. She's found a way to face complacency down and say, "Bring it, Hard!"

Using Binoculars on the Path to Hard-Easy

Remember, at the beginning of this chapter, I pointed out how, every day, several times a day, you'll find yourself at a crossroads? The Hard-Easy path and the Easy-Hard path await you. The Hard-Easy path looks unpleasant. Swamps. Quicksand. Terrifyingly steep cliffs. Hailstorms and darkness.

And the Easy-Hard path beckons with its gentle, nondisruptive trail into a sunshine-filled meadow.

But the paths go on beyond the horizon. The Easy-Hard path that started so pleasantly leads to a hard, frightening place that's oppressive, dark, unfulfilling, frustrating, and painful, while the Hard-Easy path takes you to a glorious vista surrounded by blue skies.

I desperately want you to summon your inner warrior and shout, "Bring it, Hard!" to your life. Make the Hard-Easy changes where you need them.

Chapter Recap

Key concepts and takeaways from chapter 4:

- Easy is a liar.

- Focus on the fix.
- "Many of life's failures are people who did not realize how close they were to success when they gave up." (Thomas Edison)
- Make "Bring it, Hard!" your mantra as you charge toward the obstacles that will make you stronger.
- The victim mentality—no matter how justified—is self-sabotage.
- Don't hit snooze on the complacency alarm.

Pause and Think

- What is your fix? What reward motivates you to press forward?
- What does success mean to you? What does it look like?
- Where are you confronted with disappointment, discouragement, and/or doubt? What other velociraptors are trying to hurt you?
- Where do you see complacency in your life? What is the root of it?
- Pick one velociraptor out of your pack. Identify one thing you can do to look it in the face and say, "Bring it, Hard!"

CHAPTER 5

A BRIEF WARNING ABOUT CRISIS HIGHS

Whenever possible, it's best we think before we act. Sometimes we don't get that luxury, but part of living Hard-Easy is taking that opportunity whenever we're able. Otherwise, we run the risk of being in constant crisis mode. So even if you are pumped up about living Hard-Easy now and want to sprint down that hard path, it's best to take the time to build a plan.

Reacting on impulse—even in the name of making a change for the good—can cause more harm than good.

A friend of mine who served in the army told me that all through basic training, his drill sergeant would scream at the grunts, "Make a decision! Right or wrong, just make a decision!"

That's great advice if you happen to find yourself on a mission in war-torn Somalia battling warlords in the streets with mortars exploding in the rubble near your position and automatic fire shredding the air around you.

However, those who live Easy-Hard are often reactionary in everyday scenarios—impulsively responding to problems, people, situations, or challenges without forethought, allowing the moment to drive them. Right or wrong, they act in the heat of the moment. And most of the time, it turns out to be wrong.

As a result, those who live Easy-Hard experience their lives as a never-ending churn of chaotic battles created by their own lifestyle choices. Every problem that arises in the Easy-Hard life is a fire that needs to be immediately stomped out, starting with the closest flame.

This is a crisis mentality. Every little bump in the road creates a catastrophe that calls for immediate action. There's not a spare second to think about what might be best. They'll try to sort it out later . . . maybe.

Getting High on Crises

Here's something to boggle the mind: living in crisis can actually be addictive. Many who are in constant crisis mode actually get addicted (yes, physically addicted) to the flood of hormones—adrenaline, norepinephrine, and cortisol—pumped into the bloodstream during a crisis.

Your body is pumped full of these chemicals in any fight-or-flight situation. And your body—bless its heart—can't tell whether the hormones have arrived because you're trying to escape a pack of rabid hyenas or trying to figure out how to pay your credit card debt. The result is the same—and you experience a literal high. Along with endorphins, these crisis hormones are the biochemicals responsible for the well-known runner's high—which is why I run, by the way.

Beyond the physical addiction, there's also an emotionally addictive element at work in crisis living. People in constant turmoil can come to crave the attention they get as a result. They spill the beans to anyone who will listen to their woes. But eventually, their friends tire of the perpetual predicaments and start to fall by the wayside.

Crisis addicts can become emotional drainers, consuming their victims' goodwill before moving on to their next target—someone new to drag into the orbit of their ongoing disasters. As exhausting as that sounds, it all fuels the addiction. More on these folks in chapter 19.

All of this is to say that if you're feeling the need to kamikaze into kicking complacency's ass, step back for a minute from this knee-jerk reaction so you don't sabotage yourself. Don't feed the chaos. (And if you've been reading this section and thinking that maybe it's talking about you, you should especially pump the brakes.)

Don't act before you think. In fact, finish this book before you begin razing the Easy-Hard tendencies in your life.

Chapter Recap

Key concepts and takeaways from chapter 5:

- Beware of the crisis high.
- Think before you act whenever possible.

Pause and Think

- How often are you in crisis mode?
- Think of a time when you acted impulsively in the heat of the moment. It's probably embarrassing or even painful to recall. In retrospect, how would you have acted differently if you'd taken the time to think before acting?
- Think of the last big decision you made (use whatever criteria you feel appropriate to define "big decision"). How much thought did you put into it before making it? Do you feel that this was enough?

CHAPTER 6

THE CASE OF THE INTELLIGENT IDIOT AND THE VALUE OF A WISDOM LENS

Making the best decisions requires considering the best information possible. Yet, even when we know better, we don't always make the wisest choices. Other times, two Hard-Easy choices conflict, and we must sacrifice one at the expense of the other. This chapter focuses on how to recognize these situations and make the best decisions we can in order to keep moving forward on our Hard-Easy journey.

You might think there's a direct correlation between intelligence and taking the Hard-Easy way, that the ability to take a step back, analyze a situation, and choose the Hard-Easy path is simply a matter of how smart a person is. Unfortunately, neither your intelligence nor the number of diplomas you have automatically helps you make the Hard-Easy choice. Let me show you why.

When I lived in Virginia, I met a man who worked for the surgeon general of the United States. He received his medical degree from an Ivy League school and wrote his dissertation on the evils of refined sugar in the diet. He is a brilliant man and performs impeccable research.

One day, he was describing his research to me when he suddenly stopped, looked at me, winked, and said, "Art, would you like to know a secret?" I was all ears. Perhaps he was going to give me a stock tip about a company that had invented a lucrative new sugar substitute.

Looking suspiciously over his shoulder first, he leaned toward me and whispered, "With all I know about the negative effects of sugar on our bodies, I still put two heaping tablespoons of white sugar on my cereal every morning."

His dirty little secret was out.

Ivy Leaguer. Top research doctor. Brilliant mind with deeper insight than most about the harmful effects of processed sugar.

Despite all that, his actions weren't aligned with his knowledge.

Don't Be the Intelligent Idiot

The good doctor reveals that intelligence and the accumulation of knowledge does not mean you will make the correct, most beneficial choices.

The ability to apply knowledge for your benefit and to achieve the best possible outcome—that's wisdom. True, you do need the knowledge to apply it, but knowledge and intelligence alone aren't enough.

All of us have tendencies and addictions where we become an intelligent idiot. We know the Hard-Easy way is better, but we choose the Easy-Hard way instead.

For example, I'm hugely addicted to chilled (they *have* to be chilled) Thin Mint Girl Scout Cookies. Yep. There, I said it. I'll gorge on those suckers like an amphetamine-fueled Cookie Monster until they're gone.

Should I do that?

No.

Do I do it?

All. The. Time.

You can be intelligent and know better, but that means jack if you act stupidly.

But if you're wise, you apply your knowledge in ways that yield positive results. I should definitely be wise and cease and desist from my frozen Thin Mints gorge-a-thons.

What's Your Stupidity Score?

This scoring metric of mine states, "The better we know, the dumber our stupid actions are." To illustrate this, let's figure out the stupidity scores for a doctor and a teenager both making the same poor choices.

For this metric, we'll rate an action on a scale of one to ten, and knowledge on a separate scale of one to ten. Ideally, they should match up—our actions should align with our knowledge. When advanced knowledge (knowledge derived from academics, experience, or both) aligns with choosing the action with the most beneficial outcome, you have wisdom.

Let's revisit the sugar doctor. For the purpose of this illustration, we're going to amp up his daily sugar intake to twenty times what he would consider acceptable. When it comes to the harmful effects of sugar, his knowledge is high—ten out of ten. The action of consuming heaps of sugar each day rates much lower—one out of ten. So there is a nine-point stupidity gap between his knowledge and action. They are not in alignment.

Now, take a typical teenager. Like the doctor, he consumes twenty times the daily acceptable amount. His action score is the same as the doctor's: one out of ten. However, this teenager has heard some things about too much sugar being bad for you, but that vague rumor is all he knows. His knowledge score is two out of ten. There is only a one-point stupidity gap between his actions and knowledge. His knowledge and actions are more closely aligned.

The stupidity score tells us the doctor is acting much more stupidly than the teenager. Of course, the ill effects of sugar will take their toll regardless of a person's knowledge.

Natural laws have consequences whether we're aware of a law or not. However, we can't hold the teenager accountable for his poor sugary decisions since he is not aware of the consequences. On the other hand, we can hold the doctor to a higher standard.

What Does Knowledge-Action Alignment Have to Do with Hard-Easy?

I'm afraid Peter Parker's Uncle Ben had it right: with great power comes great responsibility. But in this case, knowledge is power. With great *knowledge* comes great responsibility. The more we know, the more is expected from us in return. The more we know, the more we're able to see the difference between Hard-Easy and Easy-Hard.

Our teenager, acting in alignment with his low knowledge, couldn't understand that he was making an easy choice that would result in hard consequences down the road. Our doctor, however, knows the hard health consequences at the end of the sugary path he's on—and he's risking it anyway.

When we understand the principle and *apply* it (when we don't rank as stupid on the stupidity chart)—we can put the natural law of Hard-Easy in motion to our advantage.

Apply the Wisdom Lens to Every Decision

The more Hard-Easy paths you're able to see, the more often they will come into conflict. Sometimes you'll have two competing Hard-Easy paths in front of you, but you can only choose one. How do you know which path is best?

Wisdom.

How do you apply wisdom in the paradigm of Hard-Easy? Here's an extreme example of using wisdom to justify an Easy-Hard choice. You will see it is obvious, but I am trying to make the point clear.

Mike's Dilemma

Mike is living Hard-Easy when it comes to his personal finances. He's scrimped and saved and worked his way through grad school so he can get a higher-paying job, pay down his debt, and better support his family. He's beginning to see the fruits of those labors. He has an interview for a great job today, better than any job he interviewed for before earning his graduate degree.

For this interview, Mike must get to the sixtieth floor of the downtown high-rise.

What should he do: take the stairs or the elevator?

Mike is also trying to live Hard-Easy when it comes to his health. He's exercising regularly, trying to be less sedentary, and eating better. He has joined a local gym and even hired a fitness coach.

So the Hard-Easy choice for his health would be to arrive early and hike those stairs to get some extra exercise. At least that is what his fitness coach would encourage him to do: "Take the stairs instead of the elevator." Taking the elevator from a health perspective *seems* like the Easy-Hard option. He'll effortlessly zip up those sixty floors, but he'll have to take care of the workout later.

But what is the wisest choice for him in this scenario?

Mike applies the wisdom lens. He has knowledge and experience with both job interviews and exercise. If he hikes the stairs, he will burn a load of calories and get his heart rate up, which is great for his cardiovascular health and will thrill his fitness coach.

But how will Mike look when he walks into the interview?

Imagine you're the one interviewing Mike and he comes bursting through your door, out of breath, slicked with sweat, shirt untucked, with wet spots under his armpits and around his collar.

Yep. You'd call security.

At the very least, your first impression of him would almost certainly make you eliminate Mike from consideration for the job.

Mike's wisdom lens says, "The Easy-Hard choice for my health, taking the elevator, is the best choice in this scenario." Mike's wisdom lens allows him to see that making the Hard-Easy choice regarding his health will create a roadblock on the Hard-Easy financial path he's traveling. It tells him which path is more important at this moment.

Mike's wisdom lens has allowed him to analyze the opportunity cost of each option. The cost of getting the exercise via the stairs would likely be the loss of a job offer, along with salary, benefits, experience gained, and networking. At the very best, it would be an awkward, subpar meeting.

The cost of taking the elevator would be having to postpone a great workout, but the potential of a great interview and getting the job outweighs those exercise benefits. There is a time and a place to get that workout in; doing it in a suit and tie right before a critically important job interview that could take your career to the next level is not one of those times or places.

Again, I know this is a fairly obvious example, but in its simplicity, hopefully you can connect the dots and find parallel examples of where you need to use your wisdom lens in your own life.

The Chore Conundrum

Here's another simple example. When I offer my kids ten bucks to either weed or vacuum, they apply their wisdom lens. They'll earn ten bucks either way, but which is the wisest choice? What will earn them that money in the least amount of time?

Vacuuming.

They have knowledge of what's involved in each chore, and experience tells them which one they can get done fastest. They're not choosing between Hard-Easy or Easy-Hard; they're choosing between Hard ten dollars (weeding) and Easy ten dollars (vacuuming).

But what if I took the job they view as more difficult—weeding—and offered more money to compensate for that difficulty? Their wisdom lens might leave the house unvacuumed. In this case, they are faced with choosing between Hard-Easy and Easy-Hard. Hard-Easy (weeding) rewards them with more money, so they won't have to do as many chores to maximize their earnings. They'll focus on the fix (their payday) while crawling around in the dirt.

For me, it's not a zero-sum game with winners and losers. Regardless of what my kids choose, they learn responsibility while adding to their wisdom. My wisdom lens assures me there is nothing lost by my kids exerting control over which chore they'll do—even though they think weeding is worse.

My kids, however, will exert their control based on the outcome they desire.

Remember Mike choosing between the stairs and the elevator? He needs to exert control in order to avoid sabotaging his goals to get a higher paying job and better support his family.

So, when you think about the areas in your life over which you need to exert control, you need an honest evaluation around Hard-Easy versus Easy-Hard.

My use of the word *control* here is not accidental; it isn't merely a buzzword. To get what you really want out of life, you need to examine your Hard-Easy options to ensure a larger payoff down the line. Only then can you become who you truly want to be.

Chapter Recap

Key concepts and takeaways from chapter 6:

- Apply the wisdom lens to decisions so you don't end up becoming the intelligent idiot.
- Apply the wisdom lens when prioritizing one Hard-Easy path over another.

Pause and Think

- In what areas would you consider yourself an intelligent idiot—where you have a high stupidity score?
- Can you identify a time when two Hard-Easy paths collided? How did you decide which one to prioritize?

CHAPTER 7

§

LESSONS IN PHYSICS AND NATURAL LAWS
Flywheels, Compound Interest, and Microdecisions

Little efforts count, and it all comes down to our choices—all of them. In this chapter, we'll look at two examples of how no effort goes unrewarded, then apply that concept to living Hard-Easy.

What does it take to change?

Put another way, how long do you have to live the *hard* part of Hard-Easy before the *easy* part kicks in?

We all know this fact: living Hard-Easy does not result in insta-Easy. The Easy fairy does not appear and sprinkle you with Easy dust. You don't get teleported to the land of Easy, where money sprouts from the ground as prolifically as dandelions and french fries are the best food for your heart health. (As an aside, Easy dust sounds like a futuristic drug—or perhaps a soft-rock band from the '70s.)

Bear in mind that you can be living Hard-Easy in one or several areas of your life and simultaneously living Easy-Hard in others. It is not a zero-sum game. You might be living Hard-Easy in finances, healthy eating, and exercise but living Easy-Hard when it comes to nurturing a deep, meaningful relationship with your friends, lover, or family.

To understand the forces that govern the mechanisms of change, it's illuminating to look at three concepts: the flywheel effect, compound interest, and the accumulation of microdecisions.

The Flywheel Effect

What's a flywheel?

The basic principle has been around since caveman days. Spindles that operate on the same physics as flywheels were created by Neolithic peoples dating back five thousand to ten thousand years BC. The wheel spins around its axis, storing rotational, kinetic energy.

During the Industrial Revolution, Scottish inventor and mechanical engineer James Watt built the flywheel into his steam engine. He engineered it to produce continuous power, even when the energy source was not continuous.[14]

Huge flywheels were used on locomotives and in factories and hydroelectric plants. They take an enormous amount of energy to get moving, but once they gain momentum, they require less energy to move or accelerate. In fact, they store that rotational energy and deliver it back to the machine in a steady stream.

An object at rest tends to stay at rest. An object in motion tends to stay in motion.

In his book, *Good to Great*,[15] Jim Collins uses the flywheel effect to describe what it takes to get a business moving in a new direction. Like getting a massive flywheel in motion, getting a business or large institution to change is *hard*. But, like the flywheel, the more effort you exert in the right direction, the more the flywheel moves. At some point, the mass of the flywheel works in your favor. It becomes *easy*.

You may push the flywheel for ten hours to get it going, but once it's moving at a certain speed, it's storing and releasing kinetic energy. You can let go of the wheel, and it will turn on its own, maintaining its speed for quite a while. Or, if you need to accelerate, you can apply much less energy to generate increased rotation on the moving wheel.

Just like the physics behind the flywheel, there is a natural law at play governing our lives and decisions.

It can be hard to push on that flywheel to get it going. It may take years. And it takes a lot of pushing. But that pushing adds up and the wheel gains momentum until, one day, what was once hard to do—pushing the massive flywheel—becomes easy.

Every hard action you take in pursuit of Hard-Easy is a push on your personal flywheel. Each push builds momentum and will one day lead to easy actions.

Compound Interest

Compound interest is just the flywheel in your finances. It's adding the interest to the principal of a deposit. It's interest on your interest (which is why it's so powerfully good for you when you're earning compound interest on stocks and investments—and so devastatingly bad for you when you're paying compound interest on loans and credit cards).

In his article "Compound Interest: The Most Powerful Force in the Universe," Allan Roth recounts a story told in the *Huffington Post*[16] about June Greg, a one-hundred-year-old woman who had been a customer of her local bank for ninety-eight years. Her father had opened an account for her ninety-eight years previous and deposited $6.11 in it.

If June withdrew her money on her one-hundredth birthday, how big a wallet would she have to bring? How much cash would that money have generated over the past ninety-eight years?

It depends on the interest rate. Or, said another way, how big the flywheel driving the investment was.

Annualized Return	Value after Ninety-Eight Years
2%	$42.55
6%	$1,845.08
10%	$69,586.40
20%	$351,401,266.90

If June had kept her money in a savings account at the bank all those years and earned 2 percent, she could bring her change purse, walk away from the bank, and go buy herself a decent pair of shoes.

If her dad had put that money into bonds that yielded an average of 10 percent, she would need to bring a briefcase to the bank, and she could go buy a brand-new Corvette Stingray. (Granny must be going through a late midlife crisis.)

And if her dad had invested her $6.11 in a stock portfolio that yielded a Warren Buffet–esque 20 percent return, compounded over ninety-eight years, she would need to drive an armored truck to the bank so she could load it with almost half a billion dollars. Granny could buy an island kingdom, name it Juneva, and rule it with a wrinkly fist.

Compound interest. It's the result of small, continuous inputs that add up to a monumental output with the passage of time. While Granny cannot totally control the interest rate, she can control the investment vehicle that influences the interest rate.

Microdecisions

As you consider the ways you get your flywheel moving, don't fall into the trap of believing that only big efforts count. Your flywheel's momentum will respond to small pushes and large pushes. Remember, pennies earn interest too, so don't wait until you have one hundred dollars to add to your investment.

It works the same way with decisions. Your microdecisions count. This is the essence of the law of Hard-Easy. Every decision is an opportunity to increase the flywheel's momentum or to build and reinvest interest. In that light, there are no unimportant decisions.

One seemingly small decision can alter your trajectory. If the microdecision is Hard-Easy, it pushes on the flywheel just a little more. It puts you on a trajectory toward greater success and the Easy phase of Hard-Easy.

If, however, the microdecision is Easy-Hard, not only does it fail to push the flywheel, it also pushes you on a trajectory toward the Hard phase of Easy-Hard.

Case in point: Scott and Lori Connors's family room in Pleasant Grove, Utah.

The year was 2005. It was late March. Snow was still thick on the peaks. Ski resorts were open. But as the days warmed, it increased the danger of avalanches. As part of the Utah Department of Transportation (UDOT) Avalanche Safety Program, crews would go into canyons and fire artillery at the peaks. The shock waves would cause controlled avalanches, reducing the likelihood of one rumbling into a recreational area.

On the afternoon of March 23, a UDOT crew entered Provo Canyon and fired a 105mm howitzer.

Yep. A howitzer.

Based on their calculations, the crew thought their shot was on the mark—just like the hundreds of others they had fired. But they didn't see or hear an explosion, so they wrote the shell off as a dud.

But on the other side of the mountain in the small town of Pleasant Grove, the artillery shell exploded in the Connors's backyard.

A crater the size of a Volkswagen was scooped out of their property. It took out a shed, and the family room was shredded by shrapnel and debris. Fortunately—miraculously—no one was injured.

Someone had miscalculated, and the shell had flown three miles off course. UDOT blamed it on a tad too much gunpowder being packed into the shell. A microdecision on one side of the mountain led to a dangerously off-the-mark explosion on the other.[17]

Microdecisions matter. One extra grain of gunpowder in that shell won't propel it significantly off course. But it does not take much to suddenly have enough gunpowder to change the shell's trajectory, and suddenly you are three miles off course, and instead of protecting lives, you are threatening lives.

Lagoon

All this reminds me of a massive, smooth, round stone just past the fountains at Lagoon Amusement Park in Farmington, Utah. It's about four feet in diameter and must weigh several thousand pounds.

It rests on another stone, with water pouring from its base. When you push the mammoth stone on top and exert immense effort with both hands, it will begin to spin. The more effort, the more it spins. But once it is spinning, its own weight and momentum take over and you can easily keep it spinning with one finger. It's a tangible example of how Hard-Easy leads to Easy.

I know for a fact that these same unwavering principals can be applied in our individual lives. It is hard at first, but if we stay with it, diligently committing our daily microdecisions to our goals and visions, there will come a time when the flywheel effect takes over. From there, the energy to make good things happen is far less daunting, strenuous, or hard.

We never have a guarantee of immediate results. It takes months of a healthy diet and exercise program to see the gains. We might not see results within the first few months of striving to be a kind, selfless, tender, affectionate partner. We cannot see results within the first year or two of a financial savings plan.

But when we step back and look at our efforts from a broad perspective and at some future point, we can see that Hard did turn into Easy and that keeping Easy going is—dare I say it—easy.

Chapter Recap

Key concepts and takeaways from chapter 7:

- How do I change? Some of the laws and mechanisms that govern Hard-Easy/Easy-Hard—and govern how you can change—are the flywheel effect, compound interest, and microdecisions.
- The flywheel effect: Every Hard action you take in your life is a push on your personal flywheel. Each push builds a momentum that will one day lead to Easy results.
- Compound interest: Hard-Easy living is taking the interest on your actions and reinvesting that interest in a goal so the effort compounds over time, growing more rapidly as time goes on and compounding continues.
- Microdecisions matter.

Pause and Think

- Spend a day or two being mindfully aware of all the decisions you make—especially those you may overlook as decisions because you make them while on autopilot.
- Analyze some of the decisions you would normally categorize as minor or unimportant. How can they contribute to your flywheel's momentum?

CHAPTER 8

HIGH-PROFILE CASE EXAMPLES OF EASY CRASHING INTO HARD

We've reviewed several aspects of Hard-Easy versus Easy-Hard. Now let's put them together in some real-world examples. While you're picking out the elements we've already discussed, what other truths do you notice about the law of Hard-Easy?

Enron and Arthur Andersen

Enron began as a provider of natural gas. In 1985, after a merger, Enron owned north-south and east-west pipelines that spanned the continental United States. It was the second-largest gas-pipeline network at the time. From there, it began to invest in power plants and other energy-production ventures.

So far, so good.

But then, in the 1990s, the company shifted. Jeff Skilling, the future CEO of the company, didn't want to just produce and sell energy and natural gas. He wanted to turn natural gas into a commodity that could be traded and used as the basis for investment vehicles and financial services.

The energy company became more like an investment firm. And that's when Enron decided to live Easy-Hard.

One of their first missteps was to lobby for and get the SEC's approval for their use of something called mark-to-market accounting.

This is a common accounting practice for stocks and commodities trading but is seldom used in other types of business.

As opposed to historical accounting, which tracks past transactions (much like keeping your checkbook balanced), mark-to-market accounting uses the fair-market value of assets (or similar assets) to anticipate future earnings.

Enron was able to list anticipated future earnings—sometimes as far as twenty years down the road—as revenue for the current year.

Sound complicated? It is.

But here's an example of how it might work.

Let's say Enron builds a power plant in India and they sign a twenty-year contract. Enron will sell them $50 million of energy per year for the next twenty years. But instead of citing revenue of $50 million of revenue for year one, Enron cites $1 billion—assuming the total amount of profits for twenty years based on current market values for energy prices.

What happens if the price of energy goes down? Enron won't earn as much money. But the reality of the phantom earnings and the sinking value of energy contracts is buried deep in accounting records and smoke-and-mirrors transactions.

With mark-to-market accounting, Enron could post huge amounts of revenue, which drove stock prices sky-high. Easy, right?

But there was nowhere near that amount of real revenue coming in. And what's more, Enron started taking huge losses on various business ventures around the globe. But they couldn't let the world know they were losing money. That would drive their stock price down. Hard was making an appearance, and the Easy-Hard micro-decisions had Enron on a trajectory toward an unpleasant end.

And Enron did nothing to alter the course of their trajectory.

In 1993, CFO Andy Fastow created a labyrinthine chain of shadow companies. This accomplished two things. First, it helped Fastow hide massive liabilities and losses to keep Enron a rising rock star in the stock market. Second, it helped Fastow earn upward of $60 million for himself in shady deals.

It's all much more convoluted and complicated than that, but that's the gist of it. Enron took the easy path, citing huge revenues where they didn't exist (nor would ever exist) and combining that with hiding huge losses in entities that were illegal and propped up on the belief that Enron stock would keep rising. (They also pillaged the California energy market, but that's a story for another day.)

Enron's accounting firm, Arthur Andersen, took the easy path, too, by signing off on several questionable deals and firing or reassigning the accountants who spoke up against the deals. Arthur Andersen wanted to keep collecting their tens of millions in annual fees from Enron. And because Andersen had signed off, it perpetuated the illusion that Enron was legitimately earning all the revenue it publicly claimed it was. Investors and business partners believed Enron was a golden goose.

And the stock kept rising. In August 2000, Enron stock traded at $90.56—it's peak value. *Fortune* magazine named Enron America's Most Innovative Company for six straight years.

Then, in just about a year, things began to unravel. Bits and pieces of the accounting irregularities began to ding the company. Then it snowballed as revelation after revelation brought the company down.

By August 2001, the stock price had fallen to $42 per share. By Halloween, it was down to $15.

Still, the executive leadership expressed confidence that Enron would turn it around. Some investors, thinking they could make a killing in that turnaround by buying low now scrambled to buy Enron stock at $15 per share.

They were wrong. The accounting fraud came to light, and Enron went bankrupt, leaving thousands of investors and employees, whose pensions and 401(k)s were comprised of Enron stock, penniless.

Easy imploded and left nothing but the rubble of Hard in a spectacular corporate flameout. Arthur Andersen, the consulting firm, went down with the Enron ship for signing off on illegal, fraudulent deals—and for obstructing justice by shredding tons of Enron documents.

Enron built a fake fortune by going Easy-Hard on accounting. Arthur Andersen earned Enron's business by going Easy-Hard on oversight. Both, however, were destroyed when the Hard phase of Easy-Hard kicked in. Both companies went bankrupt, and executives from each were sentenced to prison. Not only that, but the actions of relatively few people affected many who were living honest lives and had nothing to do with perpetrating the fraud. They didn't even know it was going on, yet they lost their retirement and their jobs.

If only Enron leaders had known my cowboy friend Gordon.

And if you are wondering, mark-to-market accounting is still used to this day. However, it is far more scrutinized than before.

Watergate

It was the early 1970s in the United States. Lapels were huge, pantsuits for women and perms for men were in vogue, sideburns were long and bushy, and *The Godfather* was one of America's top movies. In 1972, Richard Nixon was completing one term as president and campaigning to be reelected for a second.

In June of 1972, months before the November elections against Democratic candidate George McGovern, something curious happened. Five burglars broke into the headquarters of the Democratic National Committee at the Watergate office complex.

Thus began the unraveling of the presidency—a process that would take years of dogged work by investigative journalists Bob Woodward and Carl Bernstein of *The Washington Post*.

What they eventually uncovered was staggering: corruption, abuse of power, covert and illegal activities, wiretapping, surveillance, coverups, and obstruction of justice—all perpetrated or approved of by President Nixon and members of his administration.

As the noose tightened around Nixon and revelation piled upon revelation, the government found itself in a constitutional crisis. Nixon fired special prosecutor Archibald Cox, who was leading the congressional investigation into the allegations of corruption.

All of this culminated a grand jury indicting several members of Nixon's administration for their crimes and finally the release of the "smoking-gun" recording that proved Nixon knew about the corruption and had given the green light.

As Congress was drawing up articles of impeachment in August 1974, President Nixon resigned from the presidency.

It all started when Nixon and his team wanted an easy way to win another term in office. They chose the Easy-Hard path of gathering intelligence to subvert their opponent's 1972 campaign. Side note: sometimes the only thing we learn from history is that we do not learn anything from history. Heavy sigh.

All that Easy led to an abrupt, Hard-induced implosion that ruined Nixon and caused him to lose the presidency he so desperately—and illegally—sought.

Did he need to go Easy-Hard?

It's difficult to say to what extent his corrupt, illegal efforts affected his second election victory. But one can surmise that Nixon didn't need to go Easy-Hard. He won the 1972 election against McGovern with 520 to 17 electoral votes.

A slaughter.

A total drubbing.

A victory so gargantuan it seems to show the American people were pretty happy with Nixon's first term and wanted him back.

But Easy sounded really good to Tricky Dick. And when it backfired into the wasteland of Hard, all that was left for Nixon was to resign in disgrace.

Tiger Woods

The man could play golf. He turned pro in 1996 at age twenty. In less than a year, he had won three PGA tour events, plus the 1997 Masters.

Oh yeah. And he won the Masters by twelve strokes.

Woods was a Jedi on the links. He holds the records for being the number-one golfer in the world for most total weeks (683) and most consecutive weeks (281).

On top of that, he fell in love.

He met Elin Nordegren in 2001. After dating for three years, they got engaged in 2003 and married in 2004.

They lived in a $39 million estate in Florida.

Any mortal who looked at Tiger Woods thought, "Man, this guy has it all."

Then, in 2009, reports of his infidelity began to surface, and we soon found out that Tiger was a serial adulterer.

He crashed his Cadillac one night after a purported fight with Elin. In the next month, more women came forward and claimed to have had affairs with Woods. A recording of Tiger calling one of his mistresses was released. Tiger admitted to all the cheating and decided to take an indefinite break from golf to sort through the wreckage of his personal life.

By 2010, he was divorced. His golf game deteriorated. His reputation suffered. Sponsors dropped him. He was arrested for a DUI.

So forget about the golf. This is the story of a relationship—of what it takes to build a caring, loving relationship on trust, love, sacrifice, and communication.

When Tiger fell in love, it seemed as though he and Elin had something special. He courted her. Romanced her. Swept her off her feet.

And then they had kids together—the ultimate expression of love, creation, and commitment.

At least it should have been.

But when it came to love and his relationship, Woods chose to live Easy-Hard. He had ample opportunities to meet and bed women all around the globe. And he did.

It was so easy for so long he thought Hard would never catch up. "I thought I could get away with whatever I wanted to," Woods admitted at a televised press conference. "I felt that I had worked hard my entire life and deserved to enjoy all the temptations around me. I felt I was entitled. Thanks to money and fame, I didn't have to go far to find them. I was wrong. I was foolish."[18]

In the span of a few months, his kingdom of Easy crumbled into the rubble of Hard.

True, this was his relationship and not directly related to his golf. However, the toxicity of his personal life spilled over into his professional life and sent him on a downward spiral that took years to recover from.

Unfortunately, there was no recovering the life he and Elin had built together. Woods's pursuit of Easy destroyed it. Just like with Enron, Nixon, and Humpty Dumpty, there was no way to put those pieces back together again.

In addition to losing his marriage and family, Tiger's public crucifixion led to a loss of respect from fans and deals with sponsors. It undoubtedly dealt a deep blow to his sense of self-worth. Tiger had undeniably done wrong, and he knew it. Worse yet, his family was paying the price, and there was nothing he could do to fix it.

He'd lost everything on the home front, so was it worth it to take the Hard path to rebuild what he could of his career?

No one would have blamed him had he said, "I'm done." He'd already undergone four knee surgeries and dealt with stress fractures in one leg and an Achilles tendon injury in the other. Shortly before his divorce was finalized, he withdrew from the Players Championship because of back pain. He had enough money to live comfortably, and it would have been easy to fade from public view and give his body a rest. But that's not how Tiger Woods—the golfer—does things.

Tiger lives Hard-Easy when it comes to golf. This mindset was much of what endeared him to fans as Tiger, the underdog, rose to fame the first time. This second rise, though, was all the more difficult because he wasn't some unknown kid. This was Tiger Woods—the golfing superstar who'd disappointed everyone and lost it all, the athletic wonder on the links whose body was falling apart. The world was watching, taking note, and making judgments.

It was a hard road, and Tiger faced many failures on it. He went to counseling and had multiple back surgeries. These led to an addiction to painkillers and a DUI in 2017. That year, he questioned whether he'd ever play professional golf again. The Easy-Hard microdecisions that led to the demise of his marriage threatened to crush his comeback.

Again, who would have blamed him if he'd thrown in the towel? He'd tried, hadn't he?

Woods credits his children for his iron determination to stay the course. Neither of his children was around to see him in his prime, and he wanted to ascend to the top again so they could see him at his best.

A friendship with another great athlete also inspired him to keep pushing down that hard path, enduring months and years of pain, doubt, and disappointment. Swimmer Michael Phelps, who had faced addiction to alcohol, gave Tiger the boost he needed. He kept fighting to alter his trajectory and push mightily to get his flywheel moving toward Hard-Easy again.

In April 2019, Woods won his fifth Masters title and fifteenth major tournament at age forty-three. His kids and Phelps were there to witness it. Without a doubt, the victory would have been sweeter with a strong family backing him up, and Woods likely has regrets, but he's focusing on what he can control *now*.

Woods's comeback teaches us that when Hard hits, even when it's the result of our own choices, we don't have to give up. And even if we've gone so far as to destroy certain aspects of our lives in the pursuit of Easy, there is always another dream to chase, and you owe it to yourself, and likely others, to chase it.

The Manager of a Convenience Store

The following example illustrates that this law applies to all. It does not care if you are famous or anonymous, rich or poor, smart or not so smart, male or female; it strikes at all.

My friend's wife is a regular at the gas-station convenience store down the road from her house. She goes there to get her daily Diet Dr Pepper. She knows most of the employees there, and they know her.

One day when she went in, the usual manager wasn't there. He had been fired.

He had been an employee of the company for several years and was supporting his family of five kids and a wife with diabetes. His insurance provided doctor's visits and insulin. They weren't a wealthy family, but they had what they needed.

But at some point, he'd gotten greedy and chosen Easy-Hard. He falsified his timesheets to get paid for hours he didn't work. And when no one noticed, he did it again. Then again. His fraud got more brazen, and he gave himself a raise. A dishonest, illegal, embezzly sort of raise.

He got caught. And he got fired.

Easy erupted into Hard, just like that.

His Easy money—along with the honest portion of the paycheck—was gone. And now he's in a world of Hard—with a family to feed, housing to pay for, car payments to make, a hard-to-overcome job record, and no insurance.

A Quick Word

There are a few interesting observations to be gleaned from all of these stories: First, the number of microdecisions required to change trajectory and start pushing the flywheel again would have been minimal on day one of the Easy-Hard journey.

If the head of Enron, Ken Lay, had looked at the proposal to use mark-to-market accounting and said, "This is not for us," that would have been it. The end. Or at least it would have made the rest of the greed and fraud that followed less likely to happen on such a magnitude and scale.

The expenditure of energy to stop that momentum at that point would have been tiny. But suppose he waited a year to try to change course. He would have had to restate earnings downward and acknowledge that the business wasn't performing as well. Stock prices would have gone down. The amount of energy needed at this juncture to reverse course and go back to Hard-Easy would have been immense.

And at some point, Enron passed an event horizon where the gravity of the scandals and illegal activities made turning back impossible.

Likewise with Nixon—if he had shut down the team who'd pitched the subversive ideas (ideas, by the way, that he really, really liked), the energy expenditure at that point would have been minimal: just uttering the word *no*.

But six months in, it would have taken much more effort and energy to turn the tide. And, eventually, the only way to stop it was to resign from the presidency.

Tiger Woods? If he'd told the first woman who flirted with him he was married and gone back to his hotel room alone, the amount of energy to accomplish that would have been relatively small. But with each step toward—and past—infidelity, the more excruciatingly difficult it became to reverse course.

The convenience-store manager who was fired could have easily halted his course if he had simply dismissed the thought of falsifying his timesheet when it first occurred to him. But as time wore on, the ability to reverse his decision became harder and harder, until it was too late.

Putting It All Together

What do all these examples mean for you?

1. Keep your flywheel moving in the right direction. Microdecisions. It's all about the microdecisions.

2. The different areas in our lives intersect and influence the others. Tiger Woods chose Easy-Hard in his relationships. But the hard consequences of his relationship path didn't stay confined within the borders of Tiger's relationships. They spilled over into his professional life and altered the Hard-Easy path he was on for golf. Natural laws don't care if we aren't aware of them.

3. Our personal path influences others' personal paths. All four examples—Enron, Richard Nixon, Tiger Woods, and the convenience-store manager—involved personal choices that had consequences beyond the individual.

4. Altering your trajectory is easy until it is hard. Would you rather try to stop a boulder at the top of a hill when it's barely started to move—or at the bottom when all forty-five tons of it are at their peak velocity? As in Newton's law of motion, to reverse Easy, it must be met with an equal and opposite Hard.

5. Friends and popularity are evidences of Easy, while Hard is often endured individually. When you live Easy, you will have many who want to be in your company. Countless individuals will be attracted to you. It does not matter if you are living Easy on the tail end of living Hard or living Easy upfront. On the other hand, when you are deep in Hard, there are few who will stick by you. In all four examples, the individuals were surrounded by family and hordes of friends. When Hard came a-knocking, they were left alone to deal with the pain and price their choices exacted.

When Kai wants to play videogames, he has plenty of friends who want to join him in person and online. But when it is time to do math homework, his friends seem to scatter as if he has a fatally contagious disease—even when many are in his class and have the same homework.

6. Our passions work for us as well as against us. When you combine passion with Hard-Easy or Easy-Hard, it amplifies the result. Enron executives had a passion for money that made the Hard phase of Easy-Hard combustible. Tiger Woods had a passion for the ladies that amplified the Hard phase of Easy-Hard when it arrived to wreak havoc on his entire life. He also had a passion for golf that amplified the Easy phase of Hard-Easy when he became one of the greatest golfers to date. Find your passion and funnel it into the Hard-Easy current—and let it amplify your return.

On Being Human and What It Means to Arrive at the Easy Phase of Hard-Easy

Long title for a short section.

This is just to say—and I'll reiterate this thought throughout the book—I don't want to give you the impression that if you live Hard-Easy in any aspect of your life you'll suddenly wake up one day and all your problems will be gone. That's not the kind of Easy I'm talking about.

We're human. That type of Easy never happens. At least until we die. And then who knows? Maybe problems don't go away then, either. Maybe our ghosts get blown all over the place in high winds.

I may have an easier time financially now because I've lived Hard-Easy my whole life, but that doesn't mean all my financial problems have gone away. I still have to budget. Save. Figure out how to invest. Some investments go bad. Sometimes the economy takes a downturn and I lose a percentage of what I've earned.

I may have lived Hard-Easy my whole life in regard to my health through diet and lots of exercise. Overall, my health and my ability to do the things I want to do physically will be easier than if I had given myself up to decades of bacon and Netflix (or cold Thin Mints and Netflix, as the case may be). But then one day I get pneumonia. Or the flu. Hard stuff happens—even in the Easy phase of the Hard-Easy sequence.

We're always in flux. The more we can get our actions flowing in the right direction in as many facets of our lives as possible, the greater our return when the Easy blossoms from the Hard.

Chapter Recap

Key concepts and takeaways from chapter 8:

- Sometimes the Hard of Easy-Hard erupts and your life and the lives of others can suddenly implode.

- To reverse Easy, it must be met with an equal and opposite Hard.
- Popularity comes with Easy, while Hard is often shouldered individually.
- Find your passion and funnel it into the Hard-Easy current—and let it amplify your return.
- Get your actions flowing in the right direction in as many facets of your life as possible.

Pause and Think

- What other examples can you think of (real or fictional) where it comes to living Hard-Easy or Easy-Hard?
- Have you ever reversed the flywheel in your life?

CHAPTER 9

IN PRAISE OF GRITS

One of the most challenging parts of living Hard-Easy is sticking with it throughout the struggle and despite the stumbling. How do we remain committed to the Hard path when we inevitably experience failure and disappointment along the way?

Grits? What do grits have to do with Hard-Easy?

While I am a fan of the delicious Southern breakfast staple, this chapter is not about food. Rather, it's about what Dr. Angela Duckworth—founder and CEO of the Character Lab and University of Pennsylvania professor—calls grit. And I am calling those who develop grit and rely upon it.[19]

Dr. Duckworth's concept of grit is a key character trait of those who live Hard-Easy.

Let me give you a brief overview of grit.

A Mystery

At age twenty-seven, Angela Duckworth left a lucrative job as a management consultant to go back to school. She became a seventh-grade math teacher.

Like most teachers, she got to know her students. And like most teachers, she gave homework, tests, and grades. And she discovered something that perplexed her. Some of her best performers on tests and homework were not her highest-IQ students. And, conversely, some of her worst-performing students happened to have high IQs.

She's not the first educator to have acquired this insight. But it did lead her to ask this: What if doing well in school and in life depends on much more than your ability to learn quickly and easily? This led her to earn a doctorate in psychology and conduct research designed to discover the answer to her core question.

She studied children and adults in a variety of challenging situations. She wanted to discover *who* would succeed and *why* they succeeded. In every situation, one characteristic emerged as a significant predictor of success: grit.

Beyond intelligence, physical attributes, social and economic factors, charisma, social smarts, talent, and everything else, grit was the denominator common to successful people no matter their age, no matter their endeavor.

What the Hell Is Grit?

Grit doesn't sound like a characteristic—it sounds like something that gets blown into my eye while I'm out working in the barn. But Duckworth defines grit as "Passion and perseverance for a very-long-term goal."[20]

Aha! Now we're talking about words in the Hard-Easy lexicon: *passion, perseverance, goal*. Remember Tiger Woods's comeback? We can apply all three of these words to that situation.

She goes on to say, "Grit is having stamina and sticking with your future, day in and day out . . . for years—and working really hard to make that future a reality."[21]

Oh yeah. We are deep into Hard-Easy territory now.

If it sounds like grit and Hard-Easy are describing the same concept, in a way, they are. They both describe the underlying natural law we've been talking about. The law says that you put in the hard work, and over time, it results in success that makes your life easier in some way.

So, problem solved. All you need is grit. (I'm not sure the Beatles would have gotten very far with that title.)

Give each kid a grit pill, or enroll them in a grit class, or have them download the Grit app, and they are assured of success.

But that's not how it works.

While Dr. Duckworth found out why some of her smart students failed and some of her less naturally intelligent kids excelled, she also discovered that science knows remarkably little about *how* to catalyze grit in an individual.

The Growth Mindset

Another researcher, Dr. Carol S. Dweck, a psychology professor at Stanford, developed a concept called the "growth mindset." Essentially, it's the idea that the ability to learn is not fixed but can change with effort.

She says that "in a fixed mindset, people believe their basic qualities, like their intelligence or talent, are simply fixed traits . . . and that talent alone creates success—without effort. In a growth mindset, people believe that their most basic abilities can be developed through dedication and hard work."[22]

To put it simply, a fixed mindset says, "I can't do this." A growth mindset says, "I can't do this *yet*."

Dr. Dweck goes on to say, "This view creates a love of learning and a resilience that is essential for great accomplishment."[23]

She conducted studies wherein school children read about the brain and how it responds and grows when faced with challenges. Children with a growth mindset, she found, were much more likely to persevere when they failed because they no longer viewed failure as a permanent condition or something that should be feared. It was a necessary stage that must be completed in order to get to success.

These kids had developed a healthy attitude about challenges and failure. They had developed grit.

Or, as we've been learning, they had begun to understand the concept of Hard-Easy.

Based on Dr. Dweck's research, I believe the fact that you're reading this book about Hard-Easy indicates that you're on the right track—that you will develop a Hard-Easy growth mindset that enables you to persevere through the challenges and failures on the hard road because you know that this sort of grit leads to the land of Easy.

Want More Out of Life? Delay Your Gratification

The concepts of grit and a growth mindset tie in nicely with another Hard-Easy concept—delayed gratification.

Remember how we talked about our Neanderthal-esque, genetically programmed cravings for instant gratification? Research recently published in *Frontiers in Psychology* confirms that the Hard-Easy concept of delayed gratification is key to reaping success down the road.

Led by Dr. William Hampton, experts from the Olson Lab at Temple University studied more than 2,500 people, testing willpower. In the study, the researchers offered money to test subjects. Subjects could take a smaller sum of money immediately or a much larger sum if they waited several weeks.

The study found that the people who put off the reward were more likely to earn more money. In fact, after education and job choice, the ability to delay gratification was the third most significant factor for determining how much money someone earned throughout their life.

While this study focuses exclusively on money and earning power, the concept of delayed gratification, or Hard-Easy, applies to every facet of your life: from Tae Kwon Do to starting a business, from becoming a better parent to playing the tuba, from eating healthier to mastering chemistry.

According to Dr. Duckworth, people who practice the art of delayed gratification do so because they have grit. According to

Dr. Dweck, their growth mindset allows them to understand the power of the word *yet* and to better understand how the choices they make today are an investment in their future.

Logotherapy

Next, we visit Viktor Frankl, a neurologist and psychiatrist born in Vienna, Austria, in 1905. He is best known for his famous book, *Man's Search for Meaning*.

In the book, Frankl recounts his experience as a Jewish prisoner in Auschwitz and in two Dachau camps, Kaufering and Türkheim, where he worked as a slave laborer and was surrounded by suffering and death. His mother and brother were murdered in Auschwitz. His wife was murdered in Bergen-Belsen. Of his immediate family, only his sister survived the Holocaust.

Because of what happened to him, he developed the psychiatric concept of logotherapy, which advocates for finding meaning in all forms of existence, no matter how brutal. Doing this, he argued, imbued one with a reason to continue living.

In the book *Logotherapy Revisited: Review of the Tenets of Viktor E. Frankl's Logotherapy*, Maria and Edward Marshall recap the basic tenets of logotherapy:

- Life has meaning under all circumstances, even the most miserable ones.
- Our main motivation for living is our will to find meaning in life.
- We have the freedom to find meaning in what we do, and what we experience, or at least in the stance we take when faced with a situation of unchangeable suffering.[24]

So, what does all this have to do with grit and Hard-Easy? Here are a few ideas.

First, despite difficult circumstances, we can always choose how we react to those circumstances.

Said Frankl:

> We who lived in concentration camps can remember the men who walked through the huts comforting others, giving away their last pieces of bread. They may have been few in number, but they offer sufficient proof that everything can be taken from a man but one thing; the last of the human freedoms—to choose one's attitude in any given set of circumstances, to choose one's own way.[25]

A second takeaway from logotherapy is the concept that grit can only be forged in the hard phase of Hard-Easy.

Said Frankl:

> Most men in a concentration camp believed that the real opportunities of life had passed. Yet, in reality, there was an opportunity and a challenge. One could make a victory of those experiences, turning life into an inner triumph, or one could ignore the challenge and simply vegetate, as did a majority of the prisoners.[26]

Frankl identifies two states of Hard-Easy and Easy-Hard: finding opportunity within challenge and finding inner triumph in spite of all the pain and difficulties surrounding you—that's Hard-Easy. Ignoring the challenge and giving in to the fate of destruction while falling into a vegetative state wherein you are acted upon instead of acting—that's Easy-Hard.

This echoes Dweck's ideas of the growth mindset: "In a growth mindset, people believe that their most basic abilities can be developed through dedication and hard work. This view creates a love of learning and a resilience that is essential for great accomplishment."[27]

When we find meaning in challenging circumstances and focus on the result, we accrue grit. When we persevere in the Hard of Hard-Easy, that grit thickens and hardens.

Those who live Easy-Hard allow life to happen to them. Those who live Hard-Easy impose their will on life to extract the most joy and satisfaction from it—for themselves and for others. They say to life, "Bring it, Hard!" No matter what life has done to them and no matter what it puts in their way, they choose to use these experiences to their advantage. They refuse to give up the Hard-Easy path that leads to their dreams. In fact, they use every obstacle and negative thing life throws at them to get stronger, smarter, and better in preparation for the steeper trails ahead.

Challenges are given equally to optimists and pessimists. One uses them to create happiness, the other misery. Optimists are propelled by joy, faith, and the belief in *yes*. Pessimists are paralyzed by fear, doubt, and the belief in *no*.

Now, I ask, is life happening *to* you or *for* you?

To Build Muscle, You Must First Break It Down

Just as muscles only grow in facing resistance, so, too, does grit only grow when the human will faces resistance.

This muscle-building metaphor is informative: the weight of resistance causes microtears in muscle fiber. But instead of each tear closing as it heals and going back to its original size, the body creates new muscle fiber to fill in the gaps, making the muscle slightly bigger when it heals. Over time and with consistent weight training, the muscle gets bigger, more defined, stronger—and able to handle heavier loads.

In fact, if you work out for a year doing squats, and you grow stronger and consistently add weight every week, something interesting happens. Something Hard-Easy.

At the end of the year, what was a struggle to lift twelve months ago now feels easy. You put in 365 days of Hard so that when you call on your body to squat and lift things at the gym, or kids at home or boxes in a storage shed, it is easier for you to accomplish. Meanwhile, your capacity to lift heavier weights increases.

Be One of the Grits

All these examples and concepts describe the mindset you need to cultivate as you seek and follow through with the Hard of Hard-Easy:

- Grit
- A growth mindset
- Delayed gratification
- The ability and willpower to determine how you will react when faced with difficult circumstances

Think about me trying to convince BigDog to cross the mountain stream on the cattle drive. I lacked sufficient levels of all those traits at first.

But thanks to a great cowboy mentor, I was able to express those traits to a sufficient degree that BigDog finally crossed the stream where I wanted him to. What was once a hard interaction with my horse became an easy one.

I'll end this chapter with one of my favorite quotes from Frankl:

> What was really needed was a fundamental change in our attitude toward life. We had to learn . . . that it did not really matter what we expected from life, but rather what life expected from us. We needed to stop asking about the meaning of life, and instead think of ourselves as those who were being questioned by life—daily and hourly. Our question must consist, not in talk and meditation, but in right action and in right conduct. Life ultimately means taking the responsibility to find the right answer to its problems and to fulfill the tasks which it constantly sets for each individual.[28]

Chapter Recap

Key concepts and takeaways from chapter 9:

- Be one of the grits.
- Natural talent, genetics, wealth, intelligence, and social status do not matter as much as we think they do; what matters is the belief that you can develop abilities, no matter how much or little you have, through dedication and hard work.
- We have the freedom—even when all other freedoms are taken—to choose how we react to the situation we're in, no matter how dire it seems.

Pause and Think

- What is the end goal you desire?
- What are some failures or problems you may run into along the way?
- How can the concepts of grit, growth mindset, and delayed gratification help you achieve that goal despite the challenges you face?

CHAPTER 10

"I CAN'T BECAUSE . . ."

The Top Excuses of All Time

We've learned a few concepts to help us persevere on the hard path no matter what, but those are no guarantee we'll stay on that path. Excuses are constant traps along our journey. While grit, a growth mindset, and delayed gratification are reliable defenses against excuses, we must know our enemy in order to use those defenses most effectively.

Benjamin Franklin.

You remember him, right? Born in Boston in 1706, Founding Father, author, printer, kite-flyer.

He said, "He that is good for making excuses is seldom good for anything else."

That's a ruthless assessment. And not too far from the truth. Making excuses is a common, self-deceptive, Easy-Hard tactic. It's easy to make excuses for our shortcomings and mistakes. It's hard to confront our weaknesses, confess our misdeeds, and commence the difficult work of change.

If you have read any of my other books, you know one of my favorite sayings is "Excuses don't change results." I learned that the hard way in a 1978 JV football game playing flanker back for Monta Vista high school. It was just like a movie: It was the fourth quarter, with just minutes left, and we were down by four. We had driven to the opponent's three-yard line. It was third down and three to go. Our coach called our signature play, which required me to go in motion and bulldoze the defensive end, clearing a lane for our quarterback to easily gain three yards and score a touchdown.

Only I screwed up.

I was preoccupied with the count and making sure I moved on the right cue. I failed to notice that the defensive end I was supposed to block had dropped back to outside linebacker. By the time I started sweeping toward the defensive end, there was no defensive end to block. I missed the block, and our QB got destroyed by the guy I missed, losing a yard.

Now it was fourth and goal from the four.

As our QB started to the sideline to get the next play, the coach stopped him and yelled for me to come over.

Normally, only the QB would run over to get the play. To say it was unusual that I had been called over as well would be an understatement. I felt a hollow pit in my stomach already from screwing up on my assignment and possibly costing us the championship. Now, as I approached the coach, I felt nervous, ready to be yelled at.

Coach didn't yell.

Instead, he calmly asked me what happened on the last play.

I started to explain in great detail how I had been concentrating on the count and how that had distracted me when I went into motion.

The coach cut me off by seizing my facemask, shaking my head, and pulling me right to his face so he had my attention. He said with eerie calmness: "Coombs, excuses do not change results. Ten other players did their job. YOU did not. We didn't score because of you. Excuses do not change results."

Then he called the exact same play we had just run. "I don't know if we will score," he said to me, "but, Coombs, I do know that YOU WILL HIT YOUR MAN."

He sent me back to the huddle with the play.

And the coach was right. I did hit my man. I drove him yards out of the play, opening a hole through which our quarterback waltzed into the end zone, sealing our championship.

My coach's mantra has stayed with me and been a guiding principle in my personal life and my work life.

Because excuses yield no results, you need to build up your excuse immune system. You need excuse-killing, white-blood-cell thoughts roaming your mind, seeking and destroying the virulent excuses that threaten to seriously damage your motivation, responsibility, and ambition—and jeopardize your ability to live Hard-Easy.

Here are eleven of the most commonly used excuses. I have heard them over and over; I have used them over and over.

1. I WANT TO CHANGE, BUT I CAN'T

Welcome to our top excuse: "I want to change, but I can't."

This has a few variations on the same theme:

"I have no willpower."

"I have no self-control."

Here is the fundamental flaw with that thinking: it presumes that practicing self-discipline is bullying yourself into doing something you do not want to do, thereby framing it as masochistic behavior. It is not.

Self-discipline is doing what you *really* want to do in the face of adversity. Suppose what we really want is x, but we're tempted to choose y at the moment because it is easier or offers instant gratification. So when you say, "I want to change, but I can't," what you are really saying is, "I want to choose the path that leads me to that deep-down x, but another part of me craves the easy of y."

Self-discipline channels the deeper part of your core integrity to override the part of your character that is weak, stressed out, and cowardly. The weak side of you screams like that toddler in the checkout line at the gas station, wanting candy *now*. Self-control is the ability to say *no* to that toddler and make the choices that propel you toward becoming your best self.

You're making choices that will impact the future you—the you two, five, and ten years from now. If you haven't already, start a relationship with your future self. Visualize future you—where you live, what you're like, how you're living a life created from the decisions you make today.

This is important in helping you conquer this excuse. Because if your future self is a stranger, you are unlikely to sacrifice for that stranger. Why would you?

When I can envision Future Art, I am more likely to transform "I want to change, but I can't" to "I want to change, and I will!" As I consistently imagine my future self and have conversations with him, I feel like I am developing a friendship with and a love for my future self, and I don't want to do anything now that would harm him.

Okay, that sounds mildly delusional, but allow me to explain. The deeper the relationship I have with Future Art, the stronger my willpower and desire to make good choices becomes.

This is basically what I did when I took my homework-dodging, video-game-loving son Kai to Walmart at 2:00 a.m. I was introducing him to Future Kai—at least the Kai of the future who would be created if he kept making Easy-Hard choices.

He met that Kai and didn't like the world he lived in.

Now, with a better relationship and understanding of his future self, Kai can connect the dots of his actions today to the impact they'll have on him five, ten, and twenty years down the road.

2. I AM ONLY HUMAN

This is one of the granddaddies of all excuses. And it's ridiculous.

This excuse supposedly absolves one of doing silly, stupid, mindless, or unkind things. According to Gary Stokes, President of Mountain Consulting and author of *Poise: A Warrior's Guide*, using this excuse is "comforting, no doubt, to people who don't want to confront their own weaknesses and bad explanations."[29]

If you take a closer look at the very words in that excuse, its merits fall apart. The keyword is *only*. We are all human. So, to me, being "only" human is the greatest compliment you can give to humans. Are we really going to suggest being "only human" is a negative condition?

To drive home the point, what metaphors do we use for people who act inhumanely?

The criminal acted like a beast when she killed the victim.

The gang members turned on each other like animals.

That man who groped me at the bar is a total pig.

We describe others as *nonhuman* when we refer to their despicable acts. We dehumanize them.

Ironically, when we describe our own foibles as being "only human," we're referring to the beastly, baser parts of us. So the very wording of the excuse contradicts its attempted meaning.

Don't use your humanity as your fall guy. In the courtroom of your personal development, never plead the Fifth. Always testify against your own mistakes instead of falsely accusing the alleged nature of your species.

"But, Art, you told us yourself that we are genetically predisposed to follow our inner Neanderthal to instant gratification! Therefore, we CAN blame our slipups on being human."

I respond by pointing at your forehead and reminding you about your prefrontal cortex, the brake pedal on the speeding car of impulsiveness.

It is true that being human includes the genetic impulse for instant gratification. But being human also involves our genetic impulse to foster society and civilization. And that includes putting the brakes on our impulsiveness, acting in unselfish ways, treating others with respect and kindness, and taking responsibility for our actions. It is all part of our up-to-the-minute, human, genetic heritage.

As Haverly Erskine says in her article for the *Democrat & Chronicle*, "I'm Only Human: An Excuse or a Reasonable Justification?":

> As humans, we do make mistakes, but it is also because we are human that we are capable of doing some incredible things. We can be amazing, wonderful, and moral. We can be loving, caring, diligent, and competent. (And luckily, a lot of people are.) Sure, we all have our weaknesses. No one is perfect. But

there's a big difference between a weakness and an enormous error in judgment. Being human should be our strength, not our excuse.[30]

Let's be clear: a slipup is when you do something accidentally or forgetfully. Repeatedly making bad decisions, however, demonstrates a deficiency in character, morals, and willpower. It also demonstrates an *unwillingness* to accept responsibility. So your "only human" mistake cannot be defined as a simple slipup if it is part of a pattern.

"I'm only human," marginalizes the strength of being human. It can never justify bad choices—from the small decisions (midnight raid on the frozen Thin Mints when I've vowed to cut unhealthy snacking out of my diet) to the revolting decisions (striking a child, hitting someone weaker, or bullying or abusing others).

That is *not* "only human." That is cowardice, the lowest of the low, and demonic weakness.

So, how do you combat this excuse?

Realize that "being human," in its purest form, implies progression. It means we are present in the moment—we are thinking, feeling, aware, and intentional beings.

When you find yourself using "I'm only human" as an excuse, let it trigger the follow-up, corrective thought: To be human is to be conscious of our thoughts, words, and actions. To be human is to deliberately make choices that maximize our pursuit of happiness to the best of our understanding and ability. To be truly human is to show others kindness, compassion, forgiveness, and mercy.

3. NATURE VERSUS NURTURE EXCUSES

What exerts the greatest influence on our behavior, choices, and human development: nature or nurture? In other words, do our genetics (nature), or our environment (nurture) make us who we are and do what we do?

You know that I am a ravenous chilled-Thin-Mint-aholic. Is it because my DNA hardwired me to gorge on the addictive cookies like a zombie feasts on the flesh of the living? Or is it because of the Thin-Mint-permissive environment I was raised in?

This has been a raging debate among psychologists and philosophers for decades. Okay, maybe not my chilled Thin Mint addiction, but the nature-versus-nurture perplexity has.

Regardless of what side of the debate you fall on, both nature and nurture give us the rationale to say, "I can't help it. I was born this way" (nature), or "I was raised this way" (nurture).

Fortunately, science helps us knock the legs out from under these excuses.

So, science ... which is it: nature or nurture?

The answer is quite clear: both.

In 2015, Dr. Beben Benyamin from the Queensland Brain Institute and researchers at the VU University of Amsterdam collaborated to review nearly every twin study completed over the past fifty years. Here's what their research, published in *Nature Genetics*,[31] found:

Researchers analyzed 2,748 standard twin studies containing 14.5 million pairs of twins. (For a guy who loves stats, that is one massively compelling control group.) These twin studies evaluated identical twins with virtually identical DNA, and nonidentical twins. They found that, on average, the variation for human traits and diseases is split almost equally.

"When visiting the nature versus nurture debate, there is overwhelming evidence that both genetic and environmental factors can influence traits and diseases," Dr. Benyamin said in a press release. "What is comforting is that, on average, about 50 percent of individual differences are genetic, and 50 percent are environmental."[32]

The study also found that this approximate 50/50 split (technically 49 percent genetics to 51 percent environment) did not apply to every trait examined. For bipolar disorder, for example, the causes were found to be approximately 70 percent genetic versus 30 percent environmental. For the development of eating disorders, the split was 60 percent environmental and 40 percent genetic. But for almost everything else, it comes down to nature *and* nurture.

This section is not meant to be an in-depth, technical discussion of heredity and genetics. I am simply trying to make the point that excuses based on nature or nurture do not give you an automatic pass for bad behavior or poor choices.

Because of my dyslexia, I know all too well how easy it is to say, "I was born this way." It was tempting to think, "I am a victim of my DNA, and there is nothing I can do about getting an education and altering the course of my future."

That was the excuse I clung to for the first twenty-five years of my life. But while I do have some limitations, I have learned that this genetic makeup cannot confine me to a life of scholastic mediocrity. Although I was, in fact, born with dyslexia, I do not have to let it hold me back.

Remember, you can't really blame either nature or nurture for your failures. So how do you overcome this excuse?

One way to beat it is to recognize the weaknesses you are trying to mask and use them as motivation to get better. For example, my dyslexia was the irritating grain of sand in the oyster that caused the oyster to create the pearl. It was the immense geologic pressure that compressed coal into a diamond. Dyslexia caused me to dig deep to find the determination to work harder, develop workarounds, utter my mantra "Bring It Hard" more times than I can count, and succeed *in spite of* my disability (more on that in chapter 21).

Every weakness can become an opportunity to become better—if you refuse to let nature/nurture excuses define your future.

4. I DON'T HAVE THE TIME OR MONEY TO CHANGE

To undercut this excuse, all you need to do is rephrase it as what it really means: I am *unwilling* to devote any of my free time or money to change.

Do you have time to Netflix binge? Do you have the money or credit cards to go shopping? Do you have time to hit the bars and clubs on the weekends? Or watch football all day on Sunday? Can you find an extra twenty dollars to play the lottery, buy a bottle of whiskey, or subscribe to a movie-streaming service?

If so, you have a pool of leisure time and money you can swap for self-evolution.

I repeatedly hear this excuse. It suggests that you struggle with self-control, desire, motivation, restraint, and direction. It also implies that your priorities are all screwed up and that you struggle to manage your time and money effectively. *Ouch.*

Often at the core of this excuse are procrastination and laziness. So, yeah, I'd rather believe the excuse than confront the truth about myself.

How do you start to conquer this excuse? When you hear yourself making it, ask yourself: "How bad do I want this change, dream, or goal?"

When you decide to divert some of your spare time and money to the Hard-Easy path you're on, it doesn't matter that it starts small. The point is that it starts. Even if you're only setting aside a few extra cents and building your savings tiny bit by tiny bit, or spending five extra minutes per day doing the hard work toward your goal, it adds up.

More importantly, you're establishing the principles and habits of discipline and saving. So when you earn more money and enjoy more free time in your life, you'll be well trained on what to do with them—save and spend wisely on those things that will bring you closer to your dreams.

5. I AM NOT READY TO CHANGE

As I interact with people, I can't tell you how many times I hear people admit they are not completely happy with their life and would like to change—but then, in the same breath, declare, "I'm just not ready to make that change right now."

What follows usually is a chain reaction of excuses that justify why they don't want to change right now. The circumstances aren't right. Their mindset isn't right. Or any of the other excuses on this list can come into play. It's a total justification nuclear meltdown, from one excuse to another.

Well, guess what? No one is ever ready to change.

To overcome this excusing, you need to realize that this gambit is not an excuse at all. Change is *always* uncomfortable and scary. What if we try but fail? We humans fight and resist change until forced by circumstance—or until we build the mojo to change.

So when you find yourself saying, "I'm not ready to change," follow that thought with "but I'm going to change anyway. Bring it hard!"

6. I DON'T KNOW HOW TO CHANGE

This excuse indicates a lack of belief and confidence in your ability to achieve your goal. In other words, you don't believe in you. Additionally, this excuse reveals the need to learn, practice, or gain the skills and knowledge to grasp what's required to change.

The key to overcoming this excuse is to add to the sentence: "I don't know how to change, but I'm going to learn how."

You possess within you the will and ability to change. Your job is to teach yourself how to drill deep enough to tap into that power. Once you do, it will be like an oil well that keeps pumping, barrel after barrel.

7. WHAT IF I FAIL?

We all fear failure. It's okay. It's a natural fear. But what separates successful people from less successful people is the ability to try despite the fear—and then learn from the mistakes of failure so they can try again.

Failure is the master teacher. Or it can be if we let it.

How do babies learn to walk? It's a long series of frustrating wobbles and occasionally painful tumbles. But they keep on going until they master it.

I love the quote by J.K. Rowling: "It is impossible to live without failing at something, unless you live so cautiously that you might as well not have lived at all."[33] The road to successful change is forever paved with potholes, roadblocks, and persistent problems. Those who fail are those who give up prematurely and refuse to rise and take accountability for their actions. Until you commit to being accountable, you are guaranteed to repeat the same pattern of failure over and over again.

Don't fear failure; invite it. Expect it. The faster you embrace failure on your quest for change, the faster you will learn, refine, and improve.

Remember Edison and the light bulb? Your greater self always lies at the end of a path of successes born from failures.

8. IT'S NOT GOING TO WORK BECAUSE NOTHING EVER WORKS OUT FOR ME

These are the people who are habitually unhappy and pessimistic and who have grown so comfortable in the victim role they believe that absolutely nothing they want will ever work out.

I want to distinguish this worldview from clinical depression and other mental illnesses, which require medical treatment and often medication. What I'm speaking about here is a habitual glass-half-empty mindset. If you happen to fall into this camp, somewhere along the line, you learned this twisted, self-destructive worldview. That's the bad news. The good news is that if it was learned, it can be unlearned.

Emerging from the habitual thinking of this chronic excuse can be extremely challenging. Those who do try to change run into the setbacks that inevitably come in the pursuit of goals. For those who believe that nothing ever works out for them, these early setbacks seem to prove they're right, and they all too quickly abandon their attempts to change.

The best way to counter this is to add the following thought to each woe-is-me thought you have: "Nothing ever works out for me . . . because I give up too quickly, but that's going to change because I know that what I'm looking for is on the other side of each obstacle I encounter. I will not give up. Bring it, hard!"

It sounds overly simplistic, but remember, as we discussed previously, words matter. Positive self-talk is a powerful way to reprogram your thoughts, actions, and, eventually—you.

9. I DON'T WANT TO CHANGE / I DON'T NEED TO CHANGE

Now and then I run into someone who says, "That's great for you and others, but I don't want to change."

If you have read this far, I can't imagine you are one of these folks. But if you are or know someone who is, what can you do to change the mind of that person when they don't see the need or have the desire to change?

Absolutely nothing!

Have you ever tried to help someone change their behavior when they had no desire or intention to change? How'd it go?

I can state with confidence that if you have tried to play the role of changer, and the changee did not want to change, you ran into a wall of resistance and frustration. You, no doubt, failed to fix the changee.

And if you yourself are the one who doesn't want to change, you can't really get around this excuse until you desire change.

Be warned: If you try to change someone who doesn't want to be changed, you risk alienating that person. You are sabotaging the love, security, and trust of the relationship . . . if there is still a relationship intact.

Bottom line: If someone doesn't see the need to change, do not waste your time and energy trying to change them. Sure, it's good to still encourage them when you can and advise them that they have resources if they ever decide to change. But you can't force it.

And if it's you who doesn't want to change—well, I doubt you're reading this, but if you are, the only way around this excuse is to see the need for a change and then desire to make it. That's your first goal—the goal upon which you can build the rest of your Hard-Easy journey.

10. I AM TOO OLD / TOO YOUNG TO CHANGE

Noah Webster completed the *American Dictionary of the English Language* when he was sixty-six. Malala Yousafzai coauthored a book at age sixteen and won the Nobel Peace Prize in 2014 at the age of seventeen.

Using the age excuse suggests a lack of perspective, understanding, and confidence. Countless women and men of all ages have accomplished unbelievable things. You are never too old or too young to have, strive for, and pursue your goals, objectives, and dreams.

Depending on your age, of course, things may be a bit more challenging for you. But that is where tenacity, willpower, and imagination can propel you. You may need to push harder and endure longer. But when the desire and grit are there, you will in fact push harder and endure longer.

To deflate this excuse, you must say, "I'm too old/young to change . . . but I will change anyway to show my age who's boss."

None of us can turn the hands of time backward or forward. But we do have today. Today, in fact, is all we ever have. This moment. This now. How will you spend your now?

11. I'LL CHANGE TOMORROW

One of the ugliest words of all time is *procrastination*—unless you're playing Scrabble.

The last-minute homework? The savings account with no deposits? The big plans to start your healthy diet and gym membership next month?

Procrastinating creates shame, stress, and anxiety. So why do we do it? There are many reasons, but the one I want to focus on is "I just don't *feel* like doing it."

Why are you waiting until you *feel* like doing it? Somewhere, you got the mistaken idea that you must be motivated before you act. As Marine Raider, author, producer, and entrepreneur Nick Koumalatsos says, "Motivation is shit."

Most successful individuals are successful due to habits that force them to put in a set number of hours a day regardless of their motivation—or whether they *feel* like doing it.

If you're procrastinating some hard task because you don't *feel* like it, just remember this: if you wait until you feel like it, it will never happen. But if you plan to change and make working on that plan a habit regardless of how you feel, you'll be able to transform to-do lists into to-done lists.

No Excuses

Remember, this is not a comprehensive list of all the excuses and permutations of rationalization we humans use to avoid blame and shame. It's just the most common I've heard or fallen prey to over the years.

As we end this chapter, I want to leave you with this thought: you must be willing to take ownership of your mistakes, and to do this, you need to recognize your favorite excuses and knock them out of your brain and vocabulary. It's not easy. If it were, we wouldn't have excuses, and everyone would be a high achiever.

The principle of Hard-Easy teaches us that the more we practice taking ownership of our mistakes, the easier it becomes. When we try to deny and hide our weaknesses, mistakes, and limitations with excuses, they become more firmly rooted in our character. And the more ingrained they become, the faster our so-called character deteriorates.

Owning and correcting our bad or mediocre behavior while balancing on the fine line of not being too critical of ourselves shows deep integrity.

Chapter Recap

Key concepts and takeaways from chapter 10:

- Keep an eye out for these excuses in your life—if you see them, shoot them on sight.

- By being aware of the most common excuse patterns our brains throw at us, we can inoculate ourselves, putting ourselves on high alert for when we try to let ourselves off the hook and go Easy-Hard.
- There's no excuse for excuses.

Pause and Think

Keep the goal from last chapter's Pause and Think in mind.

- What is step one for your goal?
- Which excuses are most tempting when you think of step one?
- How can you defeat them?

CHAPTER 11

A FEW PRACTICAL WAYS TO HELP YOU IDENTIFY AND PURGE EXCUSES

In this chapter, we'll look at a few methods for changing your brain from excuse mode to excel mode.

Stopping Excuses before They Stop You

You're at war with excuses. What kind of weapons do you have in your arsenal to help eradicate the enemy? Here are a few.

Awareness. Like an alcoholic who must first admit that they have a problem before they can begin overcoming it, you must be aware that you are guilty of making excuses. Being aware puts you in a position to do something about it.

Excuse tracker. Start keeping an excuse tracker: a spreadsheet, a little notebook, your phone—whatever. Begin with one excuse you catch yourself making and count how many times you use it over the course of two weeks. How often does the excuse help you rationalize your own destructive behavior?

Incidentally, "destructive behavior" sounds exceptionally dramatic—and it can be. But you don't have to be Amy Winehouse or Eliot Spitzer to engage in behavior that qualifies as "destructive." You may only be guilty of "mediocre behavior." But mediocre-level behavior—and the excuses that enable that behavior—hinders your progress toward great things. In that sense, mediocre behavior destroys your migration to a higher plane.

Identify triggers. What are the triggers that elicit your excuse? Location, time, or company? In your excuse tracker, write down the situation that sparked the excuse. Over a two-to-four-week period, you should be able to discern excuse patterns and their triggers.

Exorcise shame. As you identify the excuse—or excuses—you may feel guilt or shame about your weakness. Or you may feel the impulse to criticize yourself.

Don't.

When you feel bad about yourself, you are inclined to make more excuses in a flawed effort to boost your self-esteem. However, what you are really doing is obscuring your pain or discomfort with a sedative. Your pain will not only remain, it will grow worse. The only surefire remedy is figuring out how to overcome your fears and stop masking them with excuses.

But excuses look pretty sexy when you feel down on yourself. So do *not* fall into a loop of guilt and self-criticism. Remember, by ditching shame and guilt, you are not being ignorant of or embracing your faults. What you *are* doing is disconnecting yourself from counterproductive feelings. (I'll be devoting more thought to shame, so stay tuned.)

Think shift. Evolve from making excuses and justifications to generating solutions. Look deep into each challenge and failure; instead of seeing a problem, try to spot the opportunity—and then keep churning toward your goals.

Find Your Flock

Another way to fortify yourself against excuse-making is to find a flock of fellow achievers. Birds of a feather flock together, the saying goes.

Many talk about wanting to become great, yet they find themselves surrounded by excuse-making friends who tolerate mediocrity. Those closest to you should invigorate you, not exhaust you. They should encourage self-improvement, not self-destruction.

I love those bluntly candid friends who will tell me my zipper is wide open, my breath reeks of rotten squid, or my new haircut makes it look like a rabid opossum is attacking my head.

While it may be awkward and a little embarrassing at the time, those friends who will pull me aside and be candid with me are truly good friends.

Sometimes we want to avoid these outspoken friends. Humans don't want to be confronted with the painful truth. But these are exactly the friends we need, day in and day out. These are the friends who will call us out on our excuses.

Of course, saying that you want your friends to be honest with you is fine *until they're honest with you*. At first, your reaction to hearing any hard, biting truths may cause you to be a bit defensive. In fact, it may prompt you to use another excuse to justify your first excuse.

That's all perfectly natural.

Stop, take a mental break, and allow yourself some time to reflect. Instead of getting your feelings hurt or being defensive, learn to take criticism constructively. Detach yourself from the frank observation and don't take it personally.

Don't Worry about What Others Think

Okay. I get it.

I just told you to get good friends and listen to them when they point out your excuses. In other words, I just asked you to care about what they think.

And now, in this section, I'm telling you *not* to worry about what others think.

Am I being a contradictory smartass here? Or has one of my multiple personalities taken over the keyboard?

No on both counts.

I asked you to listen to friends who will torpedo your excuses and not tolerate your inclinations toward mediocrity or settling.

That's different from another human trait—seeking approval in the eyes of the wrong people for the sake of being liked or being popular.

Aesop's Fable of "The Miller, His Son, and the Ass" teaches us why the human impulse to seek approval from the crowd will hold us back:

> One day, a long, long time ago, an old miller and his son were on their way to market with an ass they wanted to sell. They walked him slowly down the dirt road, for they thought they would have a better chance to sell him if they kept him in good condition.
>
> As they walked along, a traveler laughed loudly at them. "What foolishness to walk when they might as well ride," the traveler said derisively. "The most stupid of the three is not the one you would expect it to be."
>
> The miller did not like to be laughed at, so he told his son to climb up and ride the ass.
>
> They had gone a little farther along the road when three merchants passed by. "Oho, what have we here?" they cried. "Respect old age, young man! Get down and let the old man ride."
>
> Though the miller was not tired, he made the boy get down and climbed up to ride the ass just to please the merchants.
>
> Around the next bend, they passed some women carrying market baskets loaded with vegetables and other things to sell. "Look at the old fool," exclaimed one of them. "Perched on the ass, while that poor boy has to walk."
>
> The miller felt a bit irritated, but to be agreeable, he told the boy to climb up behind him on the ass.
>
> They had no sooner started out again than a loud shout went up from another group of travelers on the road. "What a crime," cried one, "to load up a poor dumb beast like that! They look more able to carry the poor creature than he to carry them."
>
> "They must be on their way to sell the poor thing's hide," said another.
>
> The miller and his Son quickly scrambled down, and a short time later, the marketplace was thrown into an uproar as the

two came along carrying the donkey upside down, slung from a pole. A great crowd of people ran out to get a closer look at the spectacle.

The ass did not dislike being carried, but so many people came up to point at him and laugh and shout, that he began to kick and bray, and then, just as they were crossing a bridge, the ropes that held him gave way, and down he tumbled into the river.

The poor miller and his son now set out sadly for home. By trying to please everybody, the miller had pleased nobody—and lost his ass.[34]

The obvious moral of the story is that if you try to please everyone, you end up pleasing no one. You're worse off than before you started and have lost your dignity, confidence, and even your ass in the process.

Also, none of the people the miller and his son met on the road were the miller's friends—and certainly not any friends who were vested in his improvement. If the miller had been hanging around his hovel and told his friends he didn't want to go to the village to sell his ass because there was a really good episode of *Real Housewives of the Serfdom* coming on, and his friends stood up and said, "Yo, miller, stop making excuses again. Get your ass to the village. You've been talking about investing in another mill wheel for years. Now's your chance." Those would be the opinions the miller should have listened to.

But on the road, he was just interested in gaining the acceptance of the crowd so he wouldn't look stupid. And, of course, he ended up looking exceptionally stupid.

Do not do what the masses tell you. The masses sit on their asses and are masses because they think and act the way they think and act. Like asses. (I think that's from a Dr. Seuss book that never got published. Can you see my sardonic smile?)

I guess if mediocrity is your thing and you dream of one day achieving the most bland mediocrity possible, then, sure, do what the masses tell you to do. But if you want an exceptional life, act in accordance with your thinking, planning, gut, and judgment. Do those things. Shed the noise and diversions.

You Are *Not* Excused

We humans are amazingly skilled at generating creative, compelling excuses (at least compelling to us). Even today, I have to fight the inclination to make excuses.

I pray you are set free from a life of mediocrity and excuses and released into becoming the best you there is, with no regrets when it's time to check out.

Stop Excuses and Start

>Start with one yes.
>Start with one no.
>Start with one small act of kindness.
>Start with one sit-up.
>Start with cleaning one room.
>Start with one "I am sorry. I was wrong."
>Start with one payment toward a debt.
>Start with one contact deleted.
>Start with one written note of gratitude.
>Start with one "I love you."

Chapter Recap

Key concepts and takeaways from chapter 11:

- Use these tools to spot and stop excuses: being aware, using the tool tracker, identifying triggers, exorcising shame, and engaging in think-shift.
- Find your flock.

- Don't listen to those who subtly or not so subtly divert you from your dreams.
- Start.

Pause and Think

- Have any of your friends ever called you out on something? How did you react? Were they right? Did it lead to a course correction?
- Take a moment right now to start your excuse tracker. As you think about the excuses cataloged in this chapter and other excuses, name a couple you think you use quite often. Jot them down and be on the lookout for them.

CHAPTER 12

SILENCING THE TOXIC WHISPERS OF SHAME

This is my follow-up chapter on shame, which I touched upon in our excuses chapters. Shame is a powerful poison. This chapter will help you release the shame that's weighing you down and coaxing you to make Easy-Hard choices.

What Is Shame?

Shame is a corrosive, destructive force that erodes your ability to choose Hard-Easy. It constantly whispers toxic, negative messages that target our biggest insecurities. Shame sits on your shoulder when you fail and hisses that you are unfixable.

It's that hurtful, ugly feeling that spawns from how we view ourselves—by seeing all our imperfections and obsessively focusing on them. The dissonance we see between our failure selves and the better selves we wish we could be gives rise to shame.

Shame that we're not better.
Shame that we have let ourselves and others down.
Shame that we've stumbled—and stumbled again—always plagued by the same weaknesses.

One reason shame takes such a heavy toll on us is that when we experience shame, we don't just believe we've done bad things, we believe *we* are bad. And we want to hide or withdraw from others.

The shamed masses go to great lengths to mask their apparent shortcomings and failures. They desperately want others to think they have it all together when internally they feel overwhelmed by blunder and defeat.

Shame creates such strong feelings of inadequacy that it prevents you from moving forward.

Shaming Others

While we ourselves may feel shame for our own shortcomings, we can also be the purveyors of shame, causing others to feel ashamed about their failures.

There are many ways we shame: subtle sarcasm, name-calling, conveying disgust, simple eye-rolling, and ostracizing.

Shaming can make us feel superior to others. It also communicates to others that we want them to act differently.

The main ingredients of shaming are judgment, self-righteousness, and hypocrisy. It's a way to control others by using their deep-rooted craving for connection to terrorize and intimidate them, even if the intent of the person shaming is not malevolent.

The Bazooka Bubblegum Incident

As I write, I can still remember much of the shaming I experienced as a young boy. I am not trying to point the finger or blame or shame old teachers, parents, or friends. I am merely trying to demonstrate how most of us use shame from time to time as an attempt to control others—and what it feels like to be the one feeling shame.

When I was in the fourth grade at Lincoln Elementary in Cupertino, California, one of my favorite teachers had a rule that you could not chew gum in her classroom. And, usually, I was gum-free.

Back then, Bazooka Bubblegum was one cent for a single piece. Occasionally I would pinch a few nickels from my mom's purse, leave early for school, and walk to 7-Eleven, where I bought ten pieces of Bazooka Bubblegum. I would stuff my pockets and give gum to my friends throughout the day. Sometimes I would even enjoy a wad myself.

On this particular day, I was breaking my teacher's gum rule. We were all silently reading at our desks. My teacher walked up beside me and quietly asked if I was chewing gum.

Busted.

There was no getting out of this one. No quick fib would save me. For a split second, I thought of swallowing the gum and innocently saying, "Who me?" But the wad I was gnawing on was way too big for that.

I looked at her and sheepishly nodded.

Now the entire class was watching.

My teacher calmly said, "Art, please go to the wastebasket and throw out your gum, then come to the front of the class and meet me there."

I will never forget the dread that filled my heart, the ugly pit I felt in my stomach, and the panic swirling in my nine-year-old brain.

As I got up to throw my gum out, I started to hear my classmates whispering and giggling. I felt every classmate's eyes on me. I could see some pointing in my direction as I slowly walked from my desk to the wastebasket in the back of the room and then toward the front of the room, where my teacher was waiting.

When I met her at the front of the room, she calmly and lovingly (and I mean that—she was doing this with the pure intent of helping me be better at following the rules) said, "Art I am going to draw a circle on the chalkboard, and then I want you to stick your nose in the middle of it and hold it there for ten minutes."

For a moment I was kind of relieved she wasn't going to have me bend over and spank me with a ruler.

She drew the circle, then instructed me to stick my nose on the chalkboard and keep it there for ten minutes, not moving until she told me time was up.

The first few seconds were not that bad. But then shame flooded me. The hot flush of embarrassment and public disgrace seared my emotions and psyche like nothing I have ever felt before or since.

Those ten minutes were the longest of my life. In fact, as I write this, I can vividly feel the panic, stress, perspiration, and anxiety of the instant. I can even hear my classmates snickering—the echoes stretching across time to this moment.

When the ten minutes were up, I pulled away from the chalkboard, and there was a dark spot where my nose had been. I will never forget how one of the cute, popular girls called out, "Ewww, look at the board! His nose left a grease mark! Grooooossss."

I had not thought that my shame could get worse—and then it had. My public humiliation hit a low I did not think possible. There I was, singled out, publicly disgraced in front of the entire class. It was like my scarlet letter for breaking the gum rule. I wanted to cry.

The white-hot wave of shame and embarrassment still makes me tremble, even fifty years later.

Did I ever chew gum in class again?

Hell, no.

But this experience caused a lifelong behavior modification in me.

First, I hate chewing gum. I will rarely chew gum, and if I do, it is for a few minutes to freshen my breath, and then I throw it away.

And when I see—or worse yet, hear—others chew gum, I often feel frustration, annoyance, and arrogance toward them: how gross.

Don't they realize they look like a grazing, salivating, repulsive cow, and sound ten times worse? Chomp, chomp, chomp. Smack, smack, smack. I literally cannot handle it. They should be absolutely ashamed of themselves.

I generally will not say anything, but the anxiety that swells within me is palpable. That incident with my fourth-grade teacher was purely Pavlovian. It conditioned me to forever feel that people who chew gum are shameful and disgusting.

Second, from that moment on, I went to great lengths to avoid being singled out and publicly shamed. If I encountered an organization or individual who shamed others to coerce them into obedience, I avoided them at all costs.

While my teacher meant well—she really did because her motives were to make me be a better person—her method scarred me deeply. She was trying to be loving. Though she hadn't made a public announcement to the entire class saying I had messed up and would be punished, she might as well have. All the students saw, and following their basest human tendencies, began to judge, mock, and shame.

How Feeling Shame and Causing Shame Hold Us Back

While the Bazooka Bubblegum incident was successful in assuring I would never chew gum in class and for the rest of my life, it also created in me a fear—a fear that any little slipup or failure would result in the eyes of the world zeroing in on me with disapproval and disdain. This was terrifying because I didn't want to feel that degrading dread ever again.

That's how I came to understand that if you live in shame, you live in endless fear of being rejected and scorned. That leads to a life of avoidance, where you come up with strategies to escape the pain of possible rejection.

And shame left untreated grows more powerful. Unchecked, it can lead to behaviors that invite even greater shame.

Almost everyone will respond to shaming, although it will never be in a way that nourishes and fosters a trusting, healthy relationship. Shame makes us feel terrible because it convinces us that we are terrible—terrible, damaged, and worthless.

And when we are the ones shaming—no matter the motive—it prevents us from progressing to self-actualization. (Psychologist Abraham Maslow, as you may remember, postulated that self-actualization is fulfilling your talents and realizing your potential.) Shamers, much like schoolyard bullies, are often projecting the shame they feel for their shortcomings onto someone else. It's a masking device they use to hide their own feelings of inadequacy and make themselves feel better, if only for a few fleeting moments.

Shame fiercely protects itself, and what you may think is clever or inspired discipline or advice might just be shaming in disguise. Again, my teacher's motives were pure, but her methods shamed me deeply.

Social Media and the Explosion of Shame and Shaming

Social media has two problems when it comes to shame. First, it gives voice to shamers—trolls who seek to shame others. It's now possible for a multitude of shamers from around the globe to swarm like piranhas and attack their target of choice.

Second, it gives us infinite opportunities to compare ourselves with others, and more often than not, come up short when we see we don't have the perfect home, family, smile, body, income, vacation itinerary, or wardrobe, which leads to a death spiral into shame.

What's interesting about the act of comparing ourselves with others is that we become the shamers of ourselves.

Wild, right?

The problem with comparison is that there will always be someone else who's faster, smarter, stronger, richer, more beautiful, or more successful than you. Comparison will cause you to feel insecure, resent those who seem to have it all, and shame yourself for not being better.

The evil of comparing ourselves to others has one last trick up its sleeve. Since it makes us feel inadequate, it often fosters within us a desire to mask our shortcomings by belittling and shaming those who appear to be worse off than we are. In a sad and ironic twist, we now become the trolls harassing others so that we can take our mind off our failures by pointing out the weaknesses we see in others.

Every moment spent being jealous is a moment wasted.

My wife and I are building a new home. This summer, we took the opportunity to walk through some homes featured in what they call "The Parade of Homes."

The homes were ginormous and, in my opinion, extremely opulent, but the size and lavishness were not what bothered me. What bothered me was the hordes walking through and looking at how less than 1 percent of 1 percent live their lives.

Most walked away with a twinge of depression as they unwittingly started playing the comparison game. Me included.

We don't have much time on this earth. I'm in my fifties, and I'm baffled how astonishingly fast time has passed. I don't have the time or energy for jealousy.

If you're too focused on others, you can't focus on you. Instead of wasting time in the comparison game, choose to spend your time on self-improvement.

I'm teaching my youngest kids to drive. I am always telling them to "stay in your lane and focus on your car."

You shouldn't care about how fast or slow the others around you are going. Stay in your lane and stay focused. If you are worried about what others are doing, you are not focused on what you are doing.

If you focus on you, one day you'll marvel at how far you have come and the beautiful life you've traveled.

Comparison—fueled by social media, but not exclusive to it—is a breeding ground for shame and shaming. It makes us believe that the easiest way to hide our own shame is to cast shame on others. This leads to gossip, damage to self-esteem, and fractured relationships.

And it leads to more and more Easy-Hard decisions.

The History of Shame:
An Engine for Maintaining Tribal, Societal Cohesion

We are hardwired to abhor shame. It forces us to conform to group or societal rules and norms.

Back to our earliest ancestors: If someone broke the rules, they were ostracized or banished, which most likely meant death. And even if you didn't get eaten by a saber-tooth tiger after getting kicked out of the tribe, the banishment most likely felt like death anyway.

Imagine you've been cast out of your tribe of cave people. How does it feel to be hiding on a hill and looking down at your former friends and family gathered around the fire eating roast mammoth while you're stuck in the cold eating moths and raw lizards? And then you watch them after they feast, telling stories, laughing, grooming each other, and playing Throw-the-Rock-at-Thog.

Yeah, it sucks. (It probably sucked to be Thog, too, but that's a different story.)

As my Bazooka Bubblegum–chalkboard episode shows, shame can fill us with its toxic, damaging venom. Shaming words are rarely ever forgotten, and shaming, though it may bring about some behavior change, damages others and, in turn, lowers us in their regard. No one wants to be around someone who strives to make them feel ashamed.

Conquer the What-the-Hell Effect by Refusing and Diffusing Shame

So how does this all relate to Hard-Easy? You see, shame may work as a deterrent to keep others in line, but as a motivational tool, it sucks. Negative reinforcement is always counterproductive to positive behavioral change.

The uglier you feel about how you just blew your diet, the more you will want to wallow in your shameful pity with a half gallon of Häagen-Dazs Butter Pecan. It is the shame that weighs you down and drives you back to the Easy of Easy-Hard destructive behavior you are trying to overcome.

When I grab the sleeve of chilled Thin Mints, I swear to myself I will have only three, and then three turns to six and then nine. Then I rationalize I'd better eat the entire damn sleeve just to get them out of my sight.

That's why shame is one of the greatest threats to living Hard-Easy. It has the propensity to breed the what-the-hell effect.

This phrase was first used by dieting experts Janet Polivy and Peter Herman.[35] The what-the-hell effect defines a sequence of slipups that leads to shame, which then leads to deeper, more harmful slipups. Polivy and Herman's study found that dieters would feel horrible about any lapse and cave in completely. In my case, I eat a handful of Thin Mint cookies, get disgusted with myself, and gripe, "What the hell, I have already eaten six—I might as well eat the whole damn sleeve." So I do just that as I sink deeper and deeper into my own self-loathing, minty disgust.

The what-the-hell fuels living Easy-Hard. The smoker who has just one cigarette feels so horrible, he says, "What the hell. I might as well finish the pack." The gambler who loses big says, "What the hell. I am $500 in the hole. I might as well take out another $500 to win my losses back." The thief who embezzles a few hundred dollars feels horrid, then says, "What the hell. I will embezzle just a bit more."

It is not the slipup that triggers the repetitive, destructive behavior. It is the accompanying feelings of isolating shame, crippling guilt, and utter worthlessness.

Think of that!

You slipped up. So what? No need to feel shame. In fact, it's imperative you don't. Otherwise, you could be knocking on the door of the what-the-hell effect.

Let me make sure we clarify the difference between shame and guilt here. My definition of shame is "a painful humiliation or distress mixed with regret, dishonor, and self-hate." Shame is when you make yourself or others make you feel like you are a bad person. Shame creates feelings of self-loathing to the point the person shamed feels that they themselves are bad.

Guilt, on the other hand, is different. Guilt is a feeling of worry or unhappiness you get because you have done something wrong. Note the wording: Shame = I am bad. Guilt = what I did was bad. We all need a healthy amount of guilt. We all make mistakes, and guilt is that internal angst that gives us the motivation to right the wrong. You can feel guilt and have a deep sense of self-love. Guilt is, more often than not, internally motivated. Shame, more often than not, is externally motivated.

When you slip up, your internal thoughts should be *Wow I messed up. I need to do better. I will not make that mistake again.* That is healthy guilt. Shame, on the other hand, sounds like *Wow, I messed up again. I am pathetic. Why can't I get it right? I am a loser.*

Dr. Brené Brown, a research professor who has spent the past two decades studying courage, vulnerability, shame, and empathy has this to say about shame versus guilt:

> Based on my research and the research of other shame researchers, I believe that there is a profound difference between shame and guilt. I believe that guilt is adaptive and helpful—it's holding something we've done or failed to do up against our values and feeling psychological discomfort.
>
> I define shame as the intensely painful feeling or experience of believing that we are flawed and therefore unworthy of love and belonging—something we've experienced, done, or failed to do makes us unworthy of connection.
>
> I don't believe shame is helpful or productive. In fact, I think shame is much more likely to be the source of destructive, hurtful behavior than the solution or cure. I think the fear of disconnection can make us dangerous.[36]

I could not agree more. The more shame you feel, the more likely you are to spin out of control and end up in a world of isolation and self-loathing. But when you feel guilt, you have a sense of hope. You disassociate your bad choices from who you are and who you really want to be. Your choice was bad, but you are not.

If you are caught in this vicious cycle of slipups-shame-more-slipups-more-shame, it can seem like there is no way out. There is no way for you to overcome and control this destructive conduct. The slipups grow larger and more frequent. And your acceptance of this lifestyle becomes more and more comfortable and tolerant.

Soon your slipups become your drug of choice, your security and comfort, and that just fuels more feelings of shame, and you ride this roller coaster of what-the-hell into the abyss of the Hard of Easy-Hard.

So that's the bad news. What's the good news?

If you have read my book *Human Connection*, you already know I am a huge proponent of self-compassion. Healthy love of self is much more successful and persuasive than you beating yourself with the whips of self-criticism and shame.

When you mess up, train your brain to say, "Hey, man, that's totally cool. I get you. I forgive you, and we'll just pick up and try again. I got your back on this."

That's a healthy love of self.

When it comes to being shamed by others and trolls, you have to be willing to accept that other people's feelings and behavior have absolutely nothing to do with you.

When you understand and acknowledge that others have the freedom to be inclusive or separating, or caring or indifferent, and that you are not the reason for their feelings and behavior, you will no longer take others' behaviors personally.

When you let go of your need for others' approval and instead move toward empathy for yourself and others, you will ditch those false beliefs causing your feelings of shame. And you won't fall into the trap of becoming the shamer in an attempt to distract yourself from your own defeats.

Also, you must be willing to feel your true feelings rather than disguise them with anger, justification, and excuses. When you learn to be caring, empathetic, and compassionate to yourself and others, you will no longer need to seek the approval of others to validate yourself.

Self-forgiveness—not judgment, shame, or self-criticism—strengthens your willpower and the ability to leverage Hard-Easy in your life. A positive self-image fortifies willpower. The more you expect perfection of yourself, the heavier your self-judgment, shame, and unworthiness. You need to expect excellence and improvement from yourself—not perfection. No one ever achieves that, and if that's your metric for judging your success, you will always come up short.

These feelings of inadequacy undermine your ability to make good choices and your power to leverage the prefrontal cortex. Shame-fueled feelings of unworthiness drive you to unhealthy coping strategies that offer temporary comfort, like watching too much TV; eating junk food; numbing yourself with alcohol, drugs, or pornography; sleeping in too late; spending binges; and gambling.

In the End, Empathy Washes Away Shame and Shaming

"Shame corrodes the very part of us that believes we are capable of change," said Dr. Brené Brown.[37]

The best weapon we can use to fight shame is empathy. When we increase our empathy for others and for ourselves, we find we are more compassionate, understanding, and patient. We can appreciate how painful it is to be shamed in any form. We can practice short-circuiting the shame center of our brain before we shoot off our mouth, especially when we feel disgusted, angry, or hurt—by others or ourselves.

We can ask ourselves if the shaming words or deeds we are about to launch are necessary, helpful, or true. If not, with continued practice, we can decide not to launch them.

And we'll set ourselves up for making more Hard-Easy choices.

Chapter Recap

Key concepts and takeaways from chapter 12:

- Shame is a corrosive, destructive force that erodes our ability to choose Hard-Easy.
- While we may feel shame for our own shortcomings, we can also be the purveyors of shame.
- Don't give in to the temptation to compare yourself to others.
- The best weapon we can use to fight shame is empathy.
- Please don't chew gum around me.
    * Okay, I take it back. Go ahead and chew gum around me. I need to take responsibility for my own internalized damage, be more self-aware, and not shift the responsibility to those

around me for the negative emotions I feel when I hear gum being chewed. I myself am fighting to overcome the victim mentality.

Pause and Think

- Be on the lookout for shaming behaviors in yourself and in others. Learning to recognize it is necessary to avoid being someone who perpetuates it.
- Who do you most often compare yourself to? What steps can you take to limit these comparisons? Can you hide their social media posts for a while?
- Actively seek to build empathy. When you find yourself tempted to judge or shame another, genuinely try to see things from their perspective. This will likely involve being uncomfortable, but discomfort is often necessary for growth.

CHAPTER 13

INVASION OF THE BRAIN SNATCHERS
How the Quest for Instant Gratification Robs Us of Free Will and True Joy

So far, we've reviewed the basics of both instant and delayed gratification. It's time to take a closer look. In this chapter, I share two personal experiences about what the fruits of delayed gratification look like (literally!) and what the fruits of a lifetime of instant gratification look like. I also look at how technology has, over decades, fed and worsened our Neanderthal addiction for instant gratification and subverted our ability to let our brains do their best work.

Delayed gratification is deeper gratification—when it finally arrives.

Another way to say it is that Hard-Easy delivers a delicious Easy because the Hard phase ripens it on the vine, giving it a sweetness directly proportional to the degree of Hard you endure.

Imagine if your choices had "nutrition" labels. Your instant-gratification (Easy-Hard) choices are in the middle of the store and demanding your attention from the in-your-face endcaps. They're the Twinkies, chips, and Coke. The processed, packaged, heat-and-serve meals that are ready almost instantaneously. On the other hand, your delayed-gratification (Hard-Easy) choices are on the perimeter of the store. They're the produce, meat, and dairy sections. They take some skill and effort to prepare but will unquestionably lead to a healthier and longer life. Delayed gratification, by its very title, requires more time, but that time is an investment that pays off.

The Peaches of Delayed Gratification

Five years ago, I planted two peach trees in my backyard. I dropped the seeds into the soil and smoothed the dirt over them.

It looked like two dead patches of lawn in my backyard.

I watered and watered them.

Nothing.

I pulled the weeds and fertilized.

Still nothing.

Here's what I couldn't see. Beneath the surface, those seeds had sent forth tendrils and shoots. They were sinking fledgling roots into the soil—roots that, millimeter by millimeter, crawled deeper and grew thicker. They had also launched shoots toward the surface of the earth, where, in time, they would break through, unfurl small leaves, and begin to collect the sun's energy to fuel continued growth.

For a while, on the surface, it looked as if nothing was happening at all. If I had abandoned my nurturing efforts, my peach trees likely would have died. But because I persisted—sometimes longer than I wanted to or thought I should—several months later, I saw the infant trees breach the soil and seek the sky.

Those tiny peach trees still needed love and attention. I continued to water and fertilize them. I built a small fence around them so the dogs could not dig them up. I defended them from deer, rabbits, kids playing football, and the lawnmower. I sprayed them to protect them from weeds and bugs.

That was four years ago. Each year, my tiny trees grew and got stronger, and I worked hard tending to them. This year my trees began to bear fruit. In fact, they had so many peaches their limbs sagged from the weight. Every day, I had to thin the peaches so the branches wouldn't break.

The trees are not fully grown and still need pruning, weeding, and watering, but the peaches I plucked from those trees this August and September were the sweetest, juiciest peaches I've ever eaten. I made peach pies, peach muffins, peach cobblers, peach jam, and peach ice cream. I may have invented a few peach dishes. I was giving peaches to family and friends for weeks.

I had wanted those peaches five years ago when I bought the seeds. The gratification of eating that first peach was delayed by 1,825 days, give or take.

During those five years, there were days I didn't want to go out and take care of my trees. There were times I had so much on my to-do list I just wanted to skip my tree-nurturing activities. There were other times I wanted to be lazy and relax instead of pulling weeds in the summer heat.

Those were an accumulation of moments when I chose Hard-Easy. Each time I chose Hard over Easy, it nudged me closer to the moment when the peach trees would reach critical mass and begin to produce delicious fruit with less and less effort from me.

And now, with these trees, Hard is beginning to yield Easy.

With much less effort on my part, those peach trees will bear fruit for years to come. My little peach orchard testifies to the law of Hard-Easy, teaching us how sometimes it takes years for the Easy phase of Hard-Easy to manifest after devotion to Hard. But when it does, how sweet it is.

Did you know that once it begins to produce fruit, a successful peach tree will, with little maintenance, bear fruit for twelve to fourteen years?

I am fifty-nine. It makes me smile to know that I will be sitting under the shade of my peach trees when I am seventy, devouring sweet, nectar-dripping peaches. I envision holding my grandkids safe on the ladder as they pick the juiciest, sweetest peaches they will ever taste. I can see their smiles and hear their giggles as the juice runs down their chins.

Oh, the sweet joy of the Easy phase of Hard-Easy. All those moments of Hard were, in fact, hard at the time. But the intensity and duration of the Hard has made the Easy much more satisfying and euphoric once it arrived.

The Perils of Instant Gratification

This story is about Steve, a high school friend of mine.

Steve had the "it" factor. He was the BMOC (big man on campus). The ladies loved him, the guys thought he was awesome, and he seemed to have it all back then. He was the athletic, charismatic, all-the-girls-liked-him, Ferris Bueller of our school.

After graduation, Steve decided to postpone college, take a break from school, and enjoy himself for a few years. There was plenty of time for him to get a college education, he told himself. It was time for him to enjoy some "me time."

It was easy to skip the hard, tedious, expensive process of applying to colleges. It was a rush for Steve to indulge in the instant gratification of partying, not having homework or studying, and not answering to anyone or being responsible for anything.

During Steve's "me time," however, he decided to plunge into some other methods of instant gratification. He began drinking alcohol and experimenting with a variety of drugs.

"A little booze and a little weed," he would tell me. "That's all it is, Coombs. Nothing major. You should seriously give it a go. Just once. Alcohol is so relaxing, and the buzz makes you feel so good. Let's have a shot and maybe a puff, and chill."

It was always easy for me to say no. Here's why.

Part of the reason Steve followed the Easy-Hard path of instant gratification was that he didn't have a vision of where he wanted to go. He had no why—no long-term goal he was so passionate about he would delay gratification in virtually every facet of his life to achieve.

I, on the other hand, had developed a why. Despite the albatross of dyslexia that hung around my neck, I was fighting my way through college—clawing with all my might to ascend the steep peaks of academic achievement. If I worked hard now to get my degree, I could pretty much write my own ticket down the road. I had developed a vision of what I wanted, and I was not going to let dyslexia define or detour that vision. That steely determination applied to all other obstacles that might divert me from my goal. There was no way I was going to allow alcohol or pot derail what I wanted to achieve.

Steve never did get back to school. Time after time, he chose the Easy path of instant gratification. And over the years, he began to harvest the Hard that follows in Easy-Hard.

All these decades, Steve has worked jobs where he's sometimes made less than minimum wage and has had to hope for good tips to make up the difference.

He even spent a brief stint in prison for committing a crime while high. He doesn't even remember the incident because he was so smashed.

Today, I see him at high school reunions, and he's the first to admit he wrote an unbelievably tragic story arc for himself. The once BMOC who had it all and who was brimming with untapped potential, with the world at his fingertips and his whole life in front of him, is reduced to a husk of himself.

He remains single, working dead-end jobs to earn just enough to sustain himself and his addictions, which have plagued him for decades. He feels empty and depressed much of the time.

In stark contrast, people tell me I'm lucky to have a job I love doing meaningful things that improve and enrich lives and getting paid to do it.

Lucky?

Yes, I was blessed to have had loving parents. I was blessed to be raised in a home where I was nurtured and provided for. I guess you could say I was lucky. However, I was also dealt a few cards that made life extremely difficult in many ways.

I recognize we do not all have the same talents and gifts. But we all can maximize what talents we do have to the best of our ability. Everyone is fighting a battle you know nothing about. I am not trying to trivialize those who are fighting massive hardship. I am trying to encourage, persuade, and empathetically educate and motivate people from all strata of existence to dream and achieve those dreams.

I believe it is the victim mentality that will whisper to some that I had it easy, that my hardships and challenges were not nearly as big and ugly as theirs. But as we've learned, a victim mindset will not get you anywhere.

To get where I am today, I spent three years without a salary, building my company. I spent three to four nights a week after work for about two years writing each book I use as the basis for training and consulting and helping people perform better. I made many mistakes along the way, yet I tried to learn from those mistakes and apply those lessons to my next efforts.

The gratification I feel now—delayed in its arrival because it required excruciating effort over time—is deep and rich.

How is it that the one kid in high school who had everything going for him fell so short? Steve had the brains, brawn, personality, good looks, and economic backing of his parents. I was the one who thought of him as lucky and having it all when we were teenagers. What happened?

I think this is one of the key concepts Dr. Duckworth is trying to teach in her concept of grit. Sometimes raw talent can be a negative. When you are blessed with raw talent, you sometimes get lazy. You don't have to work as hard, or study as hard, or practice as hard as those around you. You may not be motivated to work hard to perfect and magnify your skills. You can rely on talent and talent alone. At least you think you can.

If you are ultra-talented yet lazy, you'll experience something interesting—and perhaps a little disconcerting. You won't maintain your head start over those who have less—or much less—talent. Those who have the combination of a little talent and a gritty work ethic will surpass you, and you will be left scratching your head, perhaps wanting to give up.

Let's chat about Michael Phelps one more time. Phelps benefits from some elite genetic gifts that give him a distinct advantage in competitive swimming. He has a natural talent for it. But he also has an astonishing work ethic—the grittiest form of grit. His natural talent didn't take him from the kiddie pool to the Olympic podium 28 times (23 for gold) all by itself. It didn't even earn him an extra day off each week. At his peak training phases, Phelps would swim almost 50 miles in a week spread over 6 days, 12 practices, and 30 to 36 hours. Phelps knew that if he didn't put in the work, someone else would.

You may have been born with natural talent, or you may have been born with limitations and challenges. Either way, you must dig deep and choose Hard to achieve your goals. There is no way around it. You must double down—and sometimes triple down, quadruple down, or quintuple down—on the work and effort you expend toward your goals. Talent without work is wasted talent. And work without enough talent doesn't overcome all—but it can get you much further than you would be without it.

You will find that *because* you chose grit over instant gratification that your performance will likely improve. And just like my peaches, that delayed gratification will be all the sweeter.

Michael Phelps and my friend Steve both made choices that affected their lives. Phelps fulfilled his potential, while Steve never even came close to reaching his. There is a clear correlation between our decisions and the results we see. Which results do you want?

Protect Your Head from the Brain Snatchers

And, now, here is our science-based argument against pursuing instant gratification.

Neuroscience teaches us that the brain has a pleasure center. No matter the source of pleasure—watching a good movie, shooting up heroin, or falling in love—the pleasure center generates the feeling of pleasure in the same way: it releases the neurotransmitter dopamine into the nucleus accumbens, a cluster of nerve cells beneath the cerebral cortex.

Addictive drugs mimic the law of Easy-Hard: they provide an easy shortcut to flood your nucleus accumbens with dopamine. In fact, addictive drugs can release two to ten times the amount of dopamine natural rewards do.

The Hard comes later. Addiction. And then tolerance. When the brain's receptors become overwhelmed, the body regulates itself by producing less dopamine or eliminating dopamine receptors. The addict requires a larger dose of the drug to trigger the same pleasurable high first experienced.[38]

Other methods of instant gratification function like drugs and snatch our brains through addiction. Pornography and gambling flood the brain's pleasure center with ultrahigh amounts of dopamine and induce addiction. Spending money and shopping can trigger it. Ditching homework and playing video games can trigger it. Pursuing sexual partners and conquests can trigger it. These instant gratifications can condition us to behave in a way that our primary motivation is seeking to recreate that pleasure rush.

Social media takes advantage of this addiction conditioning. Social media apps and platforms use a form of variable-interval-schedule conditioning. That means you don't get a reward every time you pull the slot-machine handle, but you love the rush of seeing the numbers tumble into place and the idea that just maybe you hit the jackpot. And sometimes you do win some money, but it's unpredictable when the reward might hit.

Thomas R. Zentall of the University of Kentucky has conducted several experiments using variable-interval-schedule conditioning on pigeons, showing how it reprograms your brain's chemistry, altering it so that you make suboptimal decisions (Easy-Hard decisions) in the name of instantly gratifying yourself.

He trained eight pigeons to peck at white lights for food. First, the hungry pigeons learned that if they pecked a certain light (the one on the right, for example), they would see one of two colors. Ten seconds later, the pigeon would get three food pellets. This was roughly analogous to the sure thing of money in your pocket, Zentall said.

On the other hand, if the pigeon pecked the other light (the one on the left), the light would flash either red or green. Red meant the pigeons would get ten pellets in ten seconds. Green meant the pigeons would get nothing.

Click right, and you get three pellets, guaranteed. Click left, and you see if you can hit the jackpot and get ten pellets, knowing there's a great chance you won't win anything at all, just like playing the slot machines.

Eighty-four percent of the time, the pigeons chose to gamble, pecking at the light on the left, which would give them either ten or nothing. It was the rush of the gamble that reprogrammed their brains and altered their behavior. I can hear my father saying, "Art, gambling is for the mathematically impaired."

"The pigeon is getting 50 percent more food for choosing the right side, yet the pigeon chooses the left side almost 90 percent of the time," Zentall said.[39]

Social media conditions us in the same manner.

In fact, researchers at the University of Albany found that, in addition to social media being potentially addictive (especially applications like Facebook, and Instagram), the very act of using social media may condition the brain to be at greater risk for impulse-control problems.

Julia Hormes, who led the study, said, "New notifications or the latest content on your newsfeed acts as a reward. Not being able to predict when new content is posted encourages us to check back frequently [like the pigeons who gamble for the ten pellets but often get nothing, they are still compelled to peck away]. This uncertainty about when a new reward is available is known as a 'variable interval schedule of reinforcement' and is highly effective in establishing habitual behaviors that are resistant to extinction."[40]

Hormes's interesting phrase "resistant to extinction" is just a fancy way of saying it's hard to overcome these impulsive, instant-gratification behaviors once they've started to reprogram your brain.

So as you face Easy-Hard or Hard-Easy decisions every day before you choose, remember me sitting beneath my peach trees eating my succulent, sweet peaches. And think of my friend Steve, who moves from job to job in a lonely existence because he didn't nurture his talent with hard work. Think for a moment how the decision you are about to make has the power to reprogram your brain.

Then make the Hard-Easy decision.

Chapter Recap

Key concepts and takeaways from chapter 13:

- Delayed gratification is deeper gratification.
- Each time you chose Hard-Easy over Easy-Hard, it moves your sustained efforts toward critical mass, where they will begin to produce fruitful results with less and less effort.
- Sometimes raw talent can be a negative; those who have the combination of a little talent and a gritty work ethic can surpass those who have tremendous raw talent but a lazy work ethic.
- Choosing Easy-Hard can reprogram the brain—which is part of the reason why Hard is hard.

Pause and Think

Keep your chosen goal in mind.

- What delayed-gratification reward are you working toward?
- What instant-gratification temptations do you face?
- What talents do you have that can help you achieve your goal?
- What hard work can supplement that talent?

Examine your relationship with social media.

- In what ways is your relationship healthy? Unhealthy?
- What are two small changes you could make to improve it?

CHAPTER 14

GARLIC AGAINST THE INSTANT-GRATIFICATION VAMPIRE
Defenses for When Instant Gratification Tries to Suck Your Attention Away from Hard-Easy

Modern distractions combine with our naturally short attention spans to encourage multitasking. When we attempt to multitask, we're giving in to the temptation of instant gratification. Narrowing our focus to one task at a time is delayed gratification and yields bigger rewards. I won't lie. This is hard. In this chapter, we will discuss ways to overcome these distractions and temptations and stay on the path of Hard.

If instant gratification is a vampire seeking to drain your focus and energy, what kinds of garlic, crucifixes, holy water, and sunlight can you use to repel the vampire?

Dive Deep

Focus is key. It sounds simple, but when it comes to fending off the vampire of instant gratification, focus is your wooden stake. Focus on the end goal, the post-cocoon metamorphosis. The depth of your focus directly correlates to your ability to make Hard-Easy decisions, day in and day out.

So what does "depth of focus" mean? Let's look at a few examples: one from nature, one from cinematography, and one from an associate professor of computer science at Georgetown University.

Example from Nature: The Deep-Focus Earthquake

Okay. A bit weird to be talking about earthquakes in trying to explain how to maintain your focus. But this is a special kind of earthquake. A deep-focus earthquake.

You know about earthquakes under the sea. They can occur very deep, on the floor of the ocean, and displace enough water to cause devastating tsunamis on the surface.

Deep-focus earthquakes happen even deeper than that.

They have a hypocenter (the point where the pressure finally gives—basically ground zero of the quake) deeper than three hundred kilometers (186 miles). Most occur at a place called the oceanic-continental convergent boundaries, in conjunction with subducted oceanic lithosphere.

Huh?

Basically, the quakes occur *really* deep down, where the subsurface of the tectonic plates meets the outermost shell of the earth—the last part of the earth that's still solid before you get to the molten gooey stuff that melts your face off.

What's interesting about these quakes is that they occur so deep they cause minimal surface waves. Near the hypocenter, if you could swim down there, you might feel the tremendous release of energy and shock waves. But near the top, the surface barely ripples.

It's a fascinating analogy for our brains and concentration.

When the focus is deep, the surface is never tumultuous or choppy. We are not swept away by the tsunamis of instant gratification, with their sudden release of destructive energy. We avoid those dangers and remain steady and on course above, while our creative energy and why-powered, tectonic, paradigm-shifting power keeps churning deep below.

When you think deeply, you have the ability to be more proactive as opposed to reactive. If you have read *The 7 Habits of Highly Successful People*, you know the first habit Covey inventories is being proactive. Covey clarifies that to be proactive "means more than merely taking initiative. It means that as human beings, we are responsible for our own lives. Our behavior is a function of our decisions, not our conditions."[41]

When you are in control of an expected or anticipated occurrence, you have taken proactive measures, and that requires deep thinking. When you are reactive, you are responding to something you have not anticipated or thought about.

Example from Cinematography: The Deep-Focus Shot

Photographers and cinematographers use a technique when composing a shot called "deep focus." What that means is they make the shot so that the focus remains sharp and clear in all depths of field.

To achieve deep focus in the cinematic sense, you have to adjust your lens to let in more light to allow for a longer exposure.

For humans to achieve deep focus, we need to adjust the lens of our mind to allow for more exposure. In other words, we give our minds the uninterrupted time to attain deeper, sustained, probing thoughts.

Example from a Professor: Deep Work

The name of both a concept and book by author and professor Cal Newport, "deep work" describes the ability to focus without distraction on a cognitively demanding task.[42]

People's days are often spent in a frenetic blitz of email, social media, and on-demand digital entertainment. Newport asserts that most people in today's digitally hyperconnected society have let their ability to enter into—and remain in—a realm of deep-focus atrophy. In other words, we are losing the ability to think and sustain deep thought.

Deep work is the work your brain does when allowed to chew on a problem for a sustained, dedicated amount of time—the time it takes for you to devote your attention to the problem and ignore the distractions that can dilute your focus.

How long is this, exactly, and how do you know when you've reached an appropriate depth?

I believe the time needed is going to vary from person to person. Newport suggests, "Start with the goal of having five hours per week protected on your calendar for deep work. Each session should be at least 90 minutes long."[43]

In my opinion, that's a goal you should set and work your way up to. You will not likely achieve ninety minutes of deep thought immediately. Don't sabotage yourself by thinking or pushing too hard, too fast.

Try this. Pick a subject that has been perplexing you for a while.

Now, leave your phone on your nightstand.

Phoneless, go to the backyard, take a drive to the park, sit in the basement, or just find someplace you will not be interrupted. Sit, relax, and clear your mind. Think exclusively about your perplexing thought for a solid five minutes. (And don't use your phone as a timer. Use an actual watch.)

Sound easy?

The ability to sustain deliberate focus and attention varies from person to person and subject to subject. But you will notice that your mind has a tendency to go off track. You will have to intentionally decide to refocus every eight seconds. That means in five minutes you will entertain approximately thirty-seven other thoughts you must fight off to stay lasered in on your original, perplexing subject.

Two things will jump out at you as a result of this mental workout. First, you will understand how difficult it really is to maintain a deep focus on a single topic for a full five minutes. Once you gain this understanding, I hope you are a bit more empathetic to elementary school kids.

Second, if you fight through your brain's desire to follow every eight-second distraction, you will be fascinated with the different perspectives, ideas, and depth at which you now see the issue that is (or was) so perplexing.

Or maybe you won't.

Just one plunge into the deep of deep focus may or may not be enough for your subconscious brain to deliver its insights and revelations to your conscious brain. But the habit of plunging into long stretches of deep focus will increase the likelihood that your brain starts dazzling you with amazing solutions, ideas, and prompts.

Once you have successfully completed this five-minute mental workout, try it again tomorrow but increase it to ten minutes. From there, branch out and think about your life and what you really want it to look like. Spend ten minutes on where you want to be five years from now. Are the principles I am talking about in this book ringing true? Think about the infinite possibilities.

As with any new skill, you can build up your time, focus, and depth of thought. What if you could evaluate the outcomes of different life paths, see into the future, and make choices that would enable you to achieve your wildest dreams?

What if you sustained this focused, deep thinking and combined it with deliberate actions, stubborn tenacity, and grit?

Think about your repeated, habitual actions and the consequences down the road. What will you be doing? With whom will you be doing it? Where will you be doing it? How will you be doing it? And, most importantly, *why* will you be doing it?

It is in deep thought that we plant and grow our big dreams. If you do not think it, you cannot dream it. If you do not dream it, you cannot act on it and make it your reality.

Distraction Pollution and the Era of Shallow Thinking

Given the rapid-fire existence we live today, many believe they can multitask. In fact, many pride themselves at being great multitaskers.

I hate to throw a wet blanket on the I-get-stuff-done fairy tale, but multitasking is a seductive, destructive myth. Studies have proven our human minds can only fully focus on one thought at a time; in other words, multitasking is scientifically impossible.

I know what you're thinking. "But, Art, I can peruse my social media and talk to my family at the same time. I can drive and text at the same time. I can cook, clean, help kids with homework, and do the laundry at the same time."

I would argue that you're following the Easy path of instant gratification. You're taking the smaller gift card now, rather than holding out for the bigger gift card later.

You may think you are doing all those activities simultaneously at a high level, but you are fooling yourself. However, you're not fooling those around you. Your spouse, kids, the driver whose car you rear-ended, and the white sock that is now pink all know you are not fully engaged.

In her article, "The Myth of Multitasking" in *Psychology Today*, Dr. Nancy K. Napier says:

> Much recent neuroscience research tells us that the brain doesn't really do tasks simultaneously, as we thought (hoped) it might. In fact, we just switch tasks quickly. Each time we move from hearing music to writing a text or talking to someone, there is a stop/start process that goes on in the brain.
>
> That start/stop/start process is rough on us: rather than saving time, it costs time (even very small micro seconds), it's less efficient, we make more mistakes, and over time it can be energy sapping.[44]

Let me give you a quick example. I've modified the following from Dr. Napier's article:

> Draw two horizontal lines on a piece of paper.
>   Time yourself as you do these two tasks.
>   On the first line, write: "I CAN multitask."
>   On the second line write the numbers 1–13 like those below:
>   1 2 3 4 5 6 7 8 9 10 11 12 13[45]

How much time did it take you for each task? For me, it was about ten seconds each.

Okay, you multitaskers, here is your chance to shine.

Draw two more horizontal lines. This time, alternate by writing a letter on the top line and then a number on the bottom line. Then go back up and write the next letter in the sentence on the top line and the next number on the bottom line, shifting from top to bottom, line to line. This means you write *I* and then 1, and then *c*, then the number 2, until you complete both lines.

How did you do? Were you more efficient? Were you more accurate? I know those are rhetorical questions because your attempts at doing two simple activities simultaneously just became infinitely more difficult, increasing the time it took to accomplish both tasks and radically increasing your propensity for mistakes, not to mention your frustration level.

Dana and David Dornsife of the USC College of Letters, Arts, and Sciences describe what happens in our brains while we multitask—(which really isn't multitasking; it's switch tasking):

> The prefrontal cortex of the brain begins working anytime you need to pay attention. This area of your brain helps keep your attention on a single goal and carry out the task by coordinating messages with other brain systems. Working on a single task means both sides of the prefrontal cortex are working together in harmony. Adding another task forces the left and right sides of the brain to work independently. Scientists at the Institut National de la Santé et de la Recherche Médicale (INSERM) in Paris discovered this when they asked study participants to complete two tasks at the same time while undergoing functional magnetic resonance imaging (fMRI). The results showed that the brain splits in half and causes us to forget details and make three times more mistakes when given two simultaneous goals.[46]

Beyond reducing productivity and increasing mistakes, multitasking also alters the brain itself in a negative way.

In a 2009 study at Stanford University, communications professor Clifford Nass discovered that "heavy multitaskers" performed worse at sorting relevant information from irrelevant details—a skill multitaskers consider themselves to be excellent at.

In an interview with NPR, Nass said that the negative effects of multitasking carried over into their attempts at single-focus thinking and tasks.

> The [multitaskers] we talk with continually said, "Look, when I really have to concentrate, I turn off everything and I am laser-focused." And unfortunately, they've developed habits of mind that make it impossible for them to be laser-focused. They're suckers for irrelevancy. They just can't keep on task. . . . Our brains have to be retrained to multitask and our brains . . . are remarkably plastic, remarkably adaptable. We train our brains to a new way of thinking. And then when we try to revert our brains back, our brains are plastic but they're not elastic. They don't just snap back into shape.[47]

In 2018, research also revealed that multitaskers might have reduced memory function. According to the article, "a decade of data reveals that heavy multitaskers have reduced memory."[48]

When your memory is impaired, your ability to think and sustain deep thought deteriorates. When you cannot sustain deep thought during challenges, your ability to live Hard-Easy is drastically impeded.

Big Results Require Big, Deep Thoughts

If you are going to solve big problems and create an amazingly rich and rewarding life, you must (yes, I say *must*) have big, deep, long, amazingly rich thoughts. And that, my friends, is hard. The world wants to pollute our minds with attention-deraling, idle, trivial, brain-dead thinking, and distractions, which prove to be so enticing and easy.

Truly immersing yourself in a book or simply thinking about a problem for a while is a lost art (no name pun intended).

Back in 2012, I got this crazy idea to write my first book, *Don't Just Manage—LEAD!* Just a few years before I even attempted to write this book, I thought there was no way I could possibly write a book. Madness! Utterly impossible. But I battered down the walls of that self-imposed limitation and began to write.

One of the biggest and serendipitous benefits of this endeavor was the need for me to think deep, long thoughts and to work many hours. And something amazing happened. I finished the first book, and that book led to another, and now, here we are on my third.

I have been told by some that my books have changed their lives for the better; however, the true benefactor of my deep thinking has been me. I apply the tragically forgotten skill of deep thinking across every part of my life—not just writing books. As a result, I have less anxiety, more clarity, and greater confidence while tackling challenges.

The more I exercise my gray matter to sustain a focused thought, the easier and easier it becomes. I know this will happen for you as well when you make deep focus a practice in your life.

And if you're a recovering multitasker? Take heart: "So is the damage from multitasking permanent, or will putting an end to multitasking undo the damage? Nass suggests that while further investigations are needed, the current evidence suggests that people who stop multitasking will be able to perform better."[49]

So resist the urge to multitask. You may think you are getting tons done, but the truth is, when it comes to focusing your attention, your brain can focus on only one thing at a time. Science has proven we are incapable of handling complex ideas concurrently. To be blunt, multitasking is a seductive myth that Easy wants you to believe.

Deep Thinking Is Hard

You are capable of thinking anything you want as deeply and profoundly as you want. The conceivable ideas and solutions you are capable of entertaining, pondering, and solving are endless. That is incredibly inspiring and exciting.

What sucks is that while we are capable of infinite, boundless thought, most of us now have the attention span of a goldfish.

Oh, wait. Sorry. I got that wrong.

CORRECTION: Most of us now have a attention span *shorter* than a goldfish's.

Yep. If you're still with me and haven't been distracted by something shiny over there, you heard me right. Science has proven that most humans now have an eight-second attention span, down from fifteen seconds, whereas the common goldfish has an attention span of nine.[50]

Maybe that's why three goldfish outscored you on the GMAT. And why your company outsourced your department's jobs to an aquarium in Ypsilanti.

In 2015, Microsoft commissioned a study on attention span. Researchers in Canada surveyed two thousand participants and studied the brainwaves of 112 others through electroencephalograms (EEGs). The study revealed the sad truth that a goldfish could beat us in a game of chess (okay, forgive the sarcasm, but I am trying to make a point). "Heavy multi-screeners find it difficult to filter out irrelevant stimuli," the report concluded. "They're more easily distracted by multiple streams of media."[51] The more you use social media, chat apps, IM and email tools, and devour digital content, the more your ability to maintain longstanding focus erodes. Severely.

That seems like a common-sense conclusion, but it's still startling. Incidentally, our decline in attention span has been happening since the year 2000, roughly coinciding with the advent of mobile phones and the evolution of the internet into an entertainment-on-demand technology.[52] So it would follow that if we want to regain our edge over goldfish, then, clearly, we need to invent smartphones for goldfish. Once they start watching Finflix, our attention span will be back on top!

That is sobering. If you're trying to do some deep thinking on a particular subject, you must constantly refocus your thoughts (every eight seconds) on the subject at hand.

This is why deep thought is so hard. You must deliberately make a choice every eight seconds whether to entertain a new thought or come back to the subject you started on. Like most everything in life, you cannot *not* choose. If you don't make a choice, the default is to drop your focus.

Yes, I actually just now had to consciously choose to refocus my attention on focus. Crazy, right? But it's something we're all too familiar with.

Thankfully, the more you practice deep focus while thinking deep, the better you get at quickly dismissing distractions until you're barely aware of them at all.

Your Brain Is Just One Powerful Flywheel—Just Squishier

The ability to think deep can be difficult. But just like the flywheel, once it starts turning and momentum takes over, the Hard of Hard-Easy gradually shifts to Easy.

One of the tricks I use is to turn my phone sounds completely off. It does not bing, boing, ring, or buzz. I will occasionally turn on the sound if I am expecting an urgent call or text. But 99 percent of the time, it makes no noise at all.

Another habit I have developed is to leave my phone in the car if I am having dinner with someone, attending a meeting, or going to a movie. This allows me to be utterly focused on the individuals and issues right there in front of me. I am not distracted in any way.

The ability to think deep can help you with your vocation, your sacred beliefs, your emotional and physical health, your relationships . . . you name it.

But you must train yourself to move past the distractions, extend your attention span beyond that of a goldfish, and immerse yourself in an environment that lets you plunge your mind into deep, deep thought.

Only then will you be armed with the deep focus—the garlic that repels the distracting vampire of instant gratification—to consistently achieve and overcome on the path of Hard-Easy.

Chapter Recap

Key concepts and takeaways from chapter 14:

- Focus is key.
- The depth of your focus correlates with your ability to make Hard-Easy decisions, day in and day out.
- Your thoughts are the DNA of your character and your reality—so don't have the thought DNA of a goldfish.
- The ability to think deep can be difficult, but just like the flywheel effect, once it starts turning and momentum takes over, Hard shifts to Easy.

Pause and Think

- With your big goal in mind, decide on an amount of time you can dedicate to deep focus. It might be daily or a few times each week.
- Spend the next day or two looking specifically at the times you're tempted to multitask. Whether or not you choose to follow that temptation, make note of the results you get.

CHAPTER 15

YOU NEED A PURPOSE, A PLAN, AND A VISION
In Other Words,
You Need to Become a Salmon Person

This chapter is all about purpose—the reason behind your striving toward your goals. Purpose can be a tough idea to get a handle on because it isn't as concrete or measurable as our goals. However, having an identifiable purpose is a significant indicator of whether a person will finish the journey and achieve the goal. Purpose is especially important when living Hard-Easy because the Hard-Easy path is, well, hard. Purpose keeps us going. This chapter will teach you what purpose is and guide you through the process of defining yours.

Purpose gives life meaning and direction and fosters hope for the future.

Conversely, having no purpose leaves you aimless, hollow, and hopeless.

Think of the Pacific salmon, which returns from the ocean and swims hundreds of miles upstream, ascending mountain elevations and waterfalls and fighting against the constant pressure of rapids, not to mention a gauntlet of predators—bears, eagles, seals, sea lions, and fishermen—all to reach the headwaters of the place it was born to mate and spawn the next generation of salmon.

Did you know that Idaho's chinook and sockeye salmon will travel nine hundred miles upstream—while climbing seven thousand feet!—before they finally reach their goal?

Salmon can leap as high as twelve feet out of the water to go over those waterfalls.[53] (In comparison, sometimes I can leap a few feet out of my recliner if I want one of my wife's homemade snickerdoodle cookies.)

It is their purpose that drives them. It helps them endure the rigors of the journey. They refuse to give up no matter how difficult it gets. They find ways to overcome the many obstacles blocking their way, and they push through when they're tired but still have miles to go.

And it's not like they land on the other side of the waterfall in a gentle part of the river where they rest before pushing on. No, they land in another violently strong current and rapids that threaten to push them back over the falls.

Incidentally, they make this arduous journey while fasting. That's right—they don't eat for the entirety of the journey. No time to eat, really. Because they face constant pressure, they must continue to push onward, relying on the energy stores they've spent a lifetime building in preparation for this journey.

And then, despite the difficulties, they reach their goal. (We have yet to develop a measuring tool sensitive enough to determine the psychological state of a salmon, but, if I may conjecture, I think they must feel pretty damn satisfied at having arrived. Plus, it's like a big singles bar where salmon get to use pickup lines, have a few drinks, and then pair off and spawn.)

Be the Salmon

Living Hard-Easy demands that you have a purpose in life. Purpose acts as both the anchor that keeps you grounded and the guiding star that inspires you to continue moving forward. As an added bonus, purpose is a magnet that attracts others to you. (In the same way, you'll be attracted to those with purpose and meaning in their lives.)

Those with purpose—the ones who live Hard-Easy—are positive, upbeat, and enthusiastic. You know the kind of people I'm talking about. It's the people who have purpose and who spend their lives swimming upstream to reach their goals.

In other words, salmon people. (I realize "Salmon People" sounds like a bad B movie from the 1950s, but you get the idea.)

I want to look at two types of purpose and how you develop them: individual and beyond the individual. These are not mutually exclusive purposes and can peacefully coexist and intertwine.

Tips for Deciding on Your Individual Purpose

We all have an individual purpose. Yours is unique to you and your dreams.

Perhaps you haven't figured out your purpose yet. If you fall into this camp, the question is, how do you define your purpose?

Here are a few tips that can help you accelerate your hunt for an overarching purpose.

Surround Yourself with Salmon People

Seek people you admire who have a purpose and who speak to you as friends and mentors. We thrive on those who inspire us. If you're not a salmon person, swim with them—you'll be going in the right direction, feeding off their energy, and learning how they navigate difficult waters in overcoming challenges.

Create Your Love List

Pretty straightforward here: create a list of the things you love to do.

We have all heard of and written to-do lists. They are great for chores that need to be done on a Saturday, but what I am talking about here is bigger. Much bigger. It is my experience that many individuals perfunctorily check tasks off a list just to get paid. They assume this is the way life is, but life does not have to be an endless blitz of to-do lists. I am asking you to write a "love-to-do" list. There is a big difference. Purpose requires passion. That will only happen when you swap to-dos with love-to-dos

Create Your Easy List

Where do your natural talents lie? What activities come easy to you? If you find your natural talents overlapping with the things you love to do, you may be getting close to unveiling your purpose.

Create Your Reflection List

This list looks backward on your life. When have you been the happiest and most fulfilled? Write that down. After you've completed your list, revisit it. For each entry on the list, write down what specifically about each event or era made you happy. You will probably begin to see patterns emerge regarding the things that bring you joy and fulfillment. Go back and cross-reference this list with your love and easy lists.

Draft Your Perfect-World List

This is a fun one. Complete these sentences. In my perfect world, I will be doing _____. In my perfect world, I will be achieving _____. In my perfect world, I will be the kind of person who is _____. In my perfect world, I will have _____. In my perfect world, I will affect others' lives by _____.

You can keep on adding your own perfect-world sentences to this list. Take it as far as you want. I guarantee that as you paint the vision of your perfect world, you will become more and more excited, and you'll stoke the flames of your desire to strive to create this perfect world, piece by piece.

Check in with Friends, Family, or a Mentor

You'll find it's helpful to share your lists with those close to you and those whose opinions you value. Get feedback. Talk about your lists and why you put specific things on each list. As you do, all of this—the lists, the ideas, the reflections, the chance to present your ideas to someone else—often congeals into an idea or two that may be your purpose. And if it doesn't, repeat the process until you feel you've distilled it down to a purpose that excites you, motivates you, and instills passion within you.

Create a Plan

Creating a plan sounds intimidating and scary to most because they envision a perfect, immensely detailed blueprint that anticipates every contingency and maps out every grueling step of the process. The dreaming part is fun. But creating an actual plan to achieve huge goals? Sounds daunting.

Let me tell you something that will probably alleviate your anxiety: it's okay to make an easy plan. In fact, I encourage it.

If perfection is what you consider a plan, you're making it too hard. And when it gets too hard, that becomes an excuse to blow it all off. The task becomes too daunting to even consider, so you give up before you begin. Or you start following the plan, make mistakes, and see your imperfections pile up. Now you're face-to-face with the velociraptors we discussed previously: doubt, discouragement, and disappointment. They'll block your way, and you'll end up taking zero action.

The idea of perfection is dangerous because we're bound to encounter many of our imperfections as we strive to reach our goals. It's an open invitation to those velociraptors who'll try to convince us we'll never get to perfection.

Wait! Is it contradictory to living Hard-Easy to come up with an easy plan first? Am I advocating you go Easy-Hard? And why did I make you come up with a "perfect world" list when I'm telling you to not try for perfection?

The act of finding a purpose and creating a plan is hard. If you're at this point in the process, you have already been making the Hard-Easy choices. What we're doing is simplifying the process so you can build momentum on your salmon run upstream. This will ultimately help you keep making Hard-Easy choices so you can put miles of river behind you instead of swimming in circles or giving up altogether.

And your perfect-world list? It's your dream—and part of what inspires you every step down the Hard path.

A Purpose beyond Yourself

Another important part of purpose is finding a cause beyond yourself that you can devote yourself to. In fact, some of the most rewarding purposes lie beyond the self.

If you think you're living Hard-Easy but you only focus on yourself, and your needs, and your wants, and you prioritize your time over everyone else's, then, frankly, you're not doing it right. In fact, you've deceived yourself: you're *not* living Hard-Easy. You've drifted into the land of Easy-Hard.

How?

The easiest thing in the world is to be selfish. It's our natural state.

But I'm pursuing my dreams! It's okay to be a little selfish. This whole book, you've been telling me to make the hard decisions. That's what I'm doing! I don't have time to help anyone else. Let me earn my dreams, my riches, my promotion—then I'll have time to help others. Then I'll have time to serve and mentor other people. But until then, I've got to give all my time and effort to me.

Yep. Seems counterintuitive, doesn't it?

It's definitely Hard-Easy to serve others as you're trying to accomplish and juggle all the other things in your life. Which is exactly why you need to make it part of your life.

We are surrounded by people—strangers, acquaintances, friends, and family. Yet we often get so caught up in our lives and goals we focus on ourselves to the exclusion of others. But when we expand our purpose to include helping others—when we look beyond ourselves to see and act on the needs of others—it does something absolutely amazing. It shifts the focus of our attention away from us to others, and in so doing, alleviates self-absorption and anxiety. It helps us in every other facet of our life—including pursuing our individual purpose.

In fact, a study by Canadian psychologists revealed that altruism brings true joy. The psychologists tracked 115 study participants who had high levels of social anxiety. These were the type of people who desperately try to avoid social situations because they fear them. What they found was fascinating. They asked these socially anxious people to perform acts of kindness for others. Once they began serving others, their fears and anxieties were alleviated—even if the act of service was utterly simple, like doing a roommate's dishes for them or mowing a neighbor's lawn.

As it turns out, when the socially anxious person saw how their kindness benefitted someone else, it raised their own level of happiness. Not only that, it made it easier for them to socially engage with the person they had served.

The researchers postulated that performing acts of kindness helps you live a more satisfying, engaging life. The reason, the study showed, is that people who serve others and treat others with kindness—through kind words and kind acts—see the world as a better place, which makes them happier.[54]

Lynn Alden, professor of psychology at the University of British Columbia and one of the study's authors, said that we are hardwired to value the happiness of others. "When others are happy, kind of through emotional contagion, we feel happier," she said. "It's more of an attitude change—being alert of things you can do for other people and doing them spontaneously because you want to do them. It has a side effect of making you feel good."[55]

When I hear someone say "always" or "never," my BS radar starts going off. But I am going to break that rule today.

What if Target, Nordstrom, Amazon, etc., had a product called Everlasting Happiness? Would you buy it? How much would you pay?

I am here to tell you that product exists. You can buy true happiness—as long as you buy it for someone else.

I have tested it thousands of times; it "always" works and has "never" failed. Don't believe me? Try it and see for yourself. Next time you are feeling a bit down, unexpectedly do something kind for someone else. There must be no personal gain connected to this unselfish gesture.

Then pause and check your happiness meter.

Several studies have found that giving your time and money to others will make you deeply happy, even more happy than if you spent it on yourself. More compelling is that your kindness will often start a kindness sequence that inspires lifelong happiness and altruism, with others paying it forward.

Many voices in the world will try to convince you that happiness comes to you because you get things for yourself. But it is just not true. Giving is, in fact, the surest way to make you happy.

In a world where we hear "me, me, me," I think we should be selfishly saying, "you, You, YOU!"

Your Big-Picture Plan

Now that we've talked about purpose, the next step is to develop our plan.

I'm not sure how salmon plan, but I'm betting they have some innate clock that tells them they have to be past the rapids by early September, past the waterfall by mid-September, and have ascended the seven thousand feet by the end of September. That's a plan.

Your big-picture plan to reach your big-picture goal should be constructed of small-picture goals with their own small-picture plans. I'll cover this in greater depth in chapter 17, on goals, where you will learn the core principles of goal setting and goal achieving—just as I learned them by applying them to my high school wrestling endeavors.

So I'll say this for now: an effective big-picture plan will be the lighthouse that guides your daily actions and adjusts your smaller goals—even when you have setbacks. And the small goals break down the larger goals into digestible bites that are less intimidating and help you make incremental progress.

The Small Decisions Are Actually the Big Decisions

Now that your plan is in place, you can turn your attention to the small, simple, everyday decisions that will help you carry it out. Forget the massive, earth-shaking, jumbo decisions. You're going to fill out your plan with the little stuff. Why? Because the little decisions are actually the big decisions.

I'm thinking I may have to put that phrase on a T-shirt, along with "Be a Salmon Person."

But I digress.

The easy phase of your Hard-Easy plan—the end result—should be so clear in your mind that the hard parts simply fall into place. The small decisions you plan every day will build toward it. To plan your days and weeks, use whatever "window dressing" you want to help you stay on task—your cell phone alarm, a productivity app, an old-fashioned day timer . . . whatever works for you. Whatever best facilitates your follow-through. Remember, don't make it drudgery. And when you encounter an unplanned part of your day, your purpose and big-picture plan will guide your microdecisions, tipping the scale toward the Hard-Easy.

Your Vision

Once you've got a purpose and a plan, you're ready for vision. Vision informs your strategic thinking.

Keep your eye on the prize—the long view, the land of promise. The most important part of the process is to keep your purpose or goal at the forefront.

And when you have a clear vision of that goal, you'll make it through the Hard phase of Hard-Easy to get there. Honest. There will be times when the Hard phase is just that: exceptionally hard. You might be tempted to get discouraged. But the gleaming vision of your goal will support you through it all.

Be the salmon person who pushes upstream with a vision of the glorious end of the journey, where the waters are rich, the current gentle, and the company delightful.

Chapter Recap

Key concepts and takeaways from chapter 15:

- The little decisions are actually the big decisions.
- Purpose gives life meaning and direction and fosters hope for the future.
- Be, and swim with, the Salmon People.
- Performing acts of kindness helps you live a more satisfying, engaging life.
- Find your purpose, develop your plan, and maintain your vision.

Pause and Think

- Who are the Salmon People in your life?
- Create your lists!
    * Love list
    * Easy list
    * Reflection list
    * Perfect-world list
- Who can you share your lists with? Come up with the names of two or three people who will help hold you accountable.
- What is the big goal you have in mind right now?
- What purpose will keep you working toward that goal? What is the reason you want to achieve it?
- Which way do your service scales tip—toward selfishness or selflessness? How can you bring them into better balance? (Or keep them in balance?)

CHAPTER 16

INVEST IN VALUE

A Deeper Look at Time, Assets, and the Parable of the Banker and the Fisherman

In this chapter, we take a close look at our most precious resource: time. Time is the unwavering, constant variable we can use to either reach or undermine our goals. Learning to recognize when we're using time to our best advantage will increase our ability to reach our goals.

Steve Miller had it right in his 1976 hit "Fly Like an Eagle": "Time keeps on slipin', slipin', slipin' . . . into the future . . ."[56] The clock keeps ticking, and then, eventually, for each of us, it stops.

The finite nature of time—or rather, our time as human beings on planet Earth—is a great stepping-stone for me to ask: What are you doing with your time right now? (Yes, I know you are reading this book. Don't be a smartass.) But really, how are you spending your time from day to day?

Time is your most precious resource. And unlike other any other resource in the world, this one is distributed to all in equal amounts. You can be born rich or poor, socially connected or not—we all have twenty-four hours in a day to work with. Are we really investing our time in the assets we value most? And when it comes to ranking our assets, are we ranking them correctly?

What's the Value of What You're Doing?

What makes one valuable activity more valuable than another valuable activity? And how do you measure value?

The hardest decisions in life are not between good and bad ways to spend your time. The hardest decisions in life are between two seemingly good ways to spend your time.

Hard-Easy is not just about earning money and gaining wealth. It is deeper than that. It is about making the Hard-Easy choices for the things of most value in life. The things that matter. The things that help us grow into better humans.

A meeting with my estate planner got me thinking about the value of the things I do every day.

I'm Going to Die

No big surprise there. We're all going to die.

We need to take care of some things before we die. That's why I met with an estate planner the other day.

Remember that great line from *Gladiator*? "What we do in life echoes in eternity."[57] Strangely enough, that quote could be applied to estate planning as well. (Now that I think about it, it also applies to Hard-Easy: what we do in this moment—Hard action or Easy action—echoes throughout the rest of our lives, yielding either Hard or Easy.)

For estate planning, what I prepare—or fail to prepare—in this life will echo throughout the lives of my family—kids and grandkids—for a long time. If I fail to make the proper arrangements, they will get significantly fewer of the scarce assets I have accumulated, after I die.

Conversely, if I make the proper arrangements, it will leave my family with no debt and a few valuable assets, which will allow them (if they apply the law of Hard-Easy) to leave potentially greater assets to their kids, and so on. Echoes through eternity.

Well, let me confess something to you: I've been living Easy-Hard when it comes to estate planning. I should have met with a planner thirty years ago. But as a result of writing this book, my haunting feelings of guilt over my procrastination have intensified. So, as living proof that you can start making Hard-Easy decisions later in life, I finally met with an estate planner.

He began by asking me about my assets. How much cash did I have in the bank (checking and savings)? Not as much as you would think. Do I own stock? No. Did I own bonds? No. Any precious metals? No. How about jewelry? Does my wife's ring count? How about real estate? Just a modest home. Vacation property? No. Equity in private companies? Just the small company I started and still work for today. This list went on and on, and my pitiful answers deepened my estate-planning remorse.

However, as we spoke, it got me thinking about assets.

What's an asset?

In the context of my conversation with the estate planner, it was all about wealth and the things I owned that could be turned into money.

Are those real assets?

Well, sure. But my life is filled with other assets. For me, an asset is anything that enriches me—that adds *value* to my life. So if an asset is anything of value, what assets do I have? I began making a list of every asset I could think of and categorizing them. Here's what I came up with:

TIME
- Twenty-four hours a day

RELATIONSHIPS
- Family
- Friends
- Professional
- Acquaintances

HEALTH
- Physical
- Mental
- Emotional
- Social

WEALTH
- Cash
- Stocks
- Bonds
- Real estate
- Precious metals

From there, I began to think about each asset and where it fits in a hierarchy of value—as informed by the law of Hard-Easy.

Time: The Great Equalizer

Time is the one asset everyone is given an equal amount of each day. You do not get more than anyone else. It is finite. There are no do-overs with time: once a second is spent one way, it cannot be spent another way.

All other assets you can lose, neglect, and weaken and then come back and try to restore, accumulate, grow, enlarge, and improve. But not time. You can't spend it faster than anyone else. It is constant and ever-flowing.

Time is the currency of Hard-Easy.

If each moment of time were a raindrop, a single drop wouldn't change much. But a month of constant rainfall accumulates—first watering the ground, then causing raging rivers, and eventually reshaping the landmasses.

Time is your gift each morning. How you spend it will determine the trajectory of your life. Each moment is a microcosm of what's been and what's to come.

Time is the biggest variable in the entire concept of Hard-Easy versus Easy-Hard. How are you investing it?

Wasting Time: A Definition

How do you define wasting time?

For me, it would be any activity that does not add value to your life two, five, or ten years down the road.

Sure, relaxing while you watch a football game now and then is enjoyable. And, most definitely, you need those moments of downtime to recharge your battery.

But habitually watching football all Sunday long is a bit excessive. Especially when you most likely took in two to three college games the day before and are preparing to sit in the same recliner and hunker down for the Monday-night game. Will that consistent devotion of hours to watching football add value to your life two, five, or ten years down the road? I argue no. (Unless you happen to be a football coach studying film in the pursuit of your coaching dreams.)

Of course, it's kind of easy to know you're wasting time when the activity actually looks like wasting time. But what about those activities that masquerade as productivity yet are still time wasters?

Hold that thought. And let's talk about wasting money first.

Most people know when they are wasting money. Alarm bells go off in their head when they drop money on self-indulgent, wasteful hobbies and luxuries.

But people have no alarm bells when they take their money and invest it in the stock market. It doesn't feel extravagant or wasteful. In fact, it feels quite responsible. And you can see how this might benefit you five and ten years down the road. You aren't wasting money; you are merely moving it from one asset to another.

This is the very reason a sales pitch for expensive stuff will include the angle: "It's an investment." (*This $300,000 time-share condo in Bermuda? You're not really spending money. No, you're investing in great memories with your family.*)

In my opinion, a greater danger to your wealth and savings is poor investing. Here are just a few examples among many: Joseph Pulitzer's (whom the Pulitzer Prize is named after) grandson invested the family fortune in an eight-hundred-acre citrus farm—and went bankrupt when disease devastated the trees. The ex-wife of media mogul John Werner Kluge invested all of her money in a vineyard—and lost it when the property was foreclosed.[58]

Remember Enron? Many invested their life's savings only to wind up penniless. And those who trusted Bernie Madoff and thought they were making such a wise investment were duped into financial ruin.

Now, let's apply this same logic to how we spend our time. As with wealth, the most dangerous method of losing time isn't spending it on self-indulgent, recreational activities—although those are still dangerous. Nope, one of the biggest ways to waste time is by doing seemingly productive work that's not productive at all. I call this imitation work.

I've had many days where I went to work and felt busy the entire day but accomplished nothing that would benefit me five or ten years down the road. I'm talking about emailing, reading the news, surfing social media, chatting with colleagues about the shows we're watching, and doing tasks that should be delegated to those specialized to handle such tasks: booking travel, restocking the breakroom, tackling financial reports, or updating a website.

There are plenty of office activities that make me feel busy and could arguably be called productive. But they are often not the most effective way to spend my time.

I find myself in the same predicament at the gym. Have you ever spent ninety minutes in the gym without a scripted workout? If you're like me, you can find yourself aimlessly walking from machine to machine with no real objective. Yes, you were in the gym. Yes, you lifted weights and did some cardio, but the workout was less than effective.

In both cases, the alarm bells don't go off when I'm wasting time on seemingly productive activities. It doesn't *feel* like I'm wasting time. I'm not having fun. I'm busy. I'm in a work or workout setting. I'm earning a living and investing in my health. So I head home feeling like a responsible adult who has gotten stuff done. But what have I done to close the distance between me and my goals?

When it comes to time, wealth, and health, remember that simply avoiding gratification is not enough to safeguard you. We need to install new alarms within us to spot the self-indulgence that's disguised as more virtuous activities.

Philly Cheesesteaks and Critical Mass

"Time is what we want most, but what we use worst," said William Penn, founder of the then-English province of Pennsylvania and the man who directed the planning and development of Philadelphia. I think he may have also invented the Philly cheesesteak, so major props to him.

For me, relationships are my most important asset. I must invest my time in those relationships.

True, I cannot spend 100 percent of my time developing my relationships with family and friends. I must provide the basic needs for my family first: food, water, warmth, rest, security, and safety (Maslow's hierarchy of needs). And that requires a certain amount of money.

Hence, money is crucial until you hit a critical mass.

So how much money do you need in pocket before you can start diverting your time to the other assets you value? Everyone has their number. But while you are accumulating an education and wealth, you must tend to your health and your relationships as well.

Many spend enormous amounts of time accumulating wealth, then later spend vast amounts of money trying to restore their health and relationships.

Which reminds me of a parable.

The Parable of the Fisherman and the Banker

An American investment banker was taking a much-needed vacation in a small coastal fishing village in Mexico. The banker was standing on the dock when a small boat with just one fisherman pulled up to it. The boat had several large, fresh fish in it.

The investment banker was impressed by the quality of the fish and asked the fisherman how long it had taken to catch them.

"Only a little while."

"Well," the banker said, "why don't you stay out longer and catch more fish?"

The fisherman replied he had enough to support his family's immediate needs.

The banker then asked, "But what do you do with the rest of your time?"

The fisherman replied, "I sleep late, fish a little, play with my children, take siesta with my wife, and stroll into the village each evening, where I sip wine and play guitar with my amigos."

The investment banker scoffed. "What a waste of time. Listen, I can help you earn much more money. I am a successful businessman with an MBA from Harvard University. I know exactly what you need to do.

"If you spend a few more hours each day fishing, you will come in with more fish and get more money. Then, with the additional revenue, you can buy a bigger boat. The bigger boat holds even more fish. So you can stay out all day and bring in even more fish. With the additional revenue, you can buy several boats!

"Keep on doing this, and eventually you will have a whole fleet of fishing boats. Then, instead of selling your catch to the middleman, you can sell directly to the processor. With the additional savings and revenue, you can eventually open your own cannery! Can you imagine that? Your own cannery! You will control the product, processing, and distribution. And you'll be fantastically rich. A fish mogul. Perhaps one of the richest men in Mexico."

The fisherman nodded, though not quite as enthusiastically as the banker.

"Of course," the banker said, "as you expand your business, you will have to leave this small village and move to Mexico City, which will become the hub of your enterprise."

The fisherman stroked his beard and inhaled the salt-tinged trade winds. "I see," he said. "How long will all this all take?"

"Not long at all," the banker beamed. "You can do all this—with my guidance—in a mere fifteen to twenty years."

"But what then?" asked the fisherman.

The banker laughed. "What then? Well, I'll tell you. That's the best part. When the time is right, you get to announce an IPO and take your company public. That means you sell stock shares in your company to the public and become very rich. You can make millions. Hundreds of millions."

"But what then?" asked the fisherman.

The banker looked puzzled. "Well, you'd have millions. You'd be incredibly rich. You can retire and live a life of leisure. You can move to a small coastal fishing village if you want. Then you can afford to sleep late, fish a little, be with your kids and grandkids, take siesta with your wife, and stroll to the village in the evenings where you could sip wine and play your guitar with your amigos."

Invest in the Things You Value

This parable teaches us the fallacy of our money-driven, ambitiously blind pursuit of the all-seductive shekel. We can make a living and still invest and enjoy time with our family and friends. Our money-obsessed global culture needs this message now more than ever.

It is the modest, simple things that bring true joy. And, typically, we do not have to look far to find them. They are all around us if we can find joy and gratitude in the simple things.

I remember being a poor college student. But when I reflect on those days, I don't think a lot about being poor, or eating ramen for dinner for fifty-eight straight nights, or shopping for clothes at the secondhand store. No, I remember all the crazy fun we had. We made time—between all the studying, classes, and jobs—to squeeze the most out of life.

The simple joys for me during my college years were taking a gorgeous spring afternoon and driving over Highway 17 in my baby-blue 1972 Volkswagen Beatle to Santa Cruz, where my friends and I would hit either Twin Lakes State Beach or Seabright State Beach. We would lie on the sand, soak up the ambiance, and catch the best waves around.

From there we would walk to Santa Cruz Beach Boardwalk Amusement Park. If we wanted to surf with the big boys, we could zoom over to Lighthouse Field State Beach or Steamers Lane, where the waves are world-famous among surfers. We would always stop at Togo's, a little sandwich place on our way home, and get the best roast-beef sandwich ever.

I can still feel the sting of a sunburn under my tank top and shorts, smell Coppertone sunscreen mixed with the salty sea breeze, and taste those Togo's sandwiches, capping a perfect afternoon as the sun set with vivid yellow-and-gold skies and cast our shadows behind us. It was a blast.

I have bonds with those friends to this day. And it's because I invested time in them—even when I was busy doing other important Hard-Easy things.

This is the pattern I'm talking about here, the essence of what I want to convey in this chapter. Hard-Easy isn't just about material success. It's about making the Hard-Easy decision to invest the limited time we have in those assets we value most, on a daily basis.

I love how the parable of the banker and the fisherman helps us look at the why. Like the fisherman, we should be fixated on the why.

Or, as I stated earlier in the chapter, we need to ask ourselves, "What value will this activity bring me in two, five, or ten years? Will it help develop those assets I value most?"

Parable PS

By the way, here's a little bit of science to reinforce the truths taught in our parable of the banker and the fisherman. Research shows that once your income is enough to securely meet your basic needs, having more and more money won't increase your joy. You won't be happier making another $10,000 or $10,000,000 beyond the level of living comfortably.[59]

It is important to note that sometimes Hard looks like Easy and Easy looks like Hard. Was the fisherman advocating Easy? I would argue he had clarity of purpose and was staying focused on the investment that gave him the greatest returns.

Like most everything in life, you can't shove this into a black-and-white category and call it good. So, if I had a chance to revise the parable, I would.

The fisherman said he had enough to take care of his family's immediate needs. I would say that the fisherman might want to do a little more: catch more fish to save for a rainy day—just in case he gets hurt, his boat sinks in a storm, or the fishing dries up. Providing for immediate needs almost sounds like living paycheck to paycheck. I can think of few things that would give me more anxiety than that. And that would definitely be hard.

Hardest-Easiest

Remember, time is your most precious resource. If you're going to live Hard-Easy, you may as well live Hardest-Easiest. In other words, it can be hard to make the wisest decisions, to invest time in the things of most value, when so many other things are crying for your time. But when you spend time on the things that have the most value, you will experience the biggest returns down the road.

Chapter Recap

Key concepts and takeaways from chapter 16:

- Hard-Easy is not just about earning money and gaining wealth.
- Time is your gift each morning; how you spend it will determine the trajectory of your life.
- Wasting time = any activity that will not add value to your life two, five, or ten years down the road.
- One of the biggest ways to waste time is by doing seemingly productive work that's not productive at all.

Pause and Think

- Review how you spent your time over the last two or three days. How have you spent time well (adds value in coming years)? How can you improve your time investments?
- Plan for how you will invest your time over the next two days.

CHAPTER 17

THE DECISION TO JUMP IS MADE ON THE GROUND

Or What I Learned While Plummeting 14,000 Feet to the Earth

Plans are important, but have you ever stopped to think about why plans work on a psychological level? It's all about making the hard decisions early and from a place of safety rather than waiting until the pressure is on. This concept became concrete to me when I decided to voluntarily hurl myself from a flying plane. Don't worry, I'm not going to make you go skydiving, but I would like to share what skydiving taught me about decisions, willpower, and planning.

About twenty years ago while living in Holland, I was being recruited to run a large customer-service division of Hewlett-Packard. They flew me to their headquarters in Palo Alto, California, for several interviews. As I chatted with the hiring manager I would potentially report to, he asked me if there was anything fun I might want to do with the team (there were about six of us)—something where we could get to know each other better.

I am pretty sure he was thinking of something like going to dinner, catching a show, or hitting a Golden State Warriors basketball game. For some odd reason, however, I blurted out, "Let's all go skydiving."

He didn't miss a beat. "I'll see who wants to join us, and make the arrangements," he said.

I was expecting him to laugh and say, "Good one, Art. But, really, what do you want to do?"

He answered so quickly and nonchalantly I was stunned, but I rolled with it. Too late to back out without looking like a wimpy idiot. So off we went to skydive together. For the record, this was my first, and last, skydiving experience.

Three Ways to Jump

At the time, there were three different ways you could experience your first skydiving adventure in California. First, you could jump tandem. This was where you were physically attached to the dive master's chest. The dive master did all the work, and you just went along for the ride. Once your plane hit an altitude of about thirteen thousand feet, the jump door opened, your dive master walked both of you to the edge, and you jumped. This type of jump required about twenty minutes of prep and training with your dive master, after which you were in the plane and taxying down the runway.

The second type of first-time jump was what they called a static-line jump. In this jump, your parachute was attached to a static cable within the plane so that when you jumped, your chute was automatically pulled open the moment you left the plane. Here, once the plane reached about four thousand feet, the door opened and out you went. Your chute filled with air, and you floated down to Earth. In this static-line jump, however, you did not experience the mind-blowing adrenaline rush of a free fall. It required minimal training, though.

The third type of first-time jump—and the one we all opted to do—was called an accelerated free fall. In this jump, you were assigned two dive masters. Once the plane reached about fourteen thousand feet, the plane door opened and you and both dive masters jumped from the plane. The dive masters held on to your jumpsuit on either side to ensure you did everything you were supposed to. But, essentially, you did all the work. From there the dive masters let go. You were in a free fall at the speed of 120 miles per hour, and once you pulled the cord and deployed your chute, you slowed to fifteen miles per hour.

To make this accelerated free-fall jump, we needed about eight hours of training. We were taught how to arch our backs and spread our arms and legs to gain control while free-falling through the air. To get the arch right, our instructors showed us a poster of a banana, comparing it to a skydiver. "Troops," one instructor said, "today you are all bananas. Your body should mirror a banana's shape when you are free-falling. Your head should be back, eyes looking level to the horizon, back arched, arms comfortably extended to the sides, and legs comfortable, with the soles of your shoes facing toward the sky."

They also taught us how to make sure our chute was fully deployed once we pulled our ripcord. And they instructed us how to untangle the chutes. They taught us about our reserve chute and how and when to use it. But what struck me as intriguing was the fact that they spent most of the eight hours drilling into our heads the importance of when and where the decision to jump was made.

The decision to jump was made on the ground, not on the plane.

To Jump or Not to Jump

Imagine it. You've never skydived before, and now you're up in the air, the door is open, and it's your turn to leap. Do you do it?

It's true what the instructors told us. The decision to jump is made long before you zip up your jumpsuit and strap on your parachute. And if you leave the decision till the last possible moment, like the vast majority of people if not taught otherwise, you will never jump out of the plane.

Of course, this leads to a chain reaction of problems for the divers lined up behind you. You see, the plane is packed with skydivers. They are queued up with the most experienced at the back of the line, the least experienced upfront. If you are on your first dive and you hesitate or freak out over the jump zone, it creates massive chaos and confusion for the jumpers behind you.

That's why the instructors incessantly repeat their litany during the eight hours of prejump instruction: the decision to jump is made on the ground, NOT on the plane.

To drive the point home, they showed us a video compilation of first-time jumpers and had us critique their jumps based on our training earlier that day.

In one of the examples, they showed a man who went limp and blacked out milliseconds after leaving the plane. He did regain consciousness, and all was well. But our instructor paused the video and reminded us that the decision to jump was made on the ground—not in the plane. Despite the physical effects of the man's terror, he had committed to jump, and out he went.

"If you get in the plane," our instructors said, "I promise there is only one way you are coming back to Earth. Do I make myself clear?" We all soberly nodded.

As the hours passed and the time drew closer and closer to jump, my anxiety grew. I became preoccupied with how well my parachute was being packed. The reason for this was because a few months earlier, I had heard a story about Captain Charlie Plumb. He was a U.S. Naval fighter pilot, and he told the story of being shot down in combat. He had to eject and deploy his parachute to survive.

He often reflected, he said, on the person who packed his parachute the day he was shot down. What an impact that sailor had on him! Captain Plumb had never met him, nor likely would he ever meet him. Yet this stranger had saved his life. He was forever grateful the sailor had taken his parachute-packing job seriously.

With that story fresh on my brain, I wanted to watch the young men packing my chute. I had imagined that they would be like soldiers—serious, all business, no messing around.

I hovered nearby. They noticed me in their peripheral vision and began to talk.

"Oh, man. I think I screwed up on that last one." Big stage whisper—loud enough that I could hear "Aw, what the hell. It's not like they'll complain if it doesn't open." The dudes laughed. I didn't.

Then: "Don't tell the boss, but I am way hungover from the party last night." "Oh, totally. Me too. I can hardly think straight."

They would watch me from the corner of their eyes, knowing they were making my blood pressure and heart rate skyrocket.

They both looked at me. "No worries, bro," one said. "We've got this."

Then the other said, "You know, the truth is, you don't really need a parachute to go skydiving. You only need it if you want to go skydiving twice." They laughed and high-fived. I smiled nervously. In that moment, their laidback, easygoing smack talk and joking actually made me feel more comfortable, and yet I could not hide the concern my body language was broadcasting.

The Moment of Truth

Our instructors introduced us to our two assigned dive masters, and we were suited up and strapped into our chutes. Then the dive masters ran through some basic questions, and we did a few more simulations. As I think back now, I believe they were asking me questions to assess how well my brain was working. They wanted to know if I could withstand the tension or if I was going to go ape-shit berserk in the plane.

We boarded our well-used Cessna Super Grand Caravan, with the most experienced divers at the end of the queue and least experienced at the head of the line.

The plane had a six-foot-tall exit ramp in the rear that would open in flight, allowing us easy egress. (Actually, it was kind of like being crammed in the bed of a big pickup truck with an open tailgate, so when the driver punched it, we would all tumble out, but we were at fourteen thousand feet, not four feet.)

There were about thirty jumpers sitting on the floor, packed efficiently into the main cavity. As we took off, I kept telling myself, *Well, you are in the plane now. The decision to jump has been made.* It was one of many times my brain had to outscream the other senses shouting that this was certain death. *Breathe, Art, just breathe; you will be fine. These guys are professionals and know what they are doing.*

I had been trained; I knew what I had to do once free-falling. The instructors and my dive masters were professionals through and through. I had to listen to my brain and not the volatile, powerful emotions surging through me, urging me not to jump.

Easier said than done. My other senses were so out of control it's hard to explain. In fact, if you have never been skydiving, it is impossible to convey the survival-instinct terror your body uses to try and override your brain. Yet, ironically, the rush and thrill of skydiving is directly proportional to the terror you feel before the jump.

Despite the warning my senses were sending me (*Hey, Art! You idiot! You go through with this, YOU ARE GOING TO DIE! And we're not ready to die, so sit your dumb ass down*), I was able to get my mind to do something that every other system in my body was rebelling against.

As the plane climbed in altitude, the instructors on either side of me maintained a constant chatter, telling dreadful jokes and riddles.

"Hey, Art, we want you to be successful on your first jump; if you don't succeed . . . skydiving is not your sport."

Snicker, snicker, snicker.

"Remember to pull your ripcord at four thousand feet. As long as cows look like ants, you're fine. It's when ants look like cows you know you're too late."

Har, har, har.

"Do you know the hardest thing about skydiving? The ground."

Titter, titter.

It was obvious they had told these jokes a gazillion times. It was a tactic to prevent our first-time-jumping brains from having much time to think.

As much as I would like to tell you that I was tough and did not need their head games, I did. Truth be told, my pansy-ass brain was messed up. The higher we got and the smaller the objects on the ground got, the foggier my head got. My dive masters could see it in my glazed eyes. So they had to get back in my head.

"Hey, Art, where do you live?"

"In Holland."

"Do they have a Fourth of July in Holland?"

"No."

"That's odd—is their calendar different than everyone else's?"

They laughed and laughed.

Even with their anxiety-quelling tactics, at about ten thousand feet, my heart was pounding so fast I felt like a hummingbird on crack. I was getting more and more nervous. I would try to calm myself by looking out the plane, but my dive masters screamed at me and told me to stay focused on them.

More than once they looked me in the eye to assess my mental state. To keep my focus on them, they played rock-paper-scissors with me or had thumb-wrestling matches. They knew from vast experience that I had to deliberately keep my mind on tasks other than the altitude, jostling plane, and shrinking view below me.

After about twenty minutes, we were at about fourteen thousand feet, and I was told to stand. My knees were weak, and my heart was pounding. The wind was howling. My dive masters checked my goggles and gear one last time. There was no point in pretending I wasn't petrified.

And before I knew it, I was standing inches from a massive door, looking out the back of a plane at the ground rushing past below me. We stood there waiting for the signal to jump.

This is insanely insane. You are not supposed to be standing next to an open door on an airplane while you're in flight!

Up to this point, though nervous, I had been in decent control of the battle between body and brain. I was able to make some sense of what I was dealing with. But standing on the edge, I experienced complete sensory overload.

Looking back, I now know why every other sentence in our eight hours of training was "The decision to jump is made on the ground." Because there was *no* part of me that wanted to leap out of that plane. Every fiber of my being was kicking, screaming, and begging my brain to stop. My norepinephrine and cortisol were shooting through me, and my brain kind of just shut down.

Then I heard one of my dive masters counting "One, two, three..." and they were holding each side of my jumpsuit as I was falling. I remember trying to gain some stability by running in the air. Yeah.

Just like all those Roadrunner cartoons where Wile E. Coyote sprints off the cliff and tries to run back to the cliff before he plummets.

For a second or two I panicked. But then something happened. My brain kicked in, and I remember thinking, "Arch! Arch! Arch! Art, be the banana!"

I bent my back and spread my arms and legs and, just like that, my body righted itself and I was flying. My brain said to my body, "See, idiot. You're okay."

In fact, I was better than okay. My brain and body finally agreed on something: THIS IS AMAZING!

While falling, my dive masters quickly started to run through a checklist to make sure I was mentally all there. They motioned for me to check my altimeter. They motioned for me to give them certain hand gestures to signify I was alert and knew what I was doing.

I was mentally all there and enjoying the ride.

On the Way Down

One of the biggest surprises for me was how loud it was. For some reason I wasn't expecting that.

My dive masters were inches from me, yet I could barely hear them over the screaming wind. For those who have never been skydiving, the best example I can give you is to imagine standing up in a convertible going sixty miles per hour. The sound and force of the wind is incredible. Now, make sure there are no cops around you, unless you are on the German autobahn, and ask the driver to take it up to 120 miles per hour. I promise it is a sound and sensation you will never forget.

Yes, 120 miles per hour is the speed you hit in free fall. And for some stupid reason, they call this *terminal* velocity. Seriously? Thanks for putting that in my head as I hurtle toward the ground.

Terminal velocity is the constant speed a free-falling object reaches when the resistance of the medium prevents additional acceleration.

You hit this quickly. For skydivers, terminal velocity is falling approximately 1,000 feet every 6.5 seconds. So if I jumped out at 14,000 feet and pulled my ripcord at 4,000 feet, my free fall was about 60 seconds. And what an adrenaline-fueled 60 seconds!

After I pulled the chute, I had about five minutes of a calm, peaceful, much quieter descent. I got to take in the amazing views and steer my chute to where I wanted to land.

As I approached the ground, I pulled down on my steering lines simultaneously. This slowed me down, and if I timed it correctly, it would feel like stepping down from a six-inch step. My feet hit the ground, and I just stood there, trying to comprehend what I had just done.

Just as I touched down, my adrenaline peaked. I could not wait to talk to my dive masters. I could not wait to tackle-hug my new friends. If you happen to witness a class of new divers landing, there's a reason you see everyone grinning, laughing, shouting, high-fiving, and hugging once they land. They have all just experienced a high beyond anything they have ever experienced.

And they've survived.

I remember gathering my parachute and marveling at what had just taken place and how my mind had deliberately willed my body to do something my body was convinced would bring certain death.

Later that evening, when the adrenaline subsided, just as our instructors told us it would, I became extremely fatigued and slept hard. Evidently, there's no getting around this collapse. Every chromosome in you, every evolutionary gene passed from your Neanderthal grandpappy down to you, screams that skydiving is unhealthy and insanely foolish and that you're going to die. Yet the adrenaline high is unlike anything I have ever experienced before or since. I understand full well how one could get addicted to this sport. But once the adrenaline has worn off, your body finally says, "I'm going to sleep now. Good luck trying to stop me."

Key Hard-Easy Takeaways

Here are the Hard-Easy lessons this experience taught me:

1. Commit to Acting in Spite of Fear

We all fear the unknown.

Standing at the edge of the open plane door, watching the earth rushing past far below me, I did not know how this was going to turn out. Would my parachute open? Would I die, or break my spine, or steer myself into a tree where I would be impaled on a tree limb?

As an entrepreneur, speaker, and author, I meet thousands striving to improve their lives. I regularly see firsthand how some hinder and complicate their growth by permitting anxiety, fear, and self-doubt prevent them from pursuing the life they dream of. And the sad part is that they are often not even aware they are the one holding themselves back. People will tell me they badly want x, y, or z, that they want and are ready to change, and that they will do anything to make it happen.

But for many, when it's time to step out of the plane, they're not mentally prepared to leave their comfort zone. They're not committed to pushing past the fear to do the work that creates results.

It's that inner insecurity and fear that constantly screams, "Not yet! Let's jump tomorrow! I'm not ready!" Inner uncertainty has them questioning every move they make. It is this inner voice that urges them to play it safe and not risk the pain, the embarrassment, the panic, the dread.

That day, on my first and only skydiving experience, my instructors knew that even the strongest-willed individuals would see their determination and resolve drain away before the terror of the leap into space. Had I not committed to the jump despite my fear, I would have refused. Anxiety, fear, and self-doubt would have held me back.

Let me pose a question. In a life-or-death situation, would you hesitate, procrastinate, and allow fear to take hold and stop any action? Really think about it. What would you do?

Now let's change it up a bit. What if your child, partner, or spouse was trapped in a car after an accident and the car was on fire—would you stop trying to rescue them if you couldn't open the car door? Absurd, right? Of course, you would keep trying to free them. You would try another door and then try to break a window. You would try until your life, too, was in danger. But your fear or fatigue would not be the cause for not trying, acting, and doing.

To realize the life of your dreams, you have to be as committed to saving your dreams as you are to saving your loved ones in that burning car. That sounds extreme, but it's true. You must have that same level of determination not to fail, no matter what.

Everyone I know experiences fear. What separates successful people from those who fail is their willingness to act despite the fear. The best way to deal with fear is to run headlong into it, screaming, "Bring it, Hard!" It took some courage to take that first step out of that plane. But guess what? What you are afraid of is never as bad, ugly, and ominous as you imagine it to be. In truth, taking that fourteen-thousand-foot step was one of the most liberating things I have ever done.

2. Get Comfortable with Being Uncomfortable

All the personal Hard stories I've shared have a common thread: they were all uncomfortable. Me looking out of the open plane door, me on a stubborn horse, my son Kai opting to play video games at the expense of his homework, me planting and taking care of the peach trees in my yard.

Everyone I know avoids discomfort more often than not. Me included. If you want to create and have a fascinating life, you must choose Hard upfront, and that means you must be comfortable with being uncomfortable. Yes, it is frightening at first, but you will get through it, and you'll be a better person because of it.

The million-dollar question is, are you willing to be uncomfortable? Are you willing to trade up-front Hard for the payoff of Easy somewhere down the road? If so, are you willing to do what you know you should? Are you willing to put in the extra hours? Are you willing to go without for a while? Are you willing to do what you have never done? Are you willing to do it differently than you have in the past? Are you willing to push and stretch yourself beyond your comfort zone?

If you answered yes, I will make you a promise and tell you that it's at this point that momentum builds and the Easy phase of Hard-Easy starts to take hold.

3. Willpower, Grit, and Self-Control Have a Shelf Life

My resolve to jump out of the plane was rock solid at the beginning of our instruction, but as the event drew closer, my willpower started to feel less certain.

Willpower has a shelf life.

I have found that my willpower is like the battery on my cell phone. I have a certain amount to draw on every day. Just as my battery wears down, so can my willpower and my ability to invoke self-control. I notice that refraining from temptation is easier at the beginning of the day and that my willpower weakens as the day drags on. Thus my 4:30 a.m. workout.

When the alarm goes off, it's absurdly enticing to roll over, hit snooze, and get another two hours of sleep. But if I exert my willpower, I refuse to give in to that temptation. I draw upon my will to overpower the desire to doze. I pop out of bed and get the workout done. I schedule early workouts because I need my willpower at its most potent levels.

Envision a pail full of self-control. Every time you use your self-control to resist temptation, you dip into your pail. The more you stress over and fight the temptation to do the Easy thing, the more you draw from your pail. As the day wears on, your pail of self-control gets drained, and your ability to resist temptation decreases. Think about it. Most of the ultra-stupid decisions we make that get us into hot water are made after we've been up too late. Late-night snacking, late-night gambling, late-night online purchasing, late-night drinking and partying excessively, etc.—they all become more and more of a temptation as the night rolls on. Now you know why.

Did you know there is such a thing as decision-making fatigue? The more decisions you make, and the more stressful, troubling, or complex the decision, the more it depletes your supply of self-control.

Skydiving taught me how intense decision fatigue could radically compromise my self-control, which eroded my ability to make good decisions. Jumping from a plane is hard, and my survival instinct didn't want me doing it. The more time this instinct had to work on my self-control, the less likely I was to jump. That's why I made the hard decisions early on, making sure they were good ones. I went to a reputable, accredited skydiving school with excellent instructors. I decided on the ground that I would jump out of that plane.

After the hours of a day have depleted your willpower supply, you are more likely to avoid making a decision, or you will pick the Easy-Hard route and not think it through. Essentially, you become a horrible decision-maker.

That's why you make your decision and carve it in stone early in the day, when your pail of willpower is nice and full. You don't decide when you're at the threshold of the plane at fourteen thousand feet and the willpower in your pail has evaporated.

4. Plan for Duress

The last three ideas highlight the importance of planning in advance for life's worst moments. You know, those scenarios that will or could happen but they're just so miserable to think about? Well, face that fear, get comfortable with being uncomfortable, and start making those decisions.

Duress can annihilate our willpower in a second. This duress can be physical, such as jumping from a plane, or social, such as with societal expectations. Our brains react the same way to both: fight, flight, or freeze. It takes a lot of willpower and courage to fight, and we're more likely to reach that courage and willpower if we've considered and made the decision well in advance.

Again and again, my instinct made me question my resolve to jump. I was trying to self-sabotage and get out of something I found more frightening the closer I got to following through. But I had decided to jump and was committed to doing whatever it took to make that happen.

You radically increase the probability of success when you commit—truly commit—before you are placed in the heat of battle. If you haven't decided on the ground, you won't jump once you're up in the plane.

Clearly, we cannot plan for every high-pressure situation we'll encounter in our lives, but that shouldn't stop us from making as many decisions as we can beforehand for likely tense and demanding scenarios.

For example, as a young man, my parents told me I had to make the decision not to drink alcohol or do drugs long before I got to the party. They knew the peer pressure and the cute young cheerleader holding a red plastic cup in my face would be far too much for me to withstand without a hard resolve established long before I arrived.

I made that decision early and attended many parties. It dramatically increased my ability to say, "Thanks, but no thanks." That's when I realized that as the designated driver, I got to drive the cute girl and all her hot friends home. My parents figured all that out without ever having read this Hard-Easy book—I guess they were smarter than I realized.

Life is full of high-pressure rites of passage—some joyous, some dreadful. Make as many of those important decisions as early as possible. This prevents the need to agonize over a hard decision later. The decision will still be hard, but you'll have the small comfort of sticking to a plan.

Chapter Recap

Key concepts and takeaways from chapter 17:

- To live an extraordinary life, you must be focused on and committed to taking consistent action despite misgivings and fears of the unknown.

- Living the Hard of Hard-Easy and having faith that Easy will follow can be scary; successful people feel the fear but forge ahead anyway.
- To live Hard-Easy, you need to be comfortable with being uncomfortable.
- Willpower, grit, and self-control have a shelf life.
- Decide long before you have to act.

Pause and Think

- What fears do you have associated with your dreams? Don't stop at generalizations like *failure*. Get specific. (You might just wish I'd assigned you to go skydiving instead.)
- Isolate one hard decision you will likely be called upon to make in your lifetime but which you've avoided. Do what you need to make that decision now. Remember my estate planning? This is the kind of thing I'm encouraging. (Want to jump out of that plane yet? Chances are you're facing something far more terrifying. Keep at it.)

CHAPTER 18

GOAL SETTING FOR THOSE WHO THINK THEY KNOW HOW TO SET GOALS
The Five Principles of Big-Picture Goals

There are quite possibly a billion books, podcasts, apps, speeches, and media about setting goals, and yet I am amazed at how many people not only underestimate the power of goals but fail to create them properly. You've had a big-picture goal in mind as you've read through this book. I want you to examine this goal to ensure it is framed and approached in a way that offers you the most support on your Hard-Easy journey. This chapter might sound simple, but over time, simple acts can lead to greatness. When done right, goal setting can direct and motivate you to take effective, consistent action to become the person you want to become.

When I was in the eighth grade, I joined the wrestling team. Throughout the year, I watched other wrestlers in junior high and high school win match after match, then stand on the podium to receive their medals. I idolized them and craved similar success. As the year progressed, I developed an overpowering obsession—I wanted to be one of the state's best wrestlers by the time I was a senior. I wanted to be the one taking the podium and getting the medals.

I saw it and internalized it.

I set very specific goals: the win-loss record I wanted and the various tournaments I planned to win. All that was left was for me to begin my quest and take the wrestling world by storm.

Unfortunately, the wrestling world took me by storm.

I started my wrestling career with two wins and sixteen losses. (Incidentally, both my wins were against the same opponent. I am profoundly grateful that kid was in my division.)

Despite that, I hardened my resolve, even if my goal looked like the most far-fetched goal in the history of wannabe-wrestler goals.

My overarching, big-picture goal gave me the strength to endure years of hard work. As a team, we lifted weights every morning before school from 6:00 a.m. to 7:00 a.m. Then, after school, we were in the wrestling room from 3:00 p.m. to 6:30 p.m. We worked our asses off, sweating like the foul-smelling teenage wrestlers we were. The workouts were grueling, mentally exhausting, and physically fatiguing. Many winter nights, I would walk home in the dark, frigid air, exhausted.

But I persisted morning after morning, evening after evening, day after day, year after year.

Why?

My goal. It was the engine that propelled me forward—through dark times and setbacks, through times when I was ready to quit, through times when it seemed like it was all pointless. It gave me the strength to endure.

Let's be clear. No one wrestles in high school to be popular or catch the eye of that cute cheerleader. It is a mentally and physically grueling sport with a very small, parents-only fan base. It is truly a labor of love.

Did I make it?

You'll soon find out.

But first I'd like to share the five principles of setting big-picture, long-term goals. I began learning these principles when I was pursuing my wrestling aspirations, and I've refined my understanding of them in the many years since. They're simple. They're powerful. And they work.

PRINCIPLE 1: Your Goal Must Excite You

See? I told you these principles were simple. Because there's nothing as basic and that makes as much sense as setting goals that really stoke your fire and excite you. Goals you stay up at night thinking about because you can't take your mind off them. Goals that cause you to imagine the wonderful world you will exist in if you ever accomplish those goals.

Make sure your goal is important to you and that you're not doing it to please someone else. If you are not invested in the outcome or you can't see the relevance in the big picture, you've just signed your goal's death sentence.

Let's just put it this way—if you're not that excited about your goal when the going is easy, how long will you stick with it when the going gets rough?

PRINCIPLE 2: Make It a SMART Goal

While there are many variations of what SMART stands for, here is the one I like best:

Specific
Measurable
Achievable
Relevant
Timetable

Specific

SMART goals must be clear and definable. Ambiguous goals are useless because they don't provide direction. Your goal should act as a beacon that guides, motivates, and beckons you when the dark, hard days pile on one after another. If your goal is unclear, you will lose sight of it and give in to the easy temptations of procrastination and what-the-hell mode. Make it as clear as possible so ambiguity will not blur your resolve and vision.

Measurable

You must be able to measure your goal. That way you'll know when you've succeeded or fallen short.

We measure that which is important to us. If you cannot measure it, you cannot manage it. If you cannot manage it, you cannot improve it. If you can't improve it, you won't achieve it.

I wrestled in high school. Suppose I'd made the goal to be a good wrestler but included no way to measure what *good* meant? Could I say I was a good wrestler even if I never placed in a tournament?

Now, suppose my goal was to be one of the best high school wrestlers in the state of California my senior year. That's more specific, but I'm still not able to measure that because what does "one of the best" mean? For me, it meant the top 10 percent, which is measurable.

To set a measurable goal, ask yourself, "How will I know when I've achieved it?"

Achievable

Setting reasonable, achievable goals seems like common sense, but when it comes to goal setting, sometimes we have delusions of grandeur and we bite off more than we can chew.

If your goal is so audacious there is no chance of realizing it, you will quickly give up on it, and that failure will reinforce your insecurities (we all have them).

Suppose in high school I set a goal to get a perfect score on the ACT.

Did you know that fewer than 0.2 percent of the students who take that test get a perfect score? In 2018, 1,914,817 students took the ACT, and 3,741 got a perfect score.[60]

Even if I didn't have dyslexia and the academic struggles it brought, my goal of getting a perfect ACT score would not have been realistic. With an unachievable goal, I would have failed miserably and my failure would have further reinforced my lack of academic confidence.

Goals have to be achievable. Stretchable, but still achievable.

On that note, resist the impulse to set comfortable goals that do not cause you to stretch. Obtaining a goal you didn't work hard to achieve can be disheartening and anticlimactic. By setting achievable yet demanding goals, you will feel the satisfaction that comes with accomplishing Hard-Easy.

There are almost four thousand high schools in California, so this was definitely going to stretch me. To be in the top 10 percent of all the high school wrestlers in California was going to demand many moments of uttering "Bring it, Hard!"

Also, be sure to narrow your focus—in other words, don't set too many big goals. They will become unachievable because you will have too little time to devote to any of them.

Relevant

Your goal must be relevant to you and your big picture.

Relevance is your why. Why do you want to accomplish this goal? What is your purpose? As we've previously noted, purpose is what keeps us going when things get tough. This makes relevance the fuel that keeps the SMART goal moving forward.

In high school, I wanted to prove to myself that I could set a goal and work hard for several years to achieve it. My wrestling goal aligned with the direction I wanted my life to go.

The accomplishment of my wrestling goal helped lay the foundation for the bigger, more important scholastic and then vocational goals I would set in the future.

Timetable

When your goal has a deadline, you will feel a sense of urgency that keeps you focused and moving consistently toward achievement.

It's like playing basketball and feeling the urgency of the clock ticking down to the end, knowing you only have another minute to do what it takes to win the game.

Deadlines move us.

(Incidentally, having a deadline will also give you the ability to plan your celebration for achieving the goal.)

PRINCIPLE 3: Write Down and Display Your Goals

The act of writing your goals down will make them visible and reinforceable. Post your written goal where you can see it every day. That way you won't have any excuses for ignoring or neglecting it.

When you write your goal, use the word *will* as opposed to "would like to."

Example:

"I will win the following tournaments my senior year."

NOT

"I would like to win the following tournaments my senior year."

What your mind sees, it believes.

Think about all the accomplishments in this world; they were once just thoughts. Then someone wrote the thought down, and it became a goal. A goal a person could see and begin to believe in. A goal a brain could churn on during sleep. A goal the subconscious could keep spinning like a Rubik's Cube, slowly getting the thing to align and making connections to other things—occasionally spewing forth "Aha!" moments to the conscious mind.

Listen, let's say I hop in my time machine and zoom back fifty years, where I meet young Art. "Art," I say, "just wait. In fifty years, nearly everyone in the world will have handheld phones that let you call anyone from practically anywhere—without cords!

"And guess what? That's not all. These things aren't just phones. They're also powerful computers. And they're high-resolution cameras that let you see your photos right away—you don't need to take them to get developed. Plus, they're video cameras, so you can make your own movies. They are navigation tools that give you instant maps and show you moving on them.

"And music! Don't forget the music. These phones, they are music players that hold tens of thousands of songs. But that's not all. You can talk to your phone and ask it a question, and it will answer you, like the ship's computer on *Star Trek*. You can touch the screen of your phone and move things around on it. Your phone will recognize your face. And if you don't know something, you can go to something called Google on your phone and learn virtually anything. Pretty cool, eh, Art?"

It would be about then that young Art would either laugh at me, run from me, or call the looney bin to come pick me up.

And yet we have these phones, and like every other technology that was once inconceivably cool, we take them for granted.

These smartphones began as ideas that became SMART goals that were written down.

Post your goals in obvious places to give you motivation every day. Like a compass, the sight of your goal at the beginning of each day has the power to affect what you are doing, where you are going, and what choices you make throughout the day.

PRINCIPLE 4: Develop a Plan of Action

While it is critical to focus on the big picture, you can't forget to plan out the small steps you'll need to take along the way.

Create daily or weekly to-do lists—mini-goals that get you tiny step by tiny step closer to the ultimate peak of the big-picture goal.

At the top of every to-do list, state your ultimate goal so that your daily or weekly accomplishments align and move you toward your big-picture goal.

By writing down specific actions and crossing them each off as you complete them, you'll see that you're making progress. This is essential when your goal is big, audacious, stretchable, and long-term.

Being in the top 10 percent of high school wrestlers in California during my senior year was a SMART goal, but it was the end goal. I achieved it by developing benchmark SMART goals. They included 1) be at every practice, 2) make weight each match, 3) increase my ability to lift weight, 4) increase my number of pushups, 5) win certain matches, 6) be on the podium at certain tournaments, and 7) maintain the GPA required for wrestling eligibility. Truth be told, the last one was the most difficult for me.

These smaller goals served as my roadmap to take me to the big goal. Focusing on the next small step helped me not to get overwhelmed by the hugeness of the big goal because I knew exactly how I'd get there.

PRINCIPLE 5: Endure

Recognize that part of goal setting is the ongoing necessity of recalibrating and fine-tuning.

I find that my big goals stay rather unchanged over the long haul, but the actions I take and my to-do lists shift and morph significantly. Make sure the shifting short-term goals are always in alignment with your big-picture goal. Set aside time each day, or at least each week, to review and reevaluate your goals.

Let's go back to wrestling. During my junior year, I was competing in a tournament, and I contracted bacterial cellulitis from an unclean wrestling mat through a scratch on my elbow.

Nasty!

Within twelve hours, my elbow had swollen to twenty inches in diameter.

Was my swollen, gross, pus-oozing, infected elbow a setback?
Yes.

That's just one example of why you must constantly realign your short-term goals with the big-picture goal.

While my infection kept me out of wrestling matches for several weeks that year, it did nothing to alter my big-picture goal for my senior year. It did disrupt many of my short-term wrestling goals having to do with practices and matches. My short-term goals had to shift toward treatment and recovery so I could get back to wrestling.

Enduring to the end requires diligence, vision, determination, and flexibility. I had a vision of where I wanted to go, and I was determined to find ways to overcome the obstacles that stood between me and my ultimate goal.

These five principles have worked for me over and over again as I've set my mind to accomplish hard things. And they will work for you, too.

How Did I Do?

My senior year, I finished with a record of twenty-four wins and four losses. I was recruited and went on to wrestle collegiately, so in my mind I had fulfilled my goal to be one of the best high school wrestlers in California. I wasn't *the* best, but I can safely say I was in the top 10 percent of all the California high school wrestlers at my weight my senior year. And there's no way I would have gotten there without my SMART goals and my dedication to them.

Chapter Recap

Key concepts and takeaways from chapter 18:

- Your goal must excite you.
- Make it a SMART goal.
- Write your goals and post them.
- Develop a plan of action.
- Endure.

Pause and Think

- You've kept a big goal in mind while reading this book. Take a closer look at it now.

    * Does it excite you?

- * Is it SMART?

- Once you have a goal that is exciting and SMART:

  - * Write it down and post it where you will see it often. Don't forget to use *I will*.
  - * Also, write down why the goal is important to you. How would you convey it's meaning to someone else? Refine your answer until you're satisfied with it.
  - * Make a plan of action—a series of smaller SMART goals that will keep you on track.

CHAPTER 19

THE FIVE FRIENDS YOU NEED AND THE FIVE FRIENDS YOU NEED TO AVOID

In this chapter, I'm going to tell you about ten friends—the five you need to help you live Hard-Easy and the five you need to avoid so they don't hinder your Hard-Easy efforts.

But before I get to those ten friends, I need to clarify that in these chapters, I am NOT telling you to cut ties with your current friends and recruit new, high-achieving friends.

The Power of Friends

So, at the risk of contradicting myself, I will tell you about the friends you need to help you live Hard-Easy, as well as those so-called friends who are not really friends at all because they either intentionally or unintentionally sabotage your Hard-Easy efforts.

Many studies over the past several decades have stressed the importance of a strong social network of friends as a critical factor of good health and happiness. As the Mayo Clinic states, "Friendships can have a major impact on your health and well-being. . . . Good friends are good for your health. Friends can help you celebrate good times and provide support during bad times. Friends prevent loneliness and give you a chance to offer needed companionship, too."[61] Conversely, the implication is that bad friends can be bad for your health.

If you want to live a long, happy life, having hundreds of "friends" on Instagram, Facebook, or Snapchat won't do the trick. You must have a diverse, balanced, flesh-and-blood entourage that has your back through the highs and lows.

Whether you have studied all the reports, take my word for it, or you just listen to your heart, you know you need friends. But what kind of friends?

The Five Friends You Need

The five types of friends you need in your life are the clairvoyant, the clown, the cheerleader, the cohort, and the chaperone. (Yes, all Cs. Yes, they are my titles and my definitions. I am hoping it helps you remember who they are and the role they play in your life.) By having these friends, we radically increase the probability of living happy, enriched, long, Hard-Easy lives.

1. The Clairvoyant

The clairvoyant is often quiet, influencing you more by the way they live than how they use their words. They speak loud and clear with their actions. They live kind, honest, empathetic lives, and they authentically love you no matter how stupid you can be.

This friend is anything but pretentious. They do not care about the car you drive, the orderliness of your home, or the lack of monogrammed shirts in your wardrobe. They see the real you, your true self. When your actions are debatable, they express concern, not judgment.

As Joshua Becker writes, these types of friends "know us best. They know our strengths . . . and they recognize our weaknesses. Because of their intimate knowledge of who we are, they keep us honest with each other and with ourselves."[62]

Clairvoyants inspire you to assess how you are living your life. Their sheer presence seems to compel you to evaluate your attitudes and actions to ensure they are in alignment with your ultimate goal.

Clairvoyants see the chessboard of life and look many moves ahead. At times, it seems like they can perceive the future. When you go to move your bishop, they can see it will expose your king to danger. You might see their eyebrow raised in doubt as you contemplate your poor move, and you might meet their disapproving-yet-true-friend gaze. They intuitively know the consequences you will be blessed or cursed with tomorrow based on your actions today.

This seemingly supernatural ability to put the pieces together and understand the outcomes can at times make the clairvoyant an uncomfortable friend. Sometimes we don't want to know the truth behind the clairvoyant's nonverbal and verbal cues.

While you may want to impetuously act Easy, the clairvoyant is there to calmly persuade you to act differently. They are your lighthouse in the storm. This friend can be brutally honest when needed. Yet, deep down, you know their advice is prudent. They know the truth, they live the truth, and they encourage you to do the same.

2. The Clown

With a single sarcastic word, a quick sparkle in the eye, or the perfectly timed facial expression, impression, or gesture, the clown can lighten almost any situation. They help us cope with stress and tension, make fun of the slings and arrows of outrageous fortune (see William Shakespeare, *Hamlet*, act iii, scene i), and dispel gloom with the humor we need to hear.

But they don't just lighten a dark mood—they also make the good times better. They crack you up, make you feel at ease and lighthearted, and send both of you rolling on the floor in hysterics.

This friend helps us maintain balance and perspective. The clown is the one person you can be stupid-silly with no matter what. They can discuss serious issues when needed, but they simultaneously do not take themselves too seriously.

This is the friend who helps you find the bright side of almost any situation. They like to smile and can find humor in the difficulties and in the drudgery of life. They know how to laugh, and laugh well, especially at themselves. The clown teaches you that when you can laugh at your own stupidity, you are practicing the purest form of self-acceptance and self-love.

The clown is positive, motivated, optimistic, and constantly lifts those around them. Truth be told, the clown gives you power. How do you feel when others laugh at you? Weak, embarrassed, and ashamed? When you can poke fun and laugh at yourself, you demonstrate to yourself and those around you that you are confident, relaxed, and authentic. And that, my friend, is healthy, modest, graceful power.

3. The Cheerleader

This friend is your admirer, champion, fan, and supporter. Some may suggest that to seek and foster this kind of friend is to be a borderline—or not-so-borderline—narcissist. While the clairvoyant can help us feel some productive guilt when we see the dissonance between how we're acting and how we want to be, the cheerleader makes us feel good regardless of our missteps.

The guilt you might feel from interacting with your clairvoyant is like your early warning radar. It's an in-the-moment blip that lets you know something is off course. And when you hear that blip sooner than later, you can more easily make a course correction.

The inspiring, morale-boosting encouragement you get from the cheerleader is like the fuel that propels you back on course for the long haul and toward your goals.

You need both types of motivation to improve. You need the criticism of a loving clairvoyant coach and the enthusiastic support of your biggest cheerleader. As Katherine Hurst says, "You need friends who make you feel confident about who you are, not people who induce self-doubt."[63]

My cheerleaders are sincerely happy for me when the chips fall my way. You would think that all friends would want your happiness, but that's not always the way it goes down. The friend who does not harbor a hint of jealousy when you are killing it in your new tailored suit or is excited about your promotion is your cheerleader.

I know my cheerleaders are genuinely elated when one of my books does well. They watch and relish in my triumphs without a smidgeon of resentment, and I do the same for them.

Bad, horrible, ugly days in the dog-eat-dog world can exhaust our will to go Hard-Easy. It's essential to have someone screaming into a megaphone, "WHO'S GOT SPIRIT? WHO DO? WHO DO? YOU'VE GOT SPIRIT! YOU DO! YOU DO!" while they shake pom-poms and toss your somersaulting soul high in the air.

4. The Cohort

If you are employed full-time, you are spending about half of your waking hours at work. Studies show that the more remote and friendless you are at work, the unhappier you are. That is why you should have a cohort—someone to commiserate with, grab lunch with, and hang with in the breakroom. A professional pal you relate to and trust and who can help you deal with the stress and drama in the office. Going for sushi with a trusted coworker or professional peer sure beats eating a baloney sandwich alone at your desk.

Although your cohort may be inundated with reports, meetings, and emails, they never fail to walk by your desk with a friendly "What's up?"

Your cohort doesn't necessarily need to be your best friend outside of the office; they are simply someone you are comfortable with and who you trust.

5. The Chaperone

The four kinds of friends we've discussed are all part of a healthy social community, or tribe. The clairvoyant elevates our thinking by quietly reminding us of the consequences of our actions. The clown convinces us not to take things so seriously and to laugh at our shortcomings. The cheerleader encourages us no matter what. And the cohort is there to lean on at work when we need to vent and hang out.

Last but not least is the chaperone. The chaperone is kind of like the "friend whisperer." They carefully listen to us and can understand and translate the advice of the other four types of friends. They lovingly guide us and help decipher any mixed signals the other four may occasionally send. When you are anxious, uncertain, or fearful, the chaperone will make time to listen to you. Then they will help you sort out your apprehensions and confusion and chart a course based on your goals and aspirations.

My chaperone is an old friend from high school. Because of geographical distances and our crazy-busy lives, we only chat two or three times a year. However, that infrequency doesn't matter. When we do connect, time and space are irrelevant to our relationship.

We talk, laugh, and listen to each other as if we talked daily. His guidance and reassurance rejuvenate me. His laugh is contagious and soothes any anxiety I have knotted in me. He has a way of nudging me in the direction I should go while warning me about potential pitfalls. Speaking with him revives my emotional battery and assures me I am on the right path—and if I'm not on the right path, he lovingly cautions me of that, too.

Your chaperone will do the same for you.

Five Friends Down, Five to Go

We'll now look at five more "friends" you will probably find in your life—and these are the friends you want to avoid. For every action, there is an equal and opposite reaction—and for every Hard-Easy-enabling friend, there is an equal and opposite Easy-Hard enabling friend.

Thanks to social media, we are familiar with the concept of unfriending someone. With just one click, you can eradicate someone from your friend list, saving you from a stream of pics, clips, and posts of what they had for breakfast, the birthday of their second cousin, or the new car they want to humble-brag about.

In the real world, however, it can be a bit more complicated to unfriend a friend. Relationships take time to develop; it also takes time to distance yourself should you need to.

Notice I said *distance*, not *delete*. There is a big difference. Reaching a self-awareness where you realize which friendships merit cultivating and which need distancing can be an interesting, introspective journey.

We've talked about assets and investing in those assets that are most important. My most important assets are time and relationships. If you have a friendship that enables you to live Hard-Easy, you should invest your time in it. But if the relationship is taxing your ability to live Hard-Easy and is a time-suck (your most valuable asset), consider distancing yourself from that person.

With that preamble, here are the five friends you should be wary of: the drainer, the dishonest, the dramatic, the disloyal, and the dupe. Yes, they all start with D. Stop rolling your eyes; mnemonic devices work!

Many of you will protest: "I don't have any of these types of negative friendships." Okay, slow your roll. I am betting you do have friends from this watchlist; you just haven't looked at the nature of your friendships objectively. I know I have personally fallen victim to thinking a friend was truly my friend without really seeing the overall impact of the relationship. So read with an open mind.

The Five Friends to Avoid

1. The Drainer

Drainers are all around us. They may be associates, friends, or family members. Drainers live in a constant state of *no*. Suggest a new idea or goal of yours, and the drainer will automatically reply with a no and all the reasons why it's a horrible idea.

The challenge you'll have is sorting out which friend is the drainer and which is the clairvoyant, who has your best interests in mind. One is gold; one is fool's gold.

Here is a test I use. Drainers verbalize fears rather than concerns and are typically focused on the person rather than the problem or situation.

Drainers are motivated by their own internal demons and fears. They don't grasp the law of Hard-Easy and how successful people do what they do. They are too afraid to take risks, so they try to talk you out of doing what they themselves are afraid to try.

Drainers skulk in the corners waiting for your first stumble and love to quickly pounce on you to point out what you did wrong and why you should throw in the towel. The scary part is that their draining, self-doubt-promoting advice is given in a way that seems friendly and supportive. But it undermines your character, grit, and ambition.

I call them drainers because they drain your energy instead of building it up. True friends should make you feel revitalized and uplifted. If you always feel like crap after hanging out with a particular friend, it is a sure sign they are a drainer. Friends who perpetually bring you down want you there because they are typically living Easy-Hard and want company. When you excel, it shines the spotlight on their own failures and fears.

The drainer always seems to be right; they can at times be a know-it-all. ("*Seriously? I can't believe you didn't know that you could use this one particular species of fuzzy caterpillar to brush your teeth with while camping. Everybody knows that.*")

It is taxing and demoralizing to be around someone who makes you feel like an idiot. The know-it-all drainer makes you feel dumb, lazy, and uninformed for not knowing as much as they do or being as skilled as they are at something. Conversations with the drainer are laced with plenty of dismissive phrases designed to make you feel small and them feel big: "*Weellll, Art, that's not exactly right. You see, when I was sculpting the statues for my pool, I learned a key lesson I thought you already knew: you've got to use Sicilian marble. Seriously, man. What did you think was going to happen when you bought the cheaper Florentine marble? Amateur.*"

The drainer is typically irritable, sick, worn-out, and gloomy. Your drainer finds it difficult to see the bright side of anything. It is fatiguing to rub shoulders with a relentlessly griping drainer. In their world, something is always amiss. Which is weird since, on the flip side, they're a know-it-all. You'd think they would know how to fix all the things they complain about.

You probably know your drainer because when they call you, you sometimes send them straight to voicemail. Who has room in their life for this kind of pessimism? You can try to subtly combat their gloom with a silver lining, but it rarely works. When you spend too much time with a drainer, you lose energy and may find yourself draining others' batteries in a warped attempt to recharge your own. Thus, you risk becoming a drainer as well. It's all very Dracula-like.

The problem with keeping this soul-sucking friend around is that there isn't anything you can do to help them see that they are the problem. They do not see themselves as Debbie Downer draining the life out of everyone they come in contact with. And they will sure as hell resist any candid advice you may want to give them. The habitual drainer is most comfortable when their glass is next to empty—and when you see your own as empty too.

2. The Dishonest

The dishonest friend always seems to be taking advantage of your generosity.

From time to time we are all short on cash or forget our wallet. It is in moments like this that a good friend will cover you. And if we are a trusted, good friend ourselves, we will always pay them back ASAP. They do not have to remind us.

The dishonest friend, however, always needs to borrow money. They say it is a loan and that they will pay it back, but you know better. The dishonest friend always seems to be in the bathroom when it is their turn to buy a round of drinks or to split the bill.

The dishonest friend has no respect for boundaries. They seem to be perfectly okay with borrowing your tools and clothes without permission. They may even date your ex just days after you break up.

The dishonest friend's scruples can seem jumbled and are certainly not in line with yours. At times it appears they simply want whatever you have. And they have no qualms with taking it while they smile and say, "Hey, roomie, wanna go see a movie? I went online and got us tickets. Your credit card was on file, so I just used it. You don't mind, do you?"

This friend is only your friend while you are picking up the tab in one form or another. Watch what happens when you say enough is enough and cut off their welfare check, so to speak. You won't have to distance yourself from them—they'll do it all on their own.

If the drainer is a vampire, then the dishonest is a locust, consuming your money, time, patience, and sanity.

As it says on the blog Ditch the Label, "All friendships should be equal—which means that you should receive as much as you put in, it's all based on reciprocation and mutuality. If you're putting in more than you're getting out, you should think twice about what they are asking from you."[64]

3. The Dramatic

The dramatic is a drama queen or king. They love the chaos and energy a chaotic situation creates. The dramatics whine about all the drama in their lives—when they are actually the ones causing it.

Remember, the person living Hard-Easy tends to develop the attribute of being calm and relaxed. They have a plan, and they know where they are going and why. When shit happens, they may not like it, but they adjust and deal with it, knowing it is part of the Hard-Easy journey.

But the dramatic spins up drama for drama's sake. It helps them be the center of attention, and that is exactly what a dramatic person craves.

When you have a friend who makes the birthday celebration of a friend more about themselves than the birthday friend, you know this person resents it when the eyes of the crowd are anywhere but on them.

The dramatic may ask you how your day was, and just as you start to answer, they hijack your end of the "conversation" and begin telling you about the chaos of their day.

They crave attention. Everything is bigger, sadder, or harder than you have ever imagined. If you both go fishing, no matter what you catch, it will always be a minnow compared to the whale they haul in.

When you are proud of an achievement, you get animated and want to share it with friends. Occasionally sharing a personal success story is great. However, always having to one-up everyone in the room is exhausting to everyone but the dramatic.

The perpetual need to boast is a clear sign of low self-esteem. It is important to support our friends, but if you try to fill the dramatic's need for attention, you will fail.

The need for drama is born of insecurity, and that is something your friend has got to resolve on their own. As a friend, we must help with a listening ear and a compassionate heart yet not get trapped in the necessity to always reassure them. If you are paying so much attention to your dramatic friend's drama that it negatively impacts your ability to achieve your own goals, it is time to distance yourself and stop the tumult.

4. The Disloyal

The disloyal friend is the older, uglier sibling of the dishonest friend, but instead of money and material things, they steal your trust. They say they are the wind beneath your wings, but they are really the sewage beneath your feet.

This friend may act as a friend to your face, but behind your back, they show their true colors, undercutting you, talking smack, and starting unkind rumors about you.

They may compliment you with the noncompliment: "Your kids are so well behaved—for growing up in a single-parent home." "You rock that suit—it hides your beer belly better than any of your other suits." "You are the only one I know who can look cool enough to drive that POS you drive."

This world has far too much cynicism and judgment. The friends you keep close to you should provide you a safe harbor from those storms of negativity. True friends are extremely invested in you—and let you know it! The cool thing about a real friend is that their happiness is yours, and yours theirs.

The disloyal friend can be overly competitive. "A friendship based on competitive behavior is NEVER healthy or a true friendship."[65] This only generates vengeful, jealous, resentful feelings. These feelings fuel the disloyal to lash out against you, subtly or not so subtly, when you aren't in the room. Generally, people act this way because they have low self-esteem and want to use you as a tool to make them look or feel better in front of others.

The disloyal harbors deep jealousy when good things happen to you. This is a clear sign the relationship is based on competitiveness. A real friend will always want you to succeed and be happy.

The disloyal friend loves to gossip about others behind their back. If the disloyal is gossiping to you about others in your circle behind their back, be assured they are gossiping about you behind yours.

Sometimes the malicious disloyal friend may "jokingly" insult or tease you in front of others. They may say they were only kidding and didn't mean anything by it, but don't buy it. This is an act of betrayal.

The disloyal friend always wants it their way. They want to go to their favorite restaurant, the movie of their choice, and they always listen to their playlist. When you would rather have some downtime reading in front of the fire at home, the disloyal will not care and will try to bully or guilt you into hitting the clubs until early morning.

Time is your most precious asset, and free time is rare and valuable. If your friend will not respect the way you want to spend your time, it speaks to your mismatch. Good friends learn to adjust and adapt. Disloyal friends always want it their way. If they do not adjust—or if you find that your "friend" is a back-stabber—it is time to distance yourself.

5. The Dupe

The dupe is always setting you up and not coming through. They are duping you.

This friend is regularly bailing and flaking out on your plans. Think of the dupe as Lucy holding the football for Charlie Brown—ever promising ol' Chuck she'll keep her finger on the tip of the ball so he can kick the field goal. And Charlie B. keeps on believing her, charging at the ball, thinking it will be different this time only to discover, too late, that Lucy is jerking the ball away as he swings his leg, flies through the air, and hits the ground with a grunt in a pile of dust and limbs.

The dupe seems to frequently bail on you or is always late, showing no respect for your time. These friends often wait for you to line up a lunch date and then cancel at the last minute. Go back and review your text conversations. Is it obviously one-sided? The flaky friend is talented at saying, "I am so, so sorry, but I have to bail on lunch today. Can I take a rain check?" But they never seem to claim that rain check.

The dupe also bails from moments that are deeply personal to you. You may be pouring your heart out to them about a fight with your girlfriend, and they'll flippantly take a call in the middle of your story, cutting you off so they can do something more important to them. Or you could just be telling them about your day, and they are zoned in on their Instagram, swiping through while occasionally grunting to make it sound like they're listening.

Why?

Because to them, their thoughts, ideas, and beliefs are far more important than yours. They don't want you to know it, so they string you along, pretending you're a big priority in their life.

If your friend chronically abandons you for the simple things, how can you trust them to be there for you when you really need them? Life is messy, and we all have times when we need a listening ear. The dupe is not that empathetic ear.

The dupe will rarely, if ever, remember your birthday, send you Happy New Year's wishes, or congratulate you on your anniversary. If your friend cannot acknowledge some of the important events in your life, you have to ask—Are they really a friend?

The Friend Assessment

Okay, we've covered ten types of friends. (Incidentally, I came up with these categories after much research and reflection on the various friends I've encountered in my life.)

Now it's time for you to look at your friends and see if you can spot any of the C friends (the good guys) or D friends (the not-so-friend friends) in your life. You can use the following questions to assess where you stand with your friends:

1. Am I at ease to simply be myself around my friends?
2. Of all my friends, which ones do I value most and why?
3. Who is my clairvoyant, constantly encouraging me to do better?
4. Who is my clown, helping me not to take things so seriously?
5. Who is my cheerleader, always pumping me up and telling me I am great and can do this?
6. Who is my cohort, who has my back at work and eases the stress of my professional grind?
7. Who is my chaperone, translating and interpreting other friends' advice and guiding me toward my ultimate goal?
8. What roles do I play in my friends' lives?
9. Have I ever been a D friend?
10. How can I be a better C friend?

Over the years, I have learned that the only way to have a trusted friend is to be a trusted friend. You choose your path in life and those you want to experience it with. And there are those friends who will encourage you in your Hard-Easy decisions and those who will undermine you in your Hard-Easy decisions.

And there are all those other friends, family members, and acquaintances who lie somewhere in between. Don't sever relationships with anyone in the hopes of making new friends you believe are better, but be wise in assessing which of your friends are really just wolves in sheep's clothing because they may not really be your friends at all.

Chapter Recap

Key concepts and takeaways from chapter 19:

- The five types of friends you need in your life are the clairvoyant, the clown, the cheerleader, the cohort, and the chaperone.
- There are five friends you should be wary of: the drainer, the dishonest, the dramatic, the disloyal, and the dupe.
- See if you can identify who the C friends and D friends in your life are.
- Be wise in assessing friends who are really wolves in sheep's clothing—because they may not really be your friends at all.

Pause and Think

- Complete the friend assessment.

CHAPTER 20

RELATIONSHIPS

As humans, we crave companionship, and yet, with so many marriages ending in divorce, it's clear we're not always so good at picking our partners and/or staying the course. In this chapter, we'll explore how the law of Hard-Easy applies to finding—and keeping—your special someone. As you read through it, think about the relationship you're currently in or the relationship you dream of having. How does the law of Hard-Easy apply to finding that relationship and keeping it strong?

It's fairly easy to draw a link to Hard-Easy when numbers and facts are involved. It's trickier when your heart is involved. Or is it?

Good Relationships Are Hard Work—Bad Ones Are Harder

I once believed that where true love was concerned, relationships were easy-peasy. With *real* love, you didn't have to work to create a remarkable relationship. It's *real* love, after all, and when it's real, everything else should take care of itself, right?

Alas, I have been divorced twice and married three times. (Even I roll my eyes as I write this. Am I really *that* guy? Heavy sigh. Yep, that's me.) So, while I am not a marriage therapist, I have some real-world experience that gives me a unique perspective on the subject. Given my many massive marital mistakes and the fact that we tend to learn most from our mistakes, I am here to tell you that *real* love falls under the law of Hard-Easy.

SECTION I: The Hard-Easy of Finding a Partner

Neanderthal Love

Let's revisit our Neanderthal friends. Suppose one enterprising young caveman started a Stone Age dating app called OKHominid. It's all the rage. (Granted, the "app" is using charcoal to draw on the cave wall.) One lonely Neanderthal scratches his personal ad on the wall:

> *SHMN (single hairy male Neanderthal) seeks mate who enjoys hunting mammoths, long walks by the tar pits, and propagating our gene pool through as many babies as possible. Must act quickly—our life expectancy is only 30 years at best.*[66]

As we've discussed, our brains are preprogrammed to want instant gratification. This applies to relationships. Our Neanderthal brain wants companionship and wants it NOW. And, looking back, you can see why. Sabertooth tigers lurked behind every boulder, rival tribes wanted your resources, and there were no doctors, HMOs, or medications. That biological clock was ticking for every primitive hominid.

Which means our brains are hardwired to fall in "love" with the first half-decent mate who crosses our path. Our emotions are predisposed to push us in that direction, too, if we've been unlucky in love.

You so badly want this to be *the one* that you blindly ignore or altogether miss the tell-tale signs that this is not Mr. or Ms. Right. You want love to be easy to form and easy to maintain. But that's the fallacy of Easy-Hard.

Might As Well Face It: You're Addicted to . . . Infatuation

The biochemical euphoria caused by infatuation is powerful and can make relationships go Easy-Hard in many ways: You might mistake infatuation for love and plunge into a relationship you later regret. You might be so giddy you can't bear to spend a second away from that person—and you smother that budding relationship to death. If your infatuation does mature into love, you might find yourself missing the chemical rush of the early days and look for other ways to re-create that high—which could lead to actions that doom a healthy relationship.

Remember, it's normal to get drunk with infatuation in those initial stages. As the Neanderthals have taught us, these feelings and reactions are hardwired in us and trigger our brain's reward and pleasure systems. According to Harvard's "Science in the News," physical attraction releases the chemicals dopamine, norepinephrine, and serotonin.[67] As far as your brain knows, you're literally addicted to that person, and you're constantly looking for your next fix. These feelings can come on so strong and so fast (and so *easy*) we get swept up in the biochemical euphoria of budding love.

It's easy to skip all the hard work that goes into a relationship when the infatuation makes you crazy. But things get much harder once the infatuation wears off. And depending on what Easy-Hard decisions you make during the infatuation stage, you could be facing the Hard phase before you know it.

The Myth of the Soul Mate

Finding and sustaining love is hard enough, but we often make it harder, living under the delusion that there exists in the world a one and only, a soul mate, awaiting us.

If you're one of those who believes you've got a soul mate somewhere out there (and I used to be one of you), I apologize for shattering your illusion. But the numbers back me up.

With nearly 8 billion people on this earth, if each of us did have a soul mate, statistically speaking, that one person might be living in a different country, might already be married, or might be too young, too old, or dead.

That's a discouraging notion. But many soul-mate adherents counter these ominous odds with a belief in serendipity. They are convinced the universe is going to ensure that the paths of soul mates will one day cross, that they will recognize each other, and that this will be the beginning of a charmed, fairy-tale life.

The myth of the soul mate (and the affliction of serendipity syndrome), though romantic, makes every phase of love—from dating to initial commitment to long-term commitment—harder.

Infatuation-Addiction + Soul-Mate Mania

After dating *many* candidates (sometimes it takes awhile), I would meet a woman I clicked with and with whom everything seemed right, and I would wonder, "Is she *the one*?" The chemistry, the connection, the conversation—it was all there, and things felt effortless and smooth. Within weeks I would be so convinced this was my soul mate I would start believing it was going to be happily ever after from here on out.

Those initial feelings were so powerful and all-consuming: *How can this woman not be the one? She gets me. This relationship seems so easy and natural. She shares my dreams, interests, and aspirations. She must be the one!*

That's the fallacy of Easy-Hard, stoked by our Neanderthal brains. Good chemistry and an initial sense of connection can make a relationship feel Easy—like you don't have to work at it.

With those women I thought were my soul mates, during those first several weeks, we would see each other constantly, and we would start planning a life together. All the stupid things I did, they found funny. They would tell me they had never felt this way with anyone else, and that made me feel safe.

But those adrenaline-filled, whirlwind relationships would always burn out for one reason or another. The highs and lows were like an unpredictable, unsettling, and painful roller-coaster ride. I'd be on this emotional high, and then my world would be pulled out from under me, leaving me feeling helpless and like I was spinning out of control. I hated dating. The only consistent thing about it was the inconsistent and turbulent ride my heart was on.

If you've gone through something similar, I'm sorry if I'm dredging up painful memories, but stick with me. It's hard, but confronting this particular velociraptor of disappointment will be worth it.

Looking back on those so-called "loves" that crumbled, I can see that sometimes it was a mutual hurting; other times it was one party calling it quits and imposing massive heartache on the other. I have been hurt, and I have done the hurting. What I would think was blossoming love would suddenly wilt. Someone I thought was the perfect partner just a few months earlier looked completely different now.

Certain partnerships would have been disastrous! I can definitively say, "Wow! We both dodged a bullet on that one." But that had me wondering about how I got it so wrong earlier in those relationships. How did I go from that all-consuming bliss to "What the hell am I doing?"

I could have followed the Easy-Hard path in these relationships. I could have been consumed by infatuation and dived into marriage or begun cohabitating. That part of the relationship would have been super easy. But that would have set me up for Hard down the road, when the infatuation and excitement wore off. Going through all this was part of the Hard of the Hard-Easy of real love.

Pursuing Easy-Hard in a relationship spurred by infatuation-addiction and soul-mate Mania can lead a couple to a marriage that ends in a painful divorce. What's more, echoes of the Hard reverberate throughout and after the divorce is finalized. Stress, anger, depression, loss, regret—all of it can roil within the relationship and beyond. And it can affect friends, extended families, and kids—if they've had any.

Find Someone Who Shares Most of Your Core Values

Beauty ebbs and flows. We all age. As far as the attractiveness scale, your opinion about your partner will fluctuate. However, if looking at your partner gives you a calm, peaceful, warm feeling, you've got something that will carry you through the ups and downs.

Here's how this concept has played out for my Barbie and me.

Our first date was a simple deli. Was it love at first sight? No way. But love at first sight isn't necessary. "Like at first sight" is plenty. Sure, I thought she was attractive, but she was so quiet and shy I couldn't read her. Over our many years of dating, however, I realized that her quiet, shy side was not her being aloof or weak. She is one of the strongest and kindest individuals I've ever met. I remember thinking she was attractive but also interesting, kind, and honest.

Once you have found somebody who falls in your "nice to look at" category, you must see if you share core common goals and beliefs. I don't mean trivial bullshit stuff like movies, music, clothes, and food. I mean the stuff that counts—the core values and behaviors critical to long-lasting happiness.

This is so important I suggest you make a list of your core values. Keep your list to three to four things. Again, sharing a favorite movie or tv show doesn't count. Your core values, beliefs, and behaviors should be easy for you to identify. If you cannot rattle them off, you need to be alone with yourself and sort that out because you are absolutely not prepared for the long-lasting, solid relationship you seek.

My list included kindness. If you're not kind to others, what does that say about your character and who you are, deep down? Another non-negotiable for me was humor. If I couldn't make her laugh, and I couldn't laugh while in her presence, I knew that relationship wasn't going to last. Sorry. All the rest is fluff. My wife-to-be checked both boxes.

If you and your partner do not share core values, your odds of becoming another divorce casualty go up.

In his article, "Defining Your Core Values to Develop Your Relationship," Ranil Sharma says, "It is a good idea to look at your 3–5 core values. Things like safety, trust, team, fun, loving, kindness, loyalty, respect, equality, living life to the max are common examples. It is the miss-alignment of core values that creates major disruption in relationships. If you haven't done this already with your partner then do both of yourselves a favor and try it."[68]

It's not always easy to find someone with whom you share both good chemistry and common core values. But if you do the hard work up front, the relationship will be easier to grow down the road. Easy would have you focus primarily on physical appearance and the high of infatuation; Hard has you taking the time to understand your partner's soul.

SECTION II: The Hard-Easy of Nurturing a Good Long-Term Relationship Once You're in It

Good Relationships Are Just Peachy

So, what goes into a good relationship? What ingredients do you need? Let's return to my peach-tree story.

It took years before the peach trees I planted in my backyard developed deep roots. And only after many more years did I begin to enjoy the sweetness of the fruit. I had to water and fertilize in moderation and consistently over an extended period of time. There was no way for me to accelerate the process. In fact, I might have killed the peach trees had I watered and fertilized them too often or too much. (Just as when you're infatuated, you want to water and fertilize that new fling like crazy, and yet these are the very actions that can destroy it.)

Now, sitting in my metaphorical orchard and armed with a little more knowledge and experience, I know that strong, healthy relationships take years to cultivate. Deep love takes time to grow roots and to manifest itself. We must get past the infatuation stage, take a step back, and figure out what this relationship is really all about. It's hard to do but necessary if we want to find someone we can spend the rest of our life with.

Of course, there are those couples who meet and marry within weeks and enjoy a strong and happy relationship for the rest of their lives. Sometimes these relationships are born of inner wisdom—they've each had enough experience to recognize (subconsciously or otherwise) when that person is truly a fit. And sometimes they're just lottery-lucky. (We've discussed some of the Hard-Easy issues of winning the lottery . . .) Clearly, these types of relationships are the exception, not the norm. The Law of Hard-Easy decrees, "Don't base lifelong happiness in a relationship built on luck. And don't be hasty."

But even these out-of-the-norm, lucky relationships don't flourish without nurturing. They, too, need time to germinate and to plunge their roots deep into the soil, creating a solid, strong foundation that can withstand the fury of the storms that will test their love and commitment.

Loving someone means taking time to get to know that person. Loving someone means learning to trust that person, little by little. Loving someone is seeing the good despite the bad. Loving someone is hard work.

True love is a commitment that makes life better than it already is. While love can last decades and still be a rare, exhilarating, fulfilling ride, we need to have a little patience during the first stages of a relationship, taking it slow and pumping the brakes now and then, making sure we see that "soul mate" for what they truly are.

This is who you are going to wake up with every day. This is who you will love, like, laugh with, and cry with. If you think you're going to change them and make them into someone *you* think they should be, I suggest you make the break. I've been in this kind of relationship, and I promise it will end in a painful crash months or years down the road. Life is too short. Do not waste your time or theirs. The one asset you never get back is time.

Love's Trickier Flywheel

Even those in deep, intimate relationships can demolish those relationships with just a single, stupid decision. Of course, those pivotal stupid decisions are often the result of numerous unwise microdecisions: Flirting with someone at work who is not your partner or spouse is a microdecision. Thinking about them is a microdecision. Saying yes when they ask you to grab a drink after work is a microdecision. Going clubbing with them is a microdecision. Giving them a friendly peck on the cheek is a microdecision. And all of these microdecisions can put you on a trajectory toward infidelity.

Once a relationship is damaged, it can take many more times the effort to get your flywheel back up to speed. And that's only possible if your partner, sibling, child, parent, or best friend doesn't put a wedge in your flywheel and prevent any positive momentum from building.

Hard-Easy Principles Enhance Relationships

Once you do find someone you love and want to spend the rest of your life with, the law of Hard-Easy can help you keep your relationship thriving, both emotionally and practically.

We've already compared working on love to working on my peach trees. Let's compare the Hard-Easy of love to another idea we've covered in this book: skydiving. Emotionally, the decision to jump is made on the ground. In a long-term relationship, the decision to be kind, tender, patient, and stay the course is made at the beginning. That way, when temptations, arguments, or troubles hit, you're committed to seeing things through.

Long-lasting relationships aren't made of perfect people. They are made of people who communicate, compromise, forgive, and offer understanding—people who create an environment where unconditional love can grow and thrive. All successful, long-lasting relationships endure their share of disagreements. Shit happens. You must be willing to embrace each other's imperfections to make your relationship not perfect but perfectly healthy and perfectly poised for more growth.

Finding the kind of person you can have this type of relationship with is not an easy feat. I hear those who say, "I am looking for the one person who truly gets me." In reality, they should be saying, "I want to find someone who will help with the dishes and make the bed now and then." I'm not suggesting those two goals are mutually exclusive. I'm merely saying that finding someone who does the dishes and likes the bed made in the morning (like you do) is easier and will deliver more of a long-lasting relationship than finding someone who "gets" you.

Perhaps, like me, you believed a solid, happy relationship was supposed to be effortless and that those individuals who attained it just seemed to luck out and find that one person they were totally compatible with.

Let's talk about me and my wife, Barbie. We were not "made" for each other. There was no supernatural, cosmic energy that willed us to be. The reality is that we were approximately the same age, lived close to each other, had similar interests, and were both single. If you eliminate any of those variables, we would probably not be together right now.

Loving the Good, the Bad, and the Ugly

While it's easy to love your partner for their admirable traits, the test of true love and a strong relationship is how you handle the bad and the ugly. Because we all have some ugly.

I credit the matchless peace and joy I've found with my wife of five years to her being willing to love me in spite of my broken pieces.

We are each a unique puzzle, our pieces scattered all over as we try to put them together and make ourselves whole. We can see in our partners the border pieces—clean edges forming enough of a picture that it draws us in. But it is the intricate, inner pieces that are hard to figure out. It takes time and effort to put those uneven edges together, trying a piece here, trying it there, then giving up and trying a different piece.

My wife likes my unfinished puzzle no matter how scattered my pieces and imperfect my image. True love is not the butterflies in my stomach; it's the deep-down knowledge that she will be there for me no matter what. She sees the flawed me and patiently helps me try to find where those missing pieces belong.

It's Okay to Dislike Each Other

Another key to preserving a long-lasting relationship is acknowledging that you don't always have to like each other. There will be days you are so irritated with your partner you want to get away from them and other days you want to kick their ass.

Most days, it's simply amazing, and my wife and I are in perfect sync. But sometimes we are out of sync. Relationships are not static. There is an ebb and flow. I see young or newly married couples talking about how pissed off they are at one another and then instantly start having doubts about the relationship. The couples who last will say they were mad as hell at their partner and then seem to shrug it off. Couples who've been together for years stay focused on their core beliefs and let the other stuff roll off their backs.

Doing the Little Things Is Often the Hardest Part

The big things are sexy and fun: Getting your partner a car for Christmas. Surprising them with an anniversary trip to Europe. Taking them to a fancy restaurant and giving them a big diamond for their birthday. You might do something of that magnitude once in a decade, or maybe once in a lifetime.

But when it really comes down to it, those things don't count. It's the little things—the sacrifices you don't want to make because they're, well, sacrifices. You're tired. It's not fair you have to drive carpool on what's supposed to be your night off, because your partner accidentally scheduled a girls' night out. Do you shrug your irritation off or let it fester? This is the kind of stuff that, day in and day out, can make or break a relationship.

Strong, long-term relationships require hard work—all the time. When you do the small, hard things regularly, Easy comes as a feeling of safety, togetherness, and peace.

Communication

"Communication in a relationship" may sound glib, but it's a biggie on that hard-to-do list. We sometimes forget that words can be knives and that the wounds they create can leave lifelong scars. When you give feedback, it needs to be pointed at the action or problem and not the person or personality.

Life gets messy, and it is easy to unwittingly and sometimes intentionally hurt, belittle, and insult our partner. We've all done it. No one is off the hook here. But take it from someone who has learned the hard way. Instead of launching into attack mode, tell your partner how their actions made you feel. Take a deep breath, be calm, and replace "You're such a shitty asshole for doing _____" with "When you said (or did) _____, I was surprised, confused and hurt. That is not like you."

It can be hard to do in the heat of the moment, but it will lead to Easy because it focuses on the problem, not the person. I promise that defenses will come down, vulnerability will go up, and seeds of empathy will be sown. Empathy and anger cannot coexist. One of the secrets to a long-lasting relationship is empathetic listening followed by soft, heartfelt dialogue.

Don't Let Your Relationship Get Lost in the Swirl of Life

Work, hobbies, family obligations and so forth can be all-consuming, and at times, we may find we've completely forgotten about our partner. It can be hard to carve out time for each other in this busy world.

But just like you schedule time for the gym, taking the kids to school, and getting yourself to the office, you must be proactive when it comes to scheduling time with your partner. If you aren't, relationship stress will slowly build. If you allow things to slide too long, you can be sure that Hard is going to bring you up short—and usually at the most inopportune times.

If you find it challenging to set aside regular one-on-one time with your partner, I suggest you focus on better time management. There are lots of tools out there to help with this.

Here is one little tip I have shared before, but it is so, so beneficial in making one-on-one time with my wife super effective. If I am out to dinner or a movie with my wife, I leave my phone in the car. While you are with your partner, dedicate your attention to them and them alone. Your conversations will be more in-depth, more genuine, and draw you closer as a couple.

Set Goals Together

While it's important to have individual goals and aspirations, setting goals you can work on together is essential. Setting SMART goals as a couple will strengthen your relationship. These goals could center around making and spending money, building and deepening your relationship, taking a vacation, or planning what you'll do with the house.

Keep That Spark Alive

Being with one person for years on end can begin to feel routine and even dull, particularly if nothing new is happening. So how do you combat that?

Barbie and I fight boredom by going on adventures! This can be as simple as trying out a new restaurant and spending a night up in the mountains, or as elaborate as spending a week on the Amalfi Coast. Whatever you do, get your adrenaline pumping and create memories together. There has to be lots of laughing and learning for Barbie and me. That typically means doing something neither of us has ever done. I promise that after you share a few adventures, your relationship will feel revitalized.

Light Some Candles and Play Some Barry White

Make sure physical intimacy is an important part of your long-term relationship. Sometimes you'll have crazy-passionate sex. Other times, when one or both of you are tired, it will be maintenance sex. But intimacy is critical to feeling unified. Lock your door, escape to a hotel room for a night, or come home from work when the kids are at school for a "hot lunch." It may be hard to make this a priority, but doing so is a key part of nurturing the health of the relationship.

Laughter Draws You Closer

Humor is a great way to get to know someone and to deepen a relationship. Barbie and I should know each other pretty well by now because we do a lot of laughing, finding humor in even the smallest things.

A healthy sense of humor can help you weather the worst storms. It is one of the best ways to connect with your partner. That's right. Without even realizing it, the second you release anything from a giggle to a full-blown belly laugh, you send a series of powerful messages to your partner: I like you. I feel safe with you. I accept you. I want to be with you.

Unconditional Love

Above all else, there must be love. Unconditional love.

I sometimes feel that with the term "unconditional love," emphasis is placed on *love*. But ponder for a moment the word *unconditional*. Is your love for the person you have chosen to be with unconditional?

If you don't love your partner unconditionally, what the hell is it all about?

Unconditional means being so deeply committed to your partner that 1) you don't let obstacles, challenges, or complications harm the depth or quality of the love you feel for them, or 2) deter you from sacrificing to benefit your partner and relationship. (Quick note here: unconditional love does not mean tolerating abuse, neglect, exploitation, or criminal activity. It doesn't mean codependency or ignoring warning signs or issues that create mistrust. In these instances, you may still harbor feelings of love for a person but may have to terminate the relationship.) If your partner becomes seriously ill, you face it together. If your partner loses their job, you don't pack up your stuff and leave. You can even forgive infidelity, although the trust between you and your partner may take a very long time to emerge from the scorched earth of hurt—if it ever emerges again. Still, those who genuinely, unconditionally love their partner often want to try to work together to overcome the hurt.

How do you truly know when you are in a relationship where the potential for unconditional love is strong? Easy. It's when you can't envision life without them. This is different from all-consuming infatuation. This someone who has become such a part of your life it's as if they are part of you. If you can envision a life without your partner, then get out. Stop wasting your time and theirs. It's not worth the pain, heartache, and effort. Find a partner you want to be with, not a partner you have or ought to be with.

Does having a long-term relationship with the person you can't envision life without mean you're in the perfect relationship? No. The perfect" relationship is a paradox. Why? Because it's not perfect at all. Long-lasting relationships include those who understand and adhere to the motto "Bring it, Hard!" They don't get distracted or discouraged by conflict.

There were times I wished for a "unicorn"—that perfect partner who would bring me a state of everlasting nirvana. But just like unicorns, such a partner simply does not exist. Truth be told, there are hundreds and even thousands of suitable companions strewn all over the earth, each one of them with the ability to make you equally content. They may do it in different ways, but they can do it.

So many people want instant solutions to their relationship challenges. But, like that unicorn, instant solutions just do not exist. All great relationships involve living Hard-Easy, even decades after you get married.

If only one of you is all in when it comes to building your relationship but the other person ignores, dismisses, or takes it for granted, it's not going to last. I speak from experience: if you're not giving it your all, you're living Easy, and Hard is going hunt you down sooner or later because this kind of one-sidedness is doomed to failure.

If you genuinely love your partner, nothing's too hard. Notice I said "too hard." If you want your love to be deep and lasting, you'll do the hard things to make sure the relationship gets easier down the line. Remember that it's consistency in the small romantic gestures you make today that ensures you'll find yourself in a comfortable, secure companionship tomorrow. That is when Easy settles in.

My advice? Always choose Hard when it comes to your relationships. Over time, you will have created an atmosphere that enables you to find—and keep—the partner who's your best match and who becomes your one and only.

Chapter Recap

Key concepts and takeaways from chapter 20:

- Early love is an addiction. Get through it before you make any big decisions.
- Go into a relationship with your eyes wide open.
- Hard-Easy can help keep your relationship thriving in both an emotional and a practical sense.

- It's possible to sabotage even lasting relationships when you go with Easy. Always choose Hard.

Pause and Think

- Can you envision a life without them? Do you like that vision?
- If you're dating, think about the qualities you want in a partner. Make a list of non-negotiable qualities as well as deal breakers. Go beyond physical qualities—what do you want out of a relationship? For further reading in this area, Develop Good Habits published the article "24 Best Relationship Books Every Couple Should Read Together."[69]
- If you're in a committed relationship, pay attention to the choices you make over the course of two or three days. How often are you choosing Hard?

CHAPTER 21

THE TEN COMMANDMENTS FOR ACHIEVING ACADEMIC SUCCESS FOR THOSE WITH (OR WITHOUT) DYSLEXIA

Hard-Easy Lessons for Academics

Long before I met Gordon the cowboy and heard his simple explanation of the law of Hard-Easy, I was living it. Struggling with dyslexia from elementary school on, I was tempted to take the Easy-Hard way out of pursuing higher education because of my disability. This chapter looks at how I applied some Hard-Easy concepts before I knew what to call them.

From kindergarten to third grade, students learn to read. From third grade onward, students read to learn. I am sure this is how it works for most, but for this dyslexic dude, it did not play out that way.

When I was in fourth grade at Lincoln Elementary in Cupertino, California, my teacher, Mrs. Yamaguchi, announced that we would be having a class spelling bee the following day.

I had always been a competitive young buck, so this was right up my alley. To help us prepare, Mrs. Yamaguchi gave us a long list of words. While my close friends were outside playing after school all afternoon, I studied the list until I had memorized it.

The next day, I stood by my desk, eagerly awaiting my turn. My friends breezed through their words. Then it was my turn. Mrs. Yamaguchi gave me my word. I spelled it with confidence. And I spelled it wrong. This was one of the first times in my life I recognized there was something different about me when it came to reading, spelling, and writing.

Lucky for me, my father was getting his doctorate at Stanford University in education administration. Dad and his doctoral associates put me through tons of tests: reading, psychological, IQ, and more. One day, my dad sat me down and explained, "Art, you are smart. The tests you've taken prove that. But your brain works differently than most."

While I welcomed the information, where did I go from here?

I overheard a passionate discussion between my mom and dad when I was about ten or eleven. My mother wanted to enroll me in the remedial learning classes at school. My father opposed the idea. I will never forget one of my mother's retorts: "What if Art can't tell the difference between a men's or women's bathroom? What if he walks right into a women's public restroom because he can't read the signs?" I thought, "Geez, Mom. I know the difference between men's and women's restrooms!" That was absolutely absurd!

My father came to my defense. He calmly said, "Mignon, what's most important right now is to build Art's self-esteem. If we put him in with the slow kids, he will label himself as slow, and his friends will too. He is not slow. In fact, he's smarter than most. He just struggles with reading, and reading affects all his other courses. We must keep him in the normal classes and treat him like a normal boy. We can work with him to help him overcome his dyslexia in other ways."

My mother then argued that they should restrict my athletic activities and have me spend more time doing extra reading and writing with after-school tutors. My father said, "Art is building a strong sense of self through his athletics. Those are the activities creating his positive self-image and helping to mold core leadership attributes in him. If anything, we should cut back his extra educational work and increase his athletic activities."

"You can't be serious," she said.

My father then said, "Why would we want to take our son out of the positive activities that are promoting a confident self-image? Why would we have him spend more time doing activities that reinforce his weaknesses?"

I cannot tell you how relieved I was to hear these words from my father.

Enduring the Shame

Reading was and still is extremely painful for me. I get headaches if I read too long. And reading out loud? Well, that is torture.

My Sunday school teachers wanted us to bring our Bibles to class so we could read aloud when called upon. The last thing I wanted to do was be in church, but a close second was reading out loud! Often, in situations like this, I'd listen to my peers read fluently, and then I would stumble my way through a verse. I would feel great shame well up inside me, as if I were not good enough.

Later, in college, I took a religious history class. We had a pop quiz. The answer to one of the questions was *resurrection*. I knew I had the correct answer, so I didn't think too much about it.

The next day, the teacher stood in front of the class with one of the quizzes in his hand. My quiz. How could I miss my handwriting? I was mortified. With my paper held high, he said, "Students, we have a classmate among us that is either too lazy or too stupid to be in college. They misspelled the word *resurrection*."

I felt my body shrinking into my seat. Here came that shame again. I could have died. I had heard the label *lazy* more times than I cared to remember in my educational settings. It was especially troubling because I was in a religion class that was supposed to be about love, forgiveness, acceptance, tolerance, and patience. This asshole impersonating a religious professor was being none of these. I felt confused, sad, and mad all at once. When it came to this teacher, I certainly did not learn very much about love, forgiveness, or tolerance.

Let me take a moment to offer a small plea to all the teachers out there, based on my personal experience. Please, please have a soft spot in your heart for those who struggle with reading or spelling. It does not definitively mean they are lazy or stupid. Forcing them to read out loud or pointing out simple spelling mistakes tears down their self-esteem, undermines their self-confidence, and shames and humiliates them in front of their peers.

Believing the Lie of Labels

At some point in my youth, I started allowing my dyslexia to define me. I would tell myself that I did not need to get a college degree, let alone a higher degree. Could I even be a decent college student? Heck, I hadn't been a decent high school, junior high, or elementary student! I was convinced that no one, including myself, my teachers, my friends, and possibly even my parents, would bet on me having any real success if I attended college.

So, naturally, I started to come to the conclusion that if I did not have what it took to be a decent university student, I would more than likely find myself in a less-than-advantageous vocation. I began to believe that any job, even those I wouldn't love, would be okay.

Do you recognize how I was letting the velociraptors of disappointment, discouragement, and doubt gang up on me? They were using the what-the-hell effect to trap me and convince me to surrender to their Easy-Hard master.

At the same time, I wanted to become like my father, who got his master's degree at the University of Utah and a PhD from Stanford. Plus, he always told me, "The best investment you can make is in your own education."

Fighting the Velociraptors

My father was my clairvoyant friend. He had knowledge and experience (wisdom): he was standing at the top of that metaphorical mountain, which gave him a perspective I didn't have. The clairvoyant wisdom of my father let me know I could defeat these velociraptors if only I fought fiercely enough—

"Bring it, Hard!" The battle wouldn't be easy, but neither was it impossible to win. Still, it was much easier said than done.

Fortunately, I had other role models as well. In my early twenties, my good friend Stan Pace and I would take an annual fall pilgrimage into the High Sierras.

Scholastically, you could not find two friends more diametrically opposite. But there we were. Stan was driving us down from the mountains as we approached Modesto. I remember saying to him, "You are my scholastic hero. I wish I had your educational talents."

His brow furrowed. Then he said, "You have more physical endurance than anyone I know! You just hiked me into the ground. When your wrestling coach told you to do fifty pushups, you did a hundred! You push yourself harder than anyone I have ever met. So what if you can't read as fast as I can? Use your endurance as an asset. If it takes you three times longer to read what I read, then spend the time. Don't let dyslexia define you. Don't let it beat you. Don't let it stop you from being all you can be."

It was one of those moments when you find yourself in the right place, at the right time, talking to the right person. Stan served as my chaperone and cheerleader friend all in one. He deciphered all those mixed messages cluttering my view and rearranged them into something that made sense. And he pointed out and praised my strengths and encouraged me to use those strengths to overcome my weaknesses. What he said started something within me: a belief that I could do it, and a fire to make it happen.

Daring to Dream Big

Stan was right. I had been allowing society and the scholastic establishment to determine my academic self-worth. Because my ACT, SAT, and other timed power-test scores were so low, many—including myself—underestimated what I could accomplish in college.

Could my endurance really be an academic asset? Could I be good at school and learn everything I needed to from each class?

The concept was so unbelievably bizarre to me. I had never thought about it that way before. My aim was always just for survival—trying to get at least a C average. Now I was contemplating something terrifying: putting myself in the academic world and trying to excel at it. So I enrolled at the local junior college, De Anza College, in Cupertino.

As school started, I made the decision to just go for it. But what was the *it* I actually going for? Using my endurance, learning everything, and getting the most out of my classes was a vague set of concepts, so what did I need?

I didn't know about SMART goals at the time, but for a newbie, I didn't do too bad. I decided to aim for straight As in the coming semester. This new goal was:

- **Specific:** All As
- **Measurable:** The grading scale would tell me if I'd achieved my goal. I may have rewritten the rules about *how*, but the game was still the same, and the "scoring" was still the grading scale.
- **Achievable:** For a student who strove for a C average, it might be argued that straight As was not the wisest choice. But I knew myself and my endurance. Getting straight As was absolutely within my reach if I could apply my greatest strength to my studies. My timetable also provided a safety net of sorts. If I didn't earn all As, I could go into the next semester with a new game plan and a clean slate. It is also important to note I never told my professors I was dyslexic. Again, I did not want it to define me in any way.
- **Relevant:** At the time, the relevance (the why) wasn't crystal clear to me. I wanted to prove to myself that I could do something challenging, something I'd never done before. I wanted to feel good about myself academically.
- **Timetable:** I gave myself one semester—the upcoming semester. This was a manageable chunk of time with a clear finish line several weeks away. This played well into my athletic experience. The

semester was one match after which I could review the tape of my performance and create a new plan for the next.

Even with this goal in mind, I still needed something extra. I needed an edge. I needed an academic game plan that could leverage the strength of my endurance. And that's how I developed my "scholastic ten commandments."

The education system wanted me to read and learn like their typical student, and that was how they measured, saw, and scored me. Once I realized I did not have to play the game their way and that I had strengths I could use to compensate for my weaknesses, I was off to the races.

These ten commandments focused on my strengths: endurance, relentlessness, people skills, creativity, persuasive speaking, and my perfectionist nature.

Before you say anything, yes, I know I've cited my perfectionist nature as a strength, while earlier in the book, I advocated against attempting perfection in your aspirations since perfection is virtually unattainable. Let me clarify what I mean here.

The pursuit of perfection and excellence is spurred on by looking in the mirror every day and asking, "Can I do more?" and then doing more. We should all develop this habit and push for perfection. At the same time, we must be content with progress and understand that perfection is unachievable. We should be continually striving, pushing, learning, practicing, failing, and trying again and again. It refines us and makes us better.

So, that said, here are my ten commandments. Incidentally, I believe most, if not all, of these commandments can help any student earn high marks in their college courses—no dyslexia required.

Art's Scholastic Ten Commandments

1. Never miss class.
2. Sit in the second row, just off the center, away from the door.

3. Keep lecture notes, skipping every three lines on the paper to add notes later.
4. Digitally record every lecture, if possible.
5. Listen to each lecture within twenty-four hours, filling in note details (on the three lines left open).
6. Stay one day ahead of the scheduled homework.
7. Organize study groups with other students—serious students.
8. Two to three weeks into the semester, personally meet the professor.
    a. Ask for elaboration on the last lecture.
    b. Clarify the conditions needed for an A in the class.
    c. Ask about the A+.
9. Revisit the professor, discussing his/her background, grad school, publications, and more.
10. Network with your professors, assistant professors, tutors, and classmates.

Commandment 1
Never Miss Class

This one is self-explanatory. If I was going to get straight As, it was important to be truly committed. That meant I could not miss one single class.

When I transferred from De Anza College to San Jose State University, I took an operations-management class required for my business major. It was in a large amphitheater on Monday, Wednesday, and Friday afternoons from 3:00 p.m. to 4:30 p.m. The amphitheater held about 150 people, but that semester, only fifteen students took the class. Our professor was Dr. Denzler.

One Friday, I got to class about five minutes early, like usual, and was ready to take notes. I was the only one in the auditorium. Minutes passed. No one else came. I worried that class had been canceled and I had missed the memo.

Outside, it was a stunningly gorgeous California day. The kind of day any normal kid would want to cut class and start the weekend early. Yet there I was, sitting in the last place I wanted to be—in that hot, unairconditioned auditorium. But then again, it was *exactly* where I wanted to be. I was choosing Hard-Easy.

At 3:02, I decided to wait until 3:10 and then go to the professor's office to see if he had canceled class.

Just as I was about to pack up my things, Dr. Denzler walked in. I was sure that once he saw me there alone, he would cancel the class. But he didn't. He walked in and started lecturing like every other class.

I was stunned. It was surreal. Nevertheless, he pretended like the amphitheater was full of students. I took notes and, just as he did, acted as if nothing were out of the ordinary. Imagine my surprise when several minutes into his lecture, he turned, faced the audience (me), and asked a question. I was dumbfounded. He was acting like everyone else was there.

I actually looked over my shoulder to see if anyone had come in. Nope, still just me and Dr. Denzler. What was I to do? I sheepishly raised my hand. And who do you suppose he called on? Surprise, surprise—me. Good thing I also followed commandment number six: stay one day ahead of the scheduled homework. Confidently, I answered his question.

"That is exactly right, Mr. Coombs!" he said. He kept lecturing. He asked several questions along the way. I remember saying to him, "Thanks for calling on me. I hate to dominate the class discussion, but to answer your question . . ." He smirked but never ever broke character.

This odd, one-on-one lecture went on for about forty-five minutes. Then Dr. Denzler turned and said, "Well, that should do it for today. Will you all please read the following chapters . . . ? I will see you on Monday." He gathered his papers, put them in his briefcase, and walked out the door.

Several weeks later, as the semester was winding down, I was in Dr. Denzler's office chatting with him. I took the opportunity to ask him about that Friday. "What were you thinking?" I asked.

He said, "You made a commitment to be there that day. I was on the top level of the amphitheater, overlooking the great room, when you walked in and took your seat. I watched you, and I could not believe that everyone except you had cut class. That had never happened to me in all my years of teaching. I was several minutes late on purpose. I wanted to see if you would give up and walk out. To be honest, I was hoping you would so I could also leave and do it guilt-free. But there you sat. Once I realized you were committed, I felt obligated to stay and became committed as well. I had to do my best to teach you, no matter what. So that is exactly what I did."

We laughed and reminisced about it. At one point, Dr. Denzler said to me, "You know, after that day it didn't matter how well you did on the tests, how good your essays were, or if you attended any more lectures the rest of the semester. From that day on, you were going to get an A in my class."

"Oh, sure, now you tell me!" I said.

We both chose Hard-Easy that day. Not only did I get my flywheel going strong in that class, the two of us stayed friends for years. I often think about that day and what he *really* taught me. Even if there is only one person who is committed and showing grit, that one person is important. Their grit should be met with grit in return. I would have never learned that life lesson had I not been committed to keeping commandment number one.

Commandment 2
Sit in the Second Row, Just Off the Center, Away from the Door

I did this for several reasons:

1. To record each lecture, I needed a seat that offered the best advantage. If I sat too far back, the recording would be weak.

2. Sitting in the second row was symbolic to me. I had always been one of those back-row sitters. And the reality of back-row sitters? They are less committed and less engaged in the class because they can easily sneak out or daydream or, these days, text or watch

YouTube. But the front-row sitters demonstrate their commitment to the speaker and the lesson. I was tired of being a less-committed academic loser. So I moved up front. Why the second row? I wanted to be close enough to clearly hear the teacher but not close enough for them to see that I was recording their lecture (commandment 4).

3. As mentioned above, those who choose to sit in the front are more committed, and "birds of a feather flock together." So, to be in line with commandment seven, if you want to be in a study group with those who are committed and bright, you must place yourself among them. More often than not, they are the people who will arrive early and sit close to the front.

Situating myself in the room this way gave me the best chance to get an A in that class. My physical position made me feel like the A student I wanted to be, and that confidence provided a psychological advantage.

As I look back at this rule, I see elements of Hard-Easy helping me move toward my goal. I visualized my future self and acted like him. I was mindful of the kind of friends I needed. I practiced delayed gratification by preparing for the recordings to extend the lecture outside of class time. These were all Hard-Easy choices that helped me maintain the level of grit I needed to succeed.

Commandment 3
Keep Lecture Notes, Skipping Every Three Lines

To get all As, I needed to take great notes in my lectures. As you know, writing was not a strength of mine, but I could even the odds with my endurance.

Do you remember those BIC pens—the ones with four colors: red, blue, black, and green, all in one? My kids will cringe, but yes, I took notes all through college with one of those. I had become a nerd.

I would use green during class, writing on one line and skipping the next three. Later that day I would listen to the recorded lecture, using that blank space to fill in additional information with a different color.

I am pretty sure my notes were always the most complete and colorful notes of anyone else in my class. I got a few stares in study groups whenever I pulled them out. No one ever said anything, but when a topic required some clarity, my notes were the ones the group turned to.

Commandment 4
Digitally Record Every Lecture

I needed to hear each lecture twice—or more. My dyslexia could slow me down, but if I had the lecture recorded, I could listen to it over and over. The recordings I took provided me with the time I needed to write notes that helped me learn, review, and retain the information.

Now, here's the tricky part. You'll likely need to obtain permission from the school and/or professor to record the lectures. This is the course of action I recommend now. Then, however, I didn't get permission to record. I got a mini-cassette recorder, kept it in my bag, and recorded each lecture so I could listen again after class and complete my notes.

I was absolutely breaking university rules. Most universities have some policy regarding recording in the classroom due to concerns over intellectual property rights, copyright, and privacy. In our digital age of social media, there's the added risk of potentially embarrassing audio or video clips going viral.

In retrospect, I'm guessing that if I had asked permission and explained my dyslexia, the professor would have granted me permission. And if he hadn't, I could have appealed to the Office of Disability Services.

Then again, what if all that had failed and I wasn't allowed to record?

We revere many of those who broke the law in the name of civil rights, human rights, justice, freedom from oppression, and improving the lives of themselves and others: our American forefathers, Rosa Parks, Gandhi, Susan B. Anthony, Martin Luther King, Liu Xiaobo, Aung San Suu Kyi, and Nelson Mandela, to name a few. I am *not* suggesting my cause was as great or noble as theirs. But I was fighting for my very future. I was fighting for my future family, their kids, and their kids to come. Had the school denied my right to record classes, I guarantee my life would have taken a radically different turn.

Commandment 5
Listen to Each Lecture within Twenty-Four Hours, Filling in Note Details

To get all As, I needed to get as much as I could out of each lecture. I've already discussed how my note-taking system and lecture recordings helped, but those only worked if I followed up on them after the lecture. There was still that temptation to procrastinate.

Somewhere, I had heard that for every hour you spend in the classroom, you should spend two hours studying outside the classroom. So, as a budding academic overachiever, I aimed to do three.

This is where I truly leveraged my ability to push myself, both physically and mentally. I would frequently (about every eight to fifteen seconds) find myself sitting there, thinking, "You don't need to listen to this lecture again. You got it the first time. Just think of all the fun things you could be doing instead! Haven't you done enough?" But my resolve was strong. I would choose Hard, push those thoughts from my mind, pull out my cassette recorder, and listen again, pen in hand.

One day at San Jose State, I remember having this amazing thought: "My weakness has become my strength." I had taken an area of my life that was a personal demon and wrestled it to the floor. The pathetic student I once saw in the mirror was now a student who could hang with the best of them.

Commandment 6
Stay One Day Ahead of the Scheduled Homework

Homework can be hard, and we humans like to avoid hard things. It was especially unpleasant for me. Using my physical endurance as an academic asset, I set a goal to get ahead of the homework and stay there.

This commandment had some ancillary benefits to keeping me on track to get all As. First, it appeased my competitive, type-A inclinations and gave me peace of mind. Knowing I was two or three steps ahead of the class put me at ease. If life disrupted my schedule, I was prepared. I worked hard to make sure things stayed easy later.

Second, it forced me to make studying a habit. Many of my classmates took the easy route and put off their homework, only to pull all-night cram sessions. This affected their health and the quality of work they turned in.

Third, staying ahead gave me confidence. As one of the slower students, I was always hesitant to ask questions for fear of sounding stupid. I think this is a common fear among most college students. I found that when I put energy into being ahead of the curriculum, I had better information available to me. I could ask more insightful, pertinent questions. I discovered that the more I asked and contributed to the discussion, the smarter and more educated I looked to those in my class. And the smarter I looked to others, the smarter I felt. I discovered that what had started as perception had become reality. The confidence that came from hard work helped me put the velociraptor of doubt in its place.

Fourth, I proved to myself that my mind was just like any other muscle and followed the same Hard-Easy law. I could train my brain to endure and perform better.

I never cured my dyslexia. But I can honestly say that I beat it. It no longer held its terrifying, pessimistic power over me. It no longer defined me.

Commandment 7
Organize Study Groups with Other Serious Students

I knew I couldn't achieve my goal of all As alone. I needed to surround myself with the right kinds of students. In high school, I would often get paired up with students who had the same "ho-hum" attitude I did. Birds of a feather truly do flock together. In college, I would no longer be Mr. Scholastic Ho-Hum. I would need to reach out to my classmates and create groups where we could help each other succeed. This would require consistent extra effort on my part, which would be hard, but that hard work would pay off.

I was drawn to other serious students. I noticed who arrived early each class period, who sat near the front, and who took copious notes. I found that students who had similar goals and aspirations were drawn to me as well. It felt natural to form a study group with these individuals.

During our regular meetings, we sorted out difficult concepts and brainstormed possible solutions. This form of studying was invaluable and made the path to my goal less strenuous. It gave me the ability to look at problems through the eyes of others. We would debate class concepts for hours. I discovered that I could seriously disagree with others, but we could hash those ideas out—sometimes passionately—until we arrived at what we mutually considered the best solution. This is an indispensable tool I have used with my colleagues in every organization I have been with.

Commandment 8
Two to Three Weeks into the Semester, Personally Meet Your Professor

Getting to know my professors didn't guarantee me an A, but those personal relationships helped me work toward my goal. Here's what your first meeting should look like:

1. Ask for elaboration on the last lecture.
2. Clarify the conditions needed for an A in the class.
3. Ask about the A+.

This early-semester office visit served multiple purposes:

1. It demonstrated I was serious about the subject.
2. It turned the spotlight on the professors and the subjects they loved talking about. Professors, like all of us, *love* to have someone express interest in what they love. Every professor I have ever met has been extremely passionate about their field of expertise.

    So I would go to their office and say, "Professor Jones? I want to thank you for meeting with me for a few minutes. I really enjoyed your last lecture. I am curious about one point you made. Blah, blah, blah . . . Did I understand that correctly?" Once they realized I had listened, thought about it, and showed interest in that particular point, the satisfaction in their eyes became evident!
3. I needed to make sure the professors remembered me and knew me by name before they knew any of the other students. I wanted them to call me by name in class. At the end of the semester, if a professor knew me personally, had a favorable impression of me, and I was sitting on that threshold between an A or an A-, they were more likely to give me the A.
4. I wanted to make it clear that I was truly interested in the conditions for getting an A. It firmly planted in a professor's mind that I was, indeed, an A student and that nothing short of an A was going to work for me.
5. I also let them know that the grade was not my primary motivation: excellence and learning were. I would close with this question: "Do you ever give out A+s?" Many professors initially laughed at this question. But when I did not laugh back, they sobered up. Some simply said, "Yes. But only on rare occasions." Others said, "Why do you care about an A+? It has no bearing on your GPA." Others simply said, "No."

I needed them to understand that it was not my GPA I was concerned with. It was about excellence and becoming the very best I could become.

I will never forget the end of one semester. I was at the professor's office looking at grades posted on a sheet of paper on the door. The professor had given me an A–. It was the highest grade in the class, but I had gotten As on all the tests. I immediately made an appointment to meet with the professor the next day.

We sat in his small, slightly disheveled office. We talked generally about the class. The conversation was upbeat and cordial—until I asked him about my final grade.

He was deeply offended and ardently reminded me that I had received the highest grade in the class. I remained calm and attempted to convey to him that I really did not care what grades the other students had received or how I compared to them. I did not compare myself to anyone. I only compared me to me.

With that, he became even more defensive. He reiterated that I had done very well, better than the rest of the class, and that I was definitely his top student. *But* . . . his final grade was going to stand. The defiant intonation in his voice made it clear he was not going to budge.

I paused for a few moments, gathered my thoughts, and then calmly asked, "Professor, what is it that you taught during the semester that I failed to learn?"

"That has nothing to do with it," he said. "I feel that you earned an A–, so that is what I gave you, and that is what you will get."

After a few more rounds of back and forth, I finally said, "I'm going to go. I do plan to meet with the dean and discuss this issue with him." I could tell he was shocked and irritated. As I left his office, I thanked him for a great class.

That afternoon, I made an appointment with the dean. But before the appointment, I walked by the professor's office and, to my surprise, the A– had miraculously changed into an A.

What did this experience teach me? It taught me that if you are calm and rational and have a strong conviction in what you believe, you have every right to challenge the establishment. Don't let others arbitrarily say, "This is the way it is" and accept it, especially if you know otherwise. Calmly, rationally, and articulately speak up. Let your voice be heard. Even when you're up against the so-called experts, if you believe there is a problem of some kind, step up and tactfully challenge them.

Commandment 9
Revisit the Professor, Discussing His or Her Background, Grad School, Publications, and More

To build relationships that would help me achieve my goal of all As, I couldn't leave it at a single visit of introduction. That's not how relationships are built. So I made it a point to revisit my professors often. This was hard in that I needed to take the time to schedule these meetings at the professor's convenience. This meant I sometimes had to put off other activities or obligations.

It was somewhat scary, too, since, in each case, I had to be the one to make the first move, so to speak.

It might seem like my only reason for building these relationships was to get the As, but the truth is, I enjoyed the lively, intellectual banter we often engaged in. It was stimulating and gratifying, and I reveled in my interactions with most of them.

If you'll recall, my original goal was to learn "everything" a class had to offer, but that wasn't measurable. The grade was. Building these relationships and having these conversations was bonus learning that moved the A to the A+, even if it didn't show up on my transcript that way.

This commandment of "revisiting the professor" was invaluable for me in ways that can't be measured. I was pushing hard on the flywheel, and I am happy to say that I became close friends with many of these good men and women. Not only did they take on the roles of clairvoyant, cheerleader, and chaperone friends, they also became great references later in life. I did the hard work of initiating the friendships, and Easy followed beyond my academic career.

Commandment 10
Network with Your Professors, Assistant Professors, Tutors, and Classmates

Networking is an art (no pun intended). Truth be told, I am not a natural networker. As a young man, I was shy. It took awhile, but over time I learned how to look someone in the eye, smile, extend my hand, and say hello.

Like building relationships with my professors, networking was hard and even scary, but the friendships and connections I developed helped me get the most out of my education, gave me the best chance of getting all As, and continued to help me after I'd graduated. The easy, instant-gratification choice would have been to avoid the socializing and stay within my comfort zone. But these relationships were like the peaches on my tree. They took a long time to nurture, but the gratification I received as a result of the hard work and the investment in time was absolutely worth the wait.

My Final Grades

I am often asked if I achieved my goal: did I graduate with a 4.0?
No.
Well, not completely. I ended up with a 3.8 GPA in my major, but I received a 4.0 GPA for my minor. I am also proud of the fact that I graduated from SJSU with honors. I received the following distinctions:

- President's Scholar, San Jose State University
- Dean's list, San Jose State University Business School
- Beta Gamma Sigma Business Honor Society
- Thayer Scholarship recipient, San Jose State University
- Phi Kappa Phi Honor Society

I am sure some out there reading this will think that some of my ten scholastic commandments are senseless and unnecessary. Some may even think they are replaceable with different, more powerful commandments. But as I unfailingly followed my list, I got through college by focusing on my natural strengths.

So, how many principles of the law of Hard-Easy did you spot as you read about my academic journey? I've given you some help here and there, but there are still more for you to discover. Where did you see grit? What about common excuses? You saw my plan and my vision, but what about my purpose? How did I invest the hours of my day?

Now, how many will you weave into *your* story? You can live Hard-Easy or Easy-Hard. It is your choice, your life.

Chapter Recap

Key concepts and takeaways from chapter 21:

- Defy negative labels.
- Dream big.
- Use your strengths to overcome your weaknesses.

Pause and Think

- What labels have people or institutions affixed upon you?
- Have you ever used your strengths to overcome one of your weaknesses?

CHAPTER 22

DEATH

In this final chapter, I speak of death. Wherever you fall on the religion/spirituality scale, death is universal, and our thoughts are naturally drawn to what comes next. Death is never a pleasant subject, but it is necessary to confront and reconcile our feelings of discomfort regarding it. In this chapter, we keep our focus on the now, but we must also consider how Hard-Easy affects the end.

I encourage you to see this chapter through. Do the Hard thing. Embrace the discomfort, and you'll find you feel more reconciled with the reality of death.

It was Leonardo da Vinci who said, "While I thought I was learning how to live, I have been learning how to die."

And it was my cranky tenth-grade algebra teacher who said, "Life sucks, and then you die."

One quote is indicative of a life lived Hard-Easy, one of a life lived Easy-Hard.

What does death have to do with the law of Hard-Easy? Anything?

A Note to the Faithful and the Faithless about Life beyond the Grave

Okay. Religion. Spirituality. Faith. Whether you believe in a higher power or not, the law of Hard-Easy applies to each of us in this mortal realm.

I know many have not reconciled with certainty the questions of why we are on Earth, whether or not we existed prior to this life, and whether there is a life after this one. I do not want this to get religious or preachy, I am not that way, but I personally believe the law of Hard-Easy is eternal and that we continue to exist beyond this earthly life.

And I believe we all have a greater purpose that extends beyond the mortal bounds we now experience. This earthly life is a blip of eternity and represents a small part of what we can expect.

So, if I choose to live a Hard-Easy life of integrity, kindness, and altruism, the Easy phase of Hard-Easy will not only come in this life, it will result in Easy in the next.

All major religions, to some degree, are about cheating death with the idea of an afterlife, where we experience a reward or consequence for our actions in life. Heaven, hell, karma, reincarnation, Jannah, Jahannam—the list could go on and on. Personally, I'm not sure what to call it except for the natural order of the universe.

It's easy to find the law of Hard-Easy in religion, but does this negate the law of Hard-Easy for those who don't believe in a post-mortal existence?

Of course not. Even if death is the end of all ends, each human being who exists on this planet leaves a legacy. Each life touches others, and that ripple effect exists even if those affected are never aware of the influence of others' lives on their own. In many ways, this is an afterlife, even if the existence part of that life has ended.

Learning How to Die

The end of our journey is death. It awaits us all.

"Alas, poor Yorick!" Hamlet cries, dismayed, as he holds the skull of the jester who piggybacked him and affectionately played with him when he was a child in the king's court (act v, scene i). Hamlet feels what we all feel when confronted with the reality of mortality. No matter who we are—Yorick or Alexander the Great—nothing can save us from the grave.

I am not trying to be morbid or somber but, rather, trying to let death heighten your focus on what you have today.

You have *now*.

And that knowledge should be used to live every second with joy.

Those who live Hard-Easy go to their deaths with a peace born of having lived a full, rich, joyful life.

Meanwhile, those who have lived Easy-Hard tend to fear death because they are filled with regret. It's the regret of not making wise and prudent choices; of not fostering healthy relationships with loved ones; of not living in a way that optimized physical, emotional, and psychological health.

This book is about getting you to live the absolute best life possible so that when you are near the end of your journey, you can look back with no regret. Acknowledging, accepting, and embracing your mortality is a great way to stay focused on spending every minute and every breath being the best you, you can be.

Death—The Ultimate Motivator

On June 12, 2005, Steve Jobs delivered the commencement address at Stanford University. In it, he praised death—the awareness of one's own mortality—for how it motivated him throughout his life:

> Remembering that I'll be dead soon is the most important tool I've ever encountered to help me make the big choices in life. Because almost everything—all external expectations, all pride, all fear of embarrassment or failure—these things just fall away in the face of death, leaving only what is truly important.

> Remembering that you are going to die is the best way I know to avoid the trap of thinking you have something to lose. You are already naked. There is no reason not to follow your heart.[70]

Just as Jobs says, acknowledging the reality of death—thought it's not exactly pleasant to face or ponder—is critical to living an abundant life.

I am now at an age where death is all around me. Parents, friends, and colleagues of mine have passed away. Some have lived long, happy lives, while others have been taken too soon. It seems like just yesterday we were playing ball, laughing, arguing over a Scrabble word, or asking for hot and cold clues while playing hide the thimble. And now that they're gone, I sometimes pull up their contact information on my phone and wish I could call them one more time and hear their voice.

Whenever I pull out an old photo album (back when we had actual cameras and had to drop off a roll of film and wait three weeks to see the twelve, twenty-four, or thirty-six glossy photos, which was like opening a mini time capsule), I see friends now gone—their smiles, the sparkle in their eyes, their sun-kissed cheeks, the smiles on their faces as they leaned in to blow out all the candles on their birthday cakes as we sang to them. I remember their spirit, wit, kindness, friendship, hopes, and dreams. I hear their songs, smell their cologne or perfume, and reminisce about the places and times that were uniquely ours.

I can still hear our trivial disagreements playing out in my mind, and I try to recall why I was so passionate about what now seems so petty. Oh, what I would give to have one more day with them! One more silly dance in the kitchen, one more out-of-tune karaoke in the car, one more burger or taco, one more hug, one more chance to say, "I love you."

I find death has become more of a reality than an abstraction. If I use this awareness as a motivator, as Jobs advocates, it's as if the friends and family I've lost are motivating me from beyond. I can still feel their encouragement and positive energy. It makes me feel happy and comforted to think of it that way.

Do Not Go Gentle into That Good Night

Logically, we all realize that death is an inescapable reality. Yet most people I know do not deeply contemplate their own mortality, especially the young. I imagine they spend more time thinking about upgrading their mobile phone, plunking down thousands for the latest TV, or going into debt for a new car than pondering their death.

I get it.

When I was young, death was a universe away. It was an abstract concept—a myth that only affected the elderly. That would never be me.

As a child, time seemed to crawl at a painfully slow pace, day to day, week to week, year to year. Christmas, my birthday, and the last day of school seemed to take forever to get to.

As I entered my late teens and early twenties, time seemed to pick up her pace, but it wasn't so fast yet. She sauntered in a lazy stroll.

As a full-grown adult, time began to run. Whoa! Didn't see that coming! Then it began to sprint. It was Usain Bolt accelerating year to year, defying me to keep up.

Now, as I approach my older years, time is no longer sprinting—it has sprouted wings and taken flight. Birthdays and holidays come and go so quickly I can scarcely tell them apart. It's becoming a blur as I hurtle faster and faster toward my last breath. When death is at my door, my time on earth will come to an end, and for me, it will halt its ever-furious, tiring pace.

I see how death affects us all in different ways. We all ache differently. In my experience, those who are not afraid to die are those who were not afraid to live. As I think of my own mortality and the remaining years I have on this earth, I realize how much I love life, and I want to extract as much joy and satisfaction from it as possible. To that end, I want to be healthy and live as long as possible. But I am not afraid to die. Not even close. I can truly say I have no regrets.

Some, however, concede death long before it arrives. "I'll die anyway, so what does it matter?" This is the what-the-hell effect we've touched on throughout this book.

Living Hard-Easy is a way to defy death—to look that gaunt Grim Reaper in the eye and flip him the bird. Every Hard-Easy decision says to death: "I see you waiting for me; but before I get there, I'm doing some impressive shit that will be around for a long time after I'm gone. And if that's the case, then it's like I'm not dead at all, you bony asshole."

Hard-Easy Come, Hard-Easy Go

In my younger years, there were times where I would have a close encounter with a major accident, see a friend with a serious illness, or witness a relative pass away in the prime of their life. In those moments, my own mortality would abruptly come into focus and I would feel depressed and anxious about the reality of death. But that was when I was young and had no clue about the importance of time and relationships.

Now I feel a sense of peace and calm when I ponder death. If I continue to ponder it, that calm swells to joy—joy that I'm alive and have today. If I wake up in the morning, I have tomorrow, and I have a choice as to how to spend my time and who I spend that time with.

Part of the calm I feel now is the Easy phase of Hard-Easy. Because of how I spent my time and who I spent that time with in the decades before now, I am tasting the fruit of those choices—which is why I can ponder my own death with peace.

Those who have developed a solid, robust philosophy of living and a lust for life seem to stay calm as the reality of death looms ever closer.

Death and loss are not easy. I'm not saying they are. You are forever changed after the loss of a parent, sibling, child, or spouse, which is why I'm telling you to do this now.

Finish this chapter and go make it happen: Please take the time today to appreciate each and every moment you have with your spouse, family, children, and loved ones. You never know when it is going to be your last hug, kiss, or loving goodbye. Most likely, you'll have hundreds more. But you never know. So take a few short minutes out of your busy, frenetic schedule and call that person you are thinking of and say, "I love you," "I need you," "I appreciate you," or "I'm sorry if I ever offended you or caused you pain."

Got it? Start thinking about how you're going to approach this, and I'll remind you to get to it at the end of the chapter.

You're going to do this today, and you're going to do it again tomorrow. And the next day. Try not to let a day go by when you don't take the time to reach out to those you love and tell them how important they are to you.

And when your time comes, make sure you have lived a life you are proud of. Leave this world peacefully if you're able. Your last gift to your loved ones should be one of peace and love, not one of regret and what-ifs. There should be no unfinished business. Without this peaceful, loving closure, those left behind will feel guilt.

It's much better for all involved that you take your last breath on a positive note, appreciating the grandeur of life, and that includes the wonders and mysteries of what, if anything, lies beyond.

Those who live Easy up front to avoid the later Hard die many slow painful deaths throughout their lives. Those who live Hard-Easy experience death only once.

Tecumseh, a military leader of the Shawnee tribe in the late 1700s, has been credited for saying:

> So live your life that the fear of death can never enter your heart. Trouble no one about their religion; respect others in their view, and demand that they respect yours. Love your life, perfect your life, beautify all things in your life. Seek to make your life long and its purpose in the service of your people. Prepare a noble death song for the day when you go over the great divide. Always give a word or a sign of salute when meeting or passing a friend, even a stranger, when in a lonely place.

Show respect to all people and grovel to none. When you arise in the morning give thanks for the food and for the joy of living. If you see no reason for giving thanks, the fault lies only in yourself. Abuse no one and no thing, for abuse turns the wise ones to fools and robs the spirit of its vision. When it comes your time to die, be not like those whose hearts are filled with the fear of death, so that when their time comes, they weep and pray for a little more time to live their lives over again in a different way. Sing your death song and die like a hero going home."[71]

The end of my life draws closer and closer, and I have absolutely no problem with that. My being gone is more than okay because I know that, in some small way, I will still be here to give guidance and inspiration to my kids, grandkids, and great-grandkids if they read my words, ponder my thoughts, and implement my urgings.

I have lived a long life and have been blessed, and I believe I have a responsibility to leave this world a bit better than it was before I existed.

In my twenties, thirties, and forties, I was preoccupied with things I felt were so important but which I now see were so trivial. Now, as I get older, it is clear what is essential. In large part, this book is me trying to share with you what I have learned.

It isn't easy for me to accurately express my thoughts about the importance of the concept of Hard-Easy. Still, I trust you will listen to someone who has come to understand the value of time and relationships.

We can all be great. We all have that capacity, but it takes a lot of courage, grit, and many small, consistent, hard choices to achieve it.

You can drift through a life governed by others, situations, and events beyond your control. Or you can create your life and leave your mark in this world.

Live an amazing life—however you define that. The earth we are living on is an incredible place, where you can accomplish pretty much anything and be anyone you want to be. Yet we will not be here forever. Life here is short. So do you with passion. Bring it hard so it is exciting. Make the gift of life count.

Death is not heartbreaking. Living the life you were meant to live and dying inside while living is.

The law of Hard-Easy is how you take advantage of the now so that when death calls for you, you won't cower before it but face the calm known only by those who have prepared their whole lives for the next phase of their journey.

Chapter Recap

Key concepts and takeaways from chapter 22:

- The awareness of death heightens our focus on what we have today.
- If you use this awareness as a motivator, as Steve Jobs advocates, it's as if the friends and family who have passed on are motivating you from beyond.

Pause and Think

- Take a few short minutes out of your busy, frenetic schedule and call that person you are thinking of and just say, "I love you," "I need you," "I appreciate you," or "I'm sorry if I ever offended you or caused you pain." Seriously. Go do it now.
- Do that again tomorrow. Schedule it in your planner or set a reminder in your phone.
- Do it again the next day. Make it a habit.

CONCLUSION

THIS MOMENT IS YOURS
Spend It Wisely

This is the end.

Or is it?

The Easy-Hard thing to do would be to put this book on the shelf and never revisit it. Maybe some of it sticks with you; maybe it doesn't.

But here you are, reading the conclusion, which means you're choosing Hard-Easy. Please refer back to this book as often as you can and use it to stoke your motivation, remind yourself of a tactic or principle you want to adopt or share an idea with friends, family, or coworkers.

Hopefully, the purpose and recap at the end of each chapter have helped you as you've read and will continue to aid you as you review the concepts.

With that in mind, here's the thirty-thousand-foot view of the ground we've covered in this book. (And if you do happen to find yourself plummeting toward the ground at thirty-thousand feet, remember: be the banana.)

Self-Inventory

I know that when I look in the mirror, I will see many areas of my life where I need to practice what I preach. No one is perfect, and we all need a loving, encouraging nudge now and then. So let's look in the mirror together and go down this list. If you answer no to any of the following, make a note. Then prioritize those you need to work on. Don't overwhelm yourself by trying to do everything at once.

- Are you planning sufficiently for retirement?
- Do you feel happy with the state of your health and the things you can control about it?
- Are you up to date with recommended preventative health screenings for your age group? What about visits to the dentist?
- Are you addiction-free? (Addiction is a behavior and is not limited to substance addiction.)
- Do you feel you have rock-solid relationships with your family members and close friends?
- Do you regularly express your love and gratitude for these important people?
- Do you consider yourself someone who follows through on what you start? (Think projects, books, promises, etc.)
- Do you invest time and effort in projects you feel passionate about? (The book you want to write, the business you want to start, the app you want to develop, etc.)
- Do you have an estranged relationship you feel you should repair?

If you thought of other things while reading through that list, address them head-on. That nagging feeling is there for a reason.

As a Hard-Easy practitioner, you'll recognize those small Easy-Hard actions (and inactions) that *pretend* to be inconsequential. You know how easy choice after easy choice adds up to "What the hell? It's too hard to change things now."

It's worth revisiting the danger of the what-the-hell effect and keeping it at the forefront because it is the scariest rationalization of all. When we hit that point, nothing seems to matter anymore. As bad as it is not to save money, exercise, eat right, spend quality time with loved ones, or expand your mind, it's worse to throw in the towel because you've experienced a little failure. What the hell? May as well keep making bad choices today.

When you find yourself making decisions based on a what-the-hell attitude, think of me binging on a sleeve of chilled Thin Mints and telling you, "It's not so bad. One sleeve won't kill me." What would you say to me? What about when I tear into the second sleeve with the rationalization that my diet plan is shot for today, so I might as well go all-in?

By now you'd be pointing out that my rationalizing is dangerous, and you'd not be speaking figuratively. This is what makes them so frightening. Whether it's chilled Thin Mints, smoking, avoiding homework, or fudging on your taxes, you recognize that consistent justification of these activities and others like them can put you in a place of true peril. You'd say to me, "Art! The more poor choices you make, the more comfortable you get with the danger you put yourself in. Put down the Thin Mints! Change can start *right now* if you are willing to choose Hard in this moment."

Now that you know the law of Hard-Easy, you are better equipped to magnify it in your life so it can bless you, not punish you.

This Moment Is Yours—Spend It Wisely

Given this new enlightenment and resolve, you better understand the destructive power of poor decisions. You realize that the small things are truly the big things. You comprehend that your choices matter.

Paradoxically, this harsh truth empowers you. Happiness, success, and deep joy can come to you instead by just one or two small, hard decisions taken daily. It can mean the difference between running a marathon at age sixty or fighting lung cancer, between living in the lap of luxury or on food stamps in your golden years, between rich relationships or bitter loneliness as we age.

Instead of giving me a pep talk in the midst of my chilled Thin Mint madness, I want you to direct this pep talk at yourself. Befriend your future-self and team up on present-day you. At the risk of sounding like Marty McFly and Doc Brown, future you's very existence depends on it!

What would future you advise present-day you to do? What action taken now would be most beneficial for your future self?

The Ultimate Goal

My biggest wish is for you to become your future self and to love that person. I want you to appreciate how past you made hard choices, delayed gratification, and faced down the unknown to make your dreams come true. When it comes time to face the end and whatever is next, I wish for you to meet it with no regrets. Your family will share that peace with you.

So take a few minutes every morning and talk to your future self. Really get to know that person. I know you will begin to discover ways to make the law of Hard-Easy work in your favor. With this knowledge, you will be able to make minute changes that will have massive benefits for your future self.

As with expending energy to move the flywheel, those changes will feel awkward and challenging at first—and you may not even see any discernible results. But I promise you that, over time, they will build momentum.

Once you are truly in control, you will feel a growing appreciation for the law and how it works. You will have an increase in confidence, poise, and tranquility. As the good choices mount, the flywheel will spin faster and require less effort to churn and deliver results. The Hard of Hard-Easy will be shifting to Easy.

You'll see exciting changes that encourage you to live Hard-Easy more and more.

Embrace the changes that need to be made. Race toward them. Shout those words: "Bring it, Hard!"

Today can be the day future you looks back and says, "That was the fork in the road that led me to this wonderful life."

Some days I can still hear the voice of Gordon from across the stream as BigDog refuses to cross where I want him to.

"Coombs, you can live Hard-Easy or Easy-Hard. It's your choice."

Those words changed my life. And I hope they change yours.

Make each moment a gift to future you—and when you meet that person, it will be in an extraordinary life built upon trillions of Hard-Easy decisions that put the law to work for you, not against you.

And it will be Easy awesome.

ACKNOWLEDGMENTS

It would be improper of me not to acknowledge several who have supported me through this Hard-Easy journey.

First—Chris, your efforts and contributions have been immeasurable. I do not know how to properly thank you other than saying, "Thank you."

Second—Alice, we started batting this around more than three years ago. Thanks for always being willing to help.

Third—Angela, your comments and constructive criticism made this book better. I wanted to ignore your contributions, but, deep down, I knew you were right and that I had to make changes.

Fourth—Kirk and Paul, thanks for always being a willing and able sounding board. You truly are my clairvoyant, cheerleading, chaperoning friends.

Fifth—Dave, while I might be the heart of KomBea, you are most definitely the brains. Thanks for writing the foreword. You have always been there for me with your support and friendship. Close to fifty years is a long time to be best friends. How did I get so blessed?

Last but not least—Gordon, you taught me more than you will ever know while pushing those cows that crisp fall day. Thank you for allowing this city-slicker to come along for the ride.

NOTES

1. Janet L. Jones, "How Horses See the World," *Equus*, February 2016, https://equusmagazine.com/riding/visual-discrepancies-31223.

2. Theresa Dixon Murray, "Why Do 70 Percent of Lottery Winners End Up Bankrupt?" Cleveland.com, January 14, 2016, https://www.cleveland.com/business/2016/01/why_do_70_percent_of_lottery_w.html.

3. "Study: Brain Battles Itself over Short-Term Rewards, Long-Term Goals," Princeton University, October 14, 2004, https://pr.princeton.edu/news/04/q4/1014-brain.htm.

4. Ibid.

5. "New Ally Bank Survey Links Money to Happiness," Ally, November 19, 2013, https://www.ally.com/do-it-right/trends/new-ally-bank-survey-links-money-to-happiness/.

6. Malcolm Gladwell, "Complexity and the Ten-Thousand-Hour Rule," *The New Yorker*, August 21, 2013, https://www.newyorker.com/sports/sporting-scene/complexity-and-the-ten-thousand-hour-rule.

7. "Why Specialization Can Be a Downside in Our Ever-Changing World," *The Verge*, May 30, 2019, https://www.theverge.com/2019/5/30/18563322/david-epstein-range-psychology-performance-skills-sports-career-advice-book-interview?&tag=petergasca.com.

8. Hal Erold, "True Perception," accessed August 10, 2019, https://trueperception.in/inspire/%E2%80%9CRepetition-can-be-boring-or-tedious,-which-is-why-so-few-people-ever-master-anything.%E2%80%9D---Hal-Elrod/.

9. Frank Herbert, *Dune*, London: New English Library, 1968, 14.

10. Amanda Marrazzo, "At Speech in Chrystal Lake, Kidnapping Victim Elizabeth Smart Advises Not to Let Negative Experiences Define Who You Are," *Chicago Tribune*, December 7, 2018, https://www.chicagotribune.com/suburbs/ct-met-elizabeth-smart-abduction-survivor-crystal-lake-20181207-story.html.

11. "Elizabeth Smart," Wikipedia, retrieved August 13, 2019, https://en.wikipedia.org/wiki/Elizabeth_Smart#cite_note-12.

12. Eunice Oh, "Elizabeth Smart's Advice to Jaycee Dugard: Move Forward in Life," *People*, August 28, 2009, https://people.com/celebrity/elizabeth-smarts-advice-to-jaycee-dugard-move-forward-in-life/.

13. *Elizabeth Smart Speaks at Johns Hopkins University*, May 6, 2013, Fox13 News, Salt Lake City, https://fox13now.com/2013/05/06/video-elizabeth-smart-speaks-at-johns-hopkins-university/.

14. "Flywheel," Wikipedia, accessed August 13, 2019, https://en.wikipedia.org/wiki/Flywheel.

15. Jim Collins, *Good to Great: Why Some Companies Make the Leap . . . and Others Don't* (New York: HarperBusiness, 2001).

16. CBSNews.com, June 7, 2011, https://www.cbsnews.com/news/compound-interest-the-most-powerful-force-in-the-universe/.

17. Sharon Haddock, "Shell Shocked: Errant Avalanche Bomb Rips Pleasant Grove Home," *Deseret News*, March 29, 2005, https://www.deseretnews.com/article/600121107/Shell-shocked-Errant-avalanche-bomb-rips-Pleasant-Grove-home.html.

18. "Tiger Woods' Statement: The Full Transcript," *The Guardian*, February 19, 2010, https://www.theguardian.com/sport/2010/feb/19/tiger-woods-public-statement-transcript.

19. Angela Duckworth (blog), accessed August 13, 2019, https://angeladuckworth.com/qa/.

20. Ibid.

21. Ibid.

22. Carol S. Dweck, "The Growth Mindset," in The Glossary of Education Reform, last updated August 29, 2013, https://www.edglossary.org/growth-mindset/.

23. Ibid.

24. *Logotherapy Revisited: Review of the Tenets of Viktor E. Frankl's Logotherapy* (Ontario Canada: Ottawa Institute of Logotherapy), 2012, https://books.google.com/books/about/Logotherapy_Revisited.html?id=gnZxPpqDjUUC&printsec=frontcover&source=kp_read_button#v=onepage&q&f=false.

25. "Viktor Frankl: The Human Search for Meaning," Farnum Street (blog), accessed August 13, 2019, https://fs.blog/2014/01/frankl-human-search-for-meaning/.

26. *Man's Search for Meaning* (New York: Simon & Schuster, 1984), 81.

27. Carol S. Dweck, "The Growth Mindset."

28. "Viktor Frankl: The Human Search for Meaning."

29. Gary Stokes, "How to Stop Saying, I'm Only Human," The Poised Life (blog), September 4, 2017, http://thepoisedlife.com/stop-saying-im-human/.

30. Haverly Erskine, "I'm Only Human: An Excuse or a Reasonable Justification?" May 18, 2013, *Democrat and Chronicle*, https://www.democratandchronicle.com/story/lifestyle/her/blogs/community/2011/12/02/im-only-human-an-excuse-or-a-reasonable-justification/2294911/.

31. Tinca J. C. Polderman, Beben Benyamin, Christiaan A. de Leeuw, Patrick F. Sullivan, Arjen van Bochoven, Peter M. Visscher, and Danielle Posthuma, "Meta-Analysis of the Heritability of Human Traits Based on Fifty Years of Twin Studies," *Nature Genetics*, vol. 47 (2015): 702–709.

32. Ibid.

33. J.K. Rowling (blog), "Harvard Commencement Address," June 5, 2008, https://www.jkrowling.com/harvard-commencement-address/.

34. "The Miller, His Son, and the Ass," American Literature, accessed August 15, 2019, https://americanliterature.com/author/aesop/short-story/the-miller-his-son-and-the-ass.

35. Stacy Colino, "Avoiding the What-the-Hell Health Effect," *US News*, November 15, 2017, https://health.usnews.com/wellness/mind/articles/2017-11-15/avoiding-the-what-the-hell-health-effect.

36. Brené Brown, "Shame vs. Guilt," Brené Brown (website), January 14, 2013, https://brenebrown.com/articles/2013/01/14/shame-v-guilt/.

37. Ibid.

38. "How Addiction Hijacks the Brain," Harvard Medical School, July 2011, https://www.health.harvard.edu/newsletter_article/how-addiction-hijacks-the-brain.

39. Stephanie Pappas, "Bird Brains: Pigeons Gamble Just Like Humans," LiveScience, October 13, 2010, https://www.livescience.com/8784-bird-brains-pigeons-gamble-humans.html.

40. "Craving Facebook? UAlbany Study Finds Social Media to be Potentially Addictive, Associated with Substance Abuse," University at Albany, December 9, 2014, https://www.albany.edu/news/56604.php.

41. Stephen R. Covey, *The 7 Habits of Highly Effective People: Powerful Lessons in Personal Change*, 71.

42. Cal Newport, "Resolve to Live a Deep Life," December 31, 2015, blog, https://www.calnewport.com/blog/2015/12/31/resolve-to-live-a-deep-life/.

43. Ibid.

44. Nancy K. Napier, "The Myth of Multitasking," *Psychology Today*, May 12, 2014, https://www.psychologytoday.com/us/blog/creativity-without-borders/201405/the-myth-multitasking.

45. Ibid.

46. "To Multitask or Not to Multitask," USC Dornsife, accessed August 16, 2019, https://appliedpsychologydegree.usc.edu/blog/to-multitask-or-not-to-multitask/.

47. Drake Baer, "How Multitasking Reshapes Your Brain into a Constantly Distracted State," Nebraska-City Newspress, September 26, 2014, https://www.ncnewspress.com/article/20140926/BUSINESS/309269987.

48. Sofie Bates, "A Decade of Data Reveals That Heavy Multitaskers Have Reduced Memory, Stanford Psychologist Says," *Stanford News*, October 25, 2018, https://news.stanford.edu/2018/10/25/decade-data-reveals-heavy-multitaskers-reduced-memory-psychologist-says/.

49. Kendra Cherry, "How Multitasking Affects Productivity and Brain Health," Verywell Mind, updated March 16, 2019, https://www.verywellmind.com/multitasking-2795003.

50. Kevin McSpadden, "You Now Have a Shorter Attention Span Than a Goldfish," *Time*, May 14, 2015, http://time.com/3858309/attention-spans-goldfish/.
51. Ibid.
52. Ibid.
53. See "Salmon Run," Wikipedia, accessed August 16, 2019, https://en.wikipedia.org/wiki/Salmon_run.
54. Gina Vivinetto, "The Secret to Happiness? Take Our Poll," *Today*, July 2, 2015, https://www.today.com/kindness/secret-happiness-acts-kindness-says-new-study-t30021.
55. Ibid.
56. Steve Miller Band, Capitol Records, August 13, 1976.
57. Directed by Ridley Scott (DreamWorks Pictures: May 1, 2000).
58. Esther Trattner, "How 5 of America's Richest Families Lost It All," *Moneywise*, July 3, 2019, https://moneywise.com/a/how-5-of-americas-richest-families-lost-it-all.
59. Daniel Kahneman and Angus Deaton, "High Income Improves Evaluation of Life but Not Emotional Well-Being," PNAS, September 7, 2010, https://www.pnas.org/content/early/2010/08/27/1011492107.
60. Jeremy P. Kelley, "National ACT Scores for Class of 2018 Worst in Decades, Officials Say," *Dayton Daily News*, October 17, 2018, https://www.daytondailynews.com/news/national-act-scores-for-class-2018-worst-decades-officials-say/EKA05C3FHcjN4bx8BmcC2N/.
61. Mayo Clinic Staff, "Friendships: Enrich Your Life and Improve Your Health," Mayo Clinic, accessed August 17, 2019, https://www.mayoclinic.org/healthy-lifestyle/adult-health/in-depth/friendships/art-20044860.
62. Joshua Becker, "12 Ways Friends Improve Our Lives," becoming minimalist (blog), accessed August 19, 2019, https://www.becomingminimalist.com/12-ways-friends-make-life-better/.
63. Katherine Hurst, "Best Friends Forever? 7 Essential Qualities of a Good Friend," The Law of Attraction, accessed August 19, 2019, http://www.thelawofattraction.com/essential-qualities-good-friend/.
64. "Are They Really Your Friend? 15 Signs That Suggest Otherwise," Ditch the Label (blog), accessed August 19, 2019, https://us.ditchthelabel.org/are-they-really-your-friend-15-signs-that-suggest-otherwise/.
65. Ibid.
66. Caspari R, Lee SH. "Is Human Longevity a Consequence of Cultural Change or Modern Biology?" *Am J Phys Anthropol*, 2006, 129(4): 512–17. doi:10.1002/ajpa.20360.
67. Katherine Wu, "Love, Actually: The Science behind Lust, Attraction, and Companionship," Harvard University, February 14, 2017, http://sitn.hms.harvard.edu/flash/2017/love-actually-science-behind-lust-attraction-companionship/.

68. Ranil Sharma, "Defining Your Core Values to Develop Your Relationship," accessed January 31, 2020, https://www.yogitimes.com/article/defining-core-values-couples-relationships.

69. "24 Best Relationship Books Every Couple Should Read Together," Develop Good Habits, September 30, 2019, https://www.developgoodhabits.com/best-relationship-books/.

70. Maria Forbes, "Steve Jobs: 'Death Is Very Likely the Single Best Invention of Life,'" *Forbes*, October 5, 2011, https://www.forbes.com/sites/moiraforbes/2011/10/05/steve-jobs-death-is-very-likely-the-single-best-invention-of-life/#a58454329b06.

71. "Tecumseh—'Die Like a Hero Going Home,'" November 17, 2013, https://nativeheritageproject.com/2013/11/17/tecumseh-die-like-a-hero-going-home/.

NOTE TO THE READER

Thank you so much for taking the time to read *Hard-Easy*. I hope this book resonates with you and inspires you to pay close attention to your choices and the consequences that will follow. I want you to know that I, too, am still learning this concept. I mutter "Bring it, Hard!" under my breath daily. If you've found even a small part of this read beneficial to you, it would mean a great deal if you could leave me a review on Amazon and Goodreads—and, of course, spread the word!

With sincere appreciation,
Art

Find me at www.ArtCoombs.com
Facebook: Author Arthur F. Coombs
Instagram: @arthurfcoombs
LinkedIn: www.linkedin.com/in/artcoombs
Twitter: @arthurfcoombs

ABOUT THE AUTHOR

Best-selling author, dynamic speaker, and leadership guru Arthur F. Coombs III brings decades of global expertise to readers, audiences, and corporations through his visionary and innovative practices. Founder and CEO of KomBea Corporation, Art has served for about twenty years developing and marketing tools that blend human intelligence and automation. Art's best-selling *Don't Just Manage—LEAD!* has been hailed by some of the nation's top executives. His second best-selling book, *Human Connection: How the "L" Do We Do That?*, provides a powerful formula for deep and meaningful connections with others. Before founding KomBea, Art served as EVP of Strategic Initiatives for FirstSource. As CEO and founder of Echopass Corporation, he helped build the world's premier contact-center hosting environment. Art has served as Sento Corporation's CEO, managing director and vice president of Europe for Sykes Enterprises, and worked for organizations such as Hewlett-Packard, VLSI Research, and RasterOps. His vast experience with people and organizations has led Art to share transformative principles for creating a fantastic life—principles you can now access within these pages.

www.ingramcontent.com/pod-product-compliance
Lightning Source LLC
Chambersburg PA
CBHW052102280426
43661CB00109B/1338/J